THE PEOPLE'S WEST LAKE

THE PEOPLE'S WEST LAKE

Propaganda, Nature, and Agency in Mao's China, 1949–1976

Qiliang He

University of Hawai'i Press
Honolulu

© 2023 University of Hawai'i Press
All rights reserved
Printed in the United States of America
First printing, 2023

Library of Congress Cataloging-in-Publication Data

Names: He, Qiliang, author.
Title: The people's West Lake / propaganda, nature, and agency in Mao's China, 1949–1976 / Qiliang He.
Other titles: Propaganda, nature, and agency in Mao's China, 1949–1976
Description: Honolulu : University of Hawai'i Press, [2023] | Includes bibliographical references and index.
Identifiers: LCCN 2023013319 (print) | LCCN 2023013320 (ebook) | ISBN 9780824895594 (trade paperback) | ISBN 9780824894894 (hardback) | ISBN 9780824896904 (pdf) | ISBN 9780824896911 (epub) | ISBN 9780824896928 (kindle edition)
Subjects: LCSH: Zhongguo gong chan dang—History—20th century. | Propaganda, Communist—China—History—20th century. | Communism and ecology—China—West Lake. | Human ecology—China—West Lake. | City planning—China—Hangzhou Shi. | West Lake (China)—History—20th century.
Classification: LCC DS797.88.W475 H4 2023 (print) | LCC DS797.88.W475 (ebook) | DDC 324.251/0750904—dc23/eng/20230403
LC record available at https://lccn.loc.gov/2023013319
LC ebook record available at https://lccn.loc.gov/2023013320

Cover photograph: West Lake "gentrified." Courtesy of Zhu Jiang 朱绛

University of Hawai'i Press books are printed on acid-free paper and meet the guidelines for permanence and durability of the Council on Library Resources.

This book is dedicated to Su Shi 苏轼 *(1037–1101), whose poems and prose aroused my curiosity about Hangzhou and West Lake in my childhood.*

Contents

Preface	ix
Introduction	1
Chapter One Water, Labor, and Microbes: The Campaign of Dredging West Lake in the 1950s	21
Chapter Two "Watching Fish at the Flower Harbor": Landscape, Space, and the Everydayness in Mao's China	47
Chapter Three Forests, Propaganda, and Agency: The Afforestation Movement in Hangzhou, 1950–1976	68
Chapter Four Socialist Pigs: Fertilizer, Collectivization, and Cultural Heritage in Mao-Era Hangzhou	90
Chapter Five "Ghosts as Neighbors": The Campaigns of Removing Tombs in the West Lake Region, 1956–1965	114
Conclusion	141
Abbreviations	147
Notes	149
Bibliography	171
Index	199

Preface

My journey in life and career path have converged. In the past fifteen years, I wrote about performing arts, the periodical press, fiction, and films, all of which have greatly interested me since my childhood. The subject matter of the present book, West Lake in Hangzhou, became my favorite destination when I was a teenager. The memory of my first visit to the city is still fresh. It was the Labor Day break in China in 1993, when I was a freshman at Shanghai Jiaotong University. I squeezed my way through the crowd inside a fully packed train carriage from Songjiang, Shanghai, to Hangzhou. West Lake blew me away even though I had already done a lot of preparatory work for this trip. The lake looked like a woman with ravishing beauty but unkempt hair. She was pretty but a little bit rough. Seventeen long years passed before I finally found an opportunity to revisit this scenic spot in 2010. The lake had changed a whole lot. The entire city of Hangzhou underwent "gentrification" in the 2000s, and West Lake was thoroughly renovated. This newly fashioned site did not profoundly impress me because I felt a little bemused by the mushrooming of so many new structures and tourist sites beside the lake. Despite this, my passionate love of West Lake didn't fade.

In 2013, I helped a student apply for admission to a master's program in landscape architecture. In the process, I bumped into works about landscape and its relevance to ideology. Instantly, I was thinking of West Lake and its political implications in Mao-era China (1949–1976). As I was working on two other projects, my search for the lake's meanings in post-1949 China did not begin until 2016 and 2017. Initially, I attempted to elaborate on the connectedness between the popularization of the Chinese Communist Party's (CCP's) ideologies and the (re)making of West Lake's landscape between the 1950s and 1970s. As I delved into the true complexity of the lake's history, I came to realize that landscape studies alone would not suffice for a fuller understanding of the transformations of the West Lake area in Mao's China.

Then, nonhuman studies opened up a new world for me. What has intrigued me most in nonhuman studies is a new approach to "agency." I have explored the agency of performing artists, nonelite women, and newspaper readers in my previous works. In the present book, I turn my attention to nonhuman agency. More precisely, I seek to highlight the comparability between human and nonhuman agency. West Lake, whose natural and cultural elements underwent dramatic changes in the past several decades, provides a compelling case for studying the agency of both humans and nonhuman entities. Indeed, the role of nonhuman entities in (re)shaping state policies in post-Liberation China is still understudied.

Although my quest for a better understanding of Mao-era China is a solitary journey, I'm fortunate to have gotten help from various individuals and institutions. I sincerely thank Professor Liping Wang, my academic adviser at the University of Minnesota. Her research about Hangzhou in the Qing and Republican eras has been precious to my own studies on West Lake. I would also like to thank Professors Ban Wang, Di Wang, and Poshek Fu for having read and commented on my proposals for the book manuscript a few years ago. Peter Carroll gave me critical thoughts about my presentation at the Association for Asian Studies conference meeting in 2018. His remarks somehow changed the direction of this project. Also, in 2018, I presented a paper based on Chapter 4 at a conference meeting in Minneapolis, Minnesota, where I received criticisms from Professors Mizuno Hiromi and Christ Isett. In the same year, Yan Li shared with me her scholarship on spatial reconfigurations of Beijing, which inspired me to make a comparison between Hangzhou and China's capital.

I am grateful that my friends and colleagues at Illinois State University (ISU) lent me full support over the years. In particular, I thank Lou Perez, Larissa and Ross Kennedy, Alan Lessoff, Georgia Tsouvala, Agbenyega Adedze, Tony Crubaugh, and Linda Clemmons. In addition, Dr. Christine Varga-Harris generously taught me some Russian terms I encountered in my research. The College of Arts and Sciences at ISU granted funds for my research trips a few times. During my research trips to Hangzhou in the past several years, my friends living in the "paradise on earth" gave me all kinds of assistance. I thank Tang Xiaomin, Gu Suhua, Sun Beibei, Sun Fang, Du Yuping, Wang Zhuojun, Tang Zhihao, Wang Cheng, Wang Kecheng, and Zhang Shengman. The staff members of the Zhejiang Provincial Archives, the Hangzhou Municipal Archives, and the Zhejiang Provincial Library have been helpful to my research. My friends at Zhejiang Agriculture and Forestry University, especially Ge Dandan and Zeng Wei, deserve special mention for their wholehearted support.

I appreciate that my friends and colleagues at other China-based universities shared insights and materials with me. Jiang Jin invited me to give two talks derived from this project at East China Normal University (ECNU). Li Shangyang, Professor Jiang's graduate student then, helped me locate some essential source materials. I also thank Professor Ruan Qinghua of ECNU for making arrangements for one of my talks. During the talk, I met with Liu Yanwen whose research about public works in the PRC lent me inspiration. Special thanks go to my friends at Fudan University. Indeed, my very first talk about West Lake was done in a small conference meeting in 2017, organized and sponsored by Fudan's anthropologists, Professors Pan Tianshu and Zhu Jianfeng. Dr. Zhu has been my friend since the early 2000s, when we were both in Minnesota. We still share thoughts and information. Professors Zhang Yong'an and Tao Feiya at Shanghai University invited me to give a talk about the making of a public garden in Hangzhou in 2018. Professor Xia Yun, also from Shanghai University, invited me to teach an online course on nonhuman studies for her students in 2020. I also thank my students in that class for sharing their input.

In the process of preparing this book manuscript, I gained recognition from Dr. Wu Jen-shu of Academia Sinica in Taiwan as a specialist in Hangzhou's urban history. For this reason, Dr. Wu extended an invitation to me to write an introductory chapter for his book series about cities in China. My MA student at ISU, Tan Guanhua, was a listener of my project for years. My colleagues at Hong Kong Shue Yan University have helped me at the final stage of preparing this book manuscript. I particularly thank Professor George Chuxiong Wei and Professor Selina Chan. Li Dongpeng from the Shanghai Media Group shared with me a documentary about West Lake produced in the 1950s. My friend, Zhu Jiang, generously gave me permission to use one of his photos in the book. I'm very grateful that Masako Ikeda of the University of Hawai'i Press has helped me navigate through the entire process of publication. Last but not least, there is my family: my mother, my wife, my sister, and my two kitties. I'm lucky to be supported by all of you.

Some of my articles include material that has entered some of the chapters in changed format. Chapter 2 is derived from "'Watching Fish at the Flower Harbor': Landscape, Space, and the Propaganda State in Mao's China" (*Twentieth-Century China* 46, 2, [May 2021]: 181–198). Part of Chapter 3 comes from "Afforestation, Propaganda, and Agency: The Case of Hangzhou in Mao's China" (*Modern Asian Studies* 56, 1 [2022]: 378–406).

Introduction

At the height of the Korean War (1950–1953), North Korean poet Hong Sun-ch'ol 洪淳哲 stayed in China for four months, during which time he produced a poetry anthology. Among numerous poems lauding a liberated China led by the Chinese Communist Party (CCP), Hong devoted one to West Lake (*Xihu* 西湖) in Hangzhou 杭州. Entitled "Ode to the People's West Lake" (*Gesong renmin de Xihu* 歌颂人民的西湖), the poem presents a stark contrast between the lake of the past as a plaything of "feudal landlords," "parasitic street-loafers," and "bloodsuckers," and the same body of water in "New China," which the "laboring people" (*laodong renmin* 劳动人民) own, supervise, and enjoy.[1] Similarly, Huang Yanpei 黄炎培 (1878–1965), a well-respected educator, industrialist, and political activist, ended a collection of fourteen poems about the lake with a seven-character quatrain entitled "The People's West Lake" (*Renmin Xihu* 人民西湖). In it, Huang hammered home a similar viewpoint: "The lake and the [surrounding] hills are now in the people's possession."[2]

The "people" or *renmin* 人民, the keyword in both poems, was, according to Krista Van Fleit Hang, a modifier of positions and institutions in the early years of the People's Republic of China (PRC, 1949–present) that was used to articulate a "sense of optimism over the birth of new China."[3] Throughout the PRC's history, "the people," a convenient shorthand, constituted the CCP government's source of power and had been liberally applicable to varied political contexts.[4] Aminda Smith notes that this heavily politicized but ill-defined category initially signified a collectivity "that went beyond industrial and agricultural laborers to include intellectuals, vagrants, and even the bourgeoisie."[5] However, the putative members of this collectivity did not enjoy equal standing, and more importantly, the boundary between "the people" and their foes was ever-shifting.[6] To borrow Gustave Le Bon's phrase, in the PRC, "the people" has always been "erected into a mystic entity."[7]

This "mystic entity," however, gains an added dimension—that is, internationalism—in both poems, produced as they were in the context of a global socialist movement. Placid West Lake was a symbol of the peace pursued by "the

Figure 0.1. Map of China and Zhejiang

people" of the world—as opposed to the imperialists—in Hong Sun-ch'ol's poem,[8] while Huang Yanpei underscored the lake's newly activated function as a meeting place of the people from all over the world. In this sense, the category of "the people" transcended national boundaries and came to embody socialist internationalism. Socialist internationalists not only called for the building of "a common culture that celebrated shared values, themes, and styles"[9] but also "highlighted distances between national cultures."[10] If socialist internationalism entailed both the integration of various national cultures and an emphasis on their distinctiveness, Hangzhou, where West Lake is situated, a historically cosmopolitan city and Marco Polo's (1254–1324) favorite,[11] offers an apt case study for examining the changing conceptualization of culture and nature in post-1949 China and its political implications, both domestically and internationally.

This book centers on the CCP's sustained efforts to make "the people's West Lake" of Hangzhou by reconfiguring space, reshaping the landscape (both scenic and productive), and reordering culture in the Mao Zedong era (1949–1976). It pieces together five initiatives that took place in the West Lake region between the 1950s and the 1970s: the dredging of West Lake, the construction of the public park of *Huagang guanyu* 花港观鱼 (Watching fish at the flower harbor), the afforestation movement, the development of collectivized pig farming in villages in the West Lake region, and the two campaigns to remove lakeside tombs. I argue that these projects were intended to generate visible and tangible results—a lake with a good depth, a sizable and scenic public garden, greener hills surrounding the lake, a growing swine population and rising productivity of fertilizer, and a tourist site cleansed of burial sites—whilst also being readily subject to the Party's propaganda. I thus call those programs "propaganda-campaign projects." Hence, "the people" as a modifier, like in all other cases in Mao-era China, carried dual connotations: "the people" as both the new masters of China's urban and natural spaces and yet also as those who were subject to the Party's intense ideological indoctrination. "The people" in this context were, as Giorgio Agamben puts it, both "the complex of citizens as a unitary political body" and "the members of the lower classes."[12]

Second, the CCP's endeavor to fundamentally alter the West Lake area opened up possibilities for both human and nonhuman actors to variously benefit from and undermine the political authorities' planning. Existing scholarship has highlighted human efforts to defy Party policies in Mao's China. In the case of Mao-era Hangzhou, James Gao shows that local citizens were enacting resistance to the "revolutionary changes" imposed on them[13] while also noting the self-conscious adjustment to the city's lifestyle (for example, tea consumption) on the part of the southbound CCP cadres.[14] By contrast, this book explores the "agency" of both humans and nonhumans (including water, microbes, aquatic plants, the park, pigs, trees, pests, and tombs) to affect, deflect, and undercut the CCP's sociopolitical programs, thereby diminishing the efficacy of state propaganda. Studying the agentic capacities of humankind and nonhuman entities to derail the Party-state's agenda allows for a critique of the "extraordinary tenacity" of an ahistorical divide between human culture and natural existence in both academic writing and contemporary conservation policy.[15] This book is not intended to blame the CCP's policies in Mao-era China for assaulting fixed and stable nature, which should have otherwise been impervious to transformation by external forces, thereby causing ecological degradation.[16] Instead, it historicizes the peculiar politico-cultural circumstances of the early PRC years, during which time some noticeable accomplishments were made, and predicaments arose in the process of reworking the environment in China. To borrow David Harvey's words, the sociopolitical conditions in post-1949 China had their "share of ecologically based difficulties."[17] Hence, I highlight the historicity of the complex relations between nature, politics, and culture in the massive campaign of transforming West Lake in Mao-era China.

West Lake and Hangzhou in Mao's China

Best known as the capital of the Southern Song dynasty (1127–1270), Hangzhou epitomized both the vigor and decadence of this southern empire.[18] Ever since the demise of the Southern Song, it has become a "cultural landmark in China."[19]

Meanwhile, West Lake survived severe sedimentations over a millennium thanks to numerous programs of dredging and upkeep.[20] It is thus not an overstatement to argue that West Lake has become a human-made body of water. Hence, Liping Wang reminds us of the "artificiality of West Lake landscape."[21] After the collapse of the Qing dynasty (1644–1911), Hangzhou began to capitalize on West Lake's mesmerizing beauty and the cultural imaginaries associated with the city to develop a tourist business.[22] After the completion of the Shanghai-Hangzhou railway in 1916, commercial tourism figured prominently as the backbone of the city's economy, making Hangzhou a typical "consumerist city" (*xiaofei chengshi* 消费城市) in the first half of the twentieth century. The CCP had long committed itself to the mission of turning "consumerist cities" into "productive" ones.[23] Transforming Hangzhou into a productive or industrial city did not come about as the CCP had envisioned, however. Hangzhou typified what Dean Rugg calls a "partially-changed" city in communist countries, in which ambitious projects of urban development and industrialization were conditioned by the "old historic elements" of the city.[24] To further complicate the situation, the Soviet urban planning specialist, A. C. Maxim (Muxin 穆欣), tabled a proposal in the early 1950s to "develop Hangzhou as a city for recreation, tourism, and cultural activities" and to make it "a center for international conferences ... known as 'the Geneva of the East.'" Consequently, the state suspended major investments in Hangzhou's local industry during the First Five-Year Plan period (1953–1957). As James Gao observes, none of the 697 major industrial enterprises planned for China during the First Five-Year Plan were scheduled to be built in Hangzhou.[25]

Maxim's opinion did not constitute the sole reason behind the CCP's decision to recast Hangzhou's role. Chairman Mao Zedong's 毛泽东 (1893–1976) preferences provided a special incentive for the spatial and cultural initiatives that would be proposed for the city. Ever since his sojourn in Hangzhou between December 1953 and March 1954 for the purpose of drafting the first PRC Constitution, Mao began to fall in love with the city. From 1953 to 1975, he visited Hangzhou over forty times. A complex of villas in Hangzhou became Mao's "forbidden city" outside Beijing, and he called the city his "third home."[26] Mao's favoritism prompted Hou Bo 侯波 (1924–2017), Mao's private photographer, to jokingly suggest establishing China's second or southern capital in Hangzhou.[27]

Hangzhou's status remained high throughout the Mao era. In the early 1950s, Tan Zhenlin 谭震林 (1902–1983), chairman of Zhejiang,[28] and Wang Pingyi 王平夷 (1912–1970),[29] the chief Party leader in Hangzhou, resorted to the rhetoric of "the Geneva of the East," calling for expedited construction of facilities for tourists both from home and abroad and restoration of cultural relics. To this end, high-end hotels reserved for upper-echelon leaders and foreign guests, such as

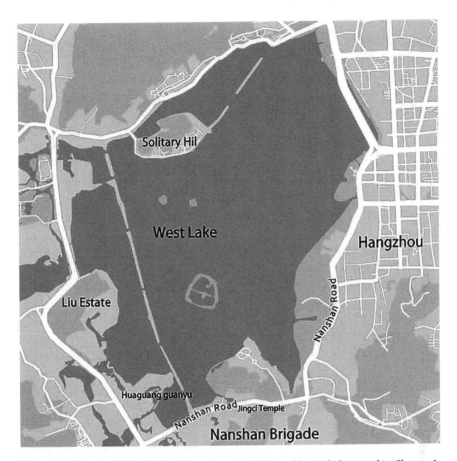

Figure 0.2. The map of West Lake. *Huagang guanyu* is the public park discussed in Chapter 2. Liu Estate or *Liuzhuang* 刘庄 was Mao's villa. The Nanshan Brigade or *Nanshan shengchan dui* 南山大队 was a model pig-breeding unit discussed in Chapter 4. Solitary Hill or *Gushan* 孤山 was the home of numerous tombs, the theme of Chapter 5.

Hangzhou Hotel (*Hangzhou fandian* 杭州饭店, established in 1956) and Liu Estate (remodeled in 1953 and 1958), mushroomed on the site of existing villas or monasteries. During the PRC's first three decades, Hangzhou hosted numerous high-profile visitors from abroad, including Chairman Kliment Voroshilov (1881–1969) of the Soviet Union, President Sukarno (1901–1970) of Indonesia, Prince Norodom Sihanouk (1922–2012) of Cambodia, and, finally, President Richard Nixon (1913–1994) of the United States. Nixon spent a night at Liu Estate on February 26, 1972, weighing words to finalize the path-breaking *Shanghai Communiqué*.[30] Hence, as a city of matchless cultural and political importance during

Mao's time, its refashioning was emblematic of the Party's initiatives to reconfigure nature and urban space in service of its political and ideological purposes.

Propaganda and the Propaganda State

Spatially (re)creating China, as Chang-tai Hung contends, played a pivotal role in popularizing the CCP's agenda of building "Mao's New World" after 1949.[31] Hence, rebuilding cities, such as Beijing, constituted a vital part of the Party's effort to make the PRC a propaganda state.[32] Admittedly, Hung gains insights from Peter Kenez as he asserts that the PRC was a more effective propaganda state than the Soviet Union.[33] In Kenez's words, the Soviet Union was a "propaganda state" because of "the extraordinarily significant role played by indoctrination in forming the state and in executing policy."[34] David Brandenberger further complicates the notion of the propaganda state by suggesting that the efficacy of propaganda be assessed from three different perspectives, "production, projection, and popular reception." For Brandenberger, the inconsistencies among the three led to the lack of efficiency in propagating the communist ideology in Stalin's Russia and ultimately undermined the working of the propaganda state.[35] Among these three dimensions, "production" has been central to the scholarly inquiry of those specializing in studies on the CCP and the PRC. For them, "propaganda," a word with negative connotations in English, was unquestioningly picked up in the context of Chinese politics and culture because *xuanchuan* 宣传, the Chinese term that is typically translated as "propaganda," denotes "propagate[ing] what one believes to be true, with overtones of propagating an orthodoxy."[36] More recently, Kirk Denton traces the origins of *xuanchuan* in China to the *Book of Songs* (*Shijing* 诗经), insofar as its poets endeavored to use "cultural texts to influence people and their ethical behavior." In light of a historical dimension, Denton argues, *xuanchuan* or propaganda has thus not been viewed as "anomalous" or "nefarious" in the PRC.[37]

Denton also detects a growing trend in the recent scholarship on Mao's China that rejects the "use of the term propaganda and instead treats Mao era texts as literature, or drama, or film, or art."[38] Denton's observation testifies to a shift from the production of the communist ideology to its circulation and reception at the grassroots level ("popular reception" in Brandenberger's schema), as scholars have increasingly found that it was impossible for the PRC regime to create and disseminate a uniform and universalizing "official" or "state" culture.[39] As Barbara Mittler cogently puts it, "[t]he question . . . appears to be less 'What does propaganda do to the people?' than 'What do people do to propaganda?'"[40] Much attention has been directed at the gulf between the norms and values propagated by the upper-echelon authorities and how the local, lower-ranking cadres and the masses selectively, inconsistently, and superficially received such messages. Here it is worth noting a critical aspect of propaganda as determined by Peter Kenez: that propaganda is not so much to convince "people to do what they did not want to do" as to define what the political system is in a communist regime.[41]

For Kenez and his like-minded scholars, propaganda is language-centric. For example, propaganda in the Soviet Union in the 1920s entailed creating a "new political language," in which it was demanded that the masses acquire fluency.[42] In other words, workers and peasants were compelled to learn the practice of "speaking Bolshevik,"[43] a language with "no native speakers."[44] Although Chang-tai Hung begins to shift away from this language-centered paradigm, he similarly points out that the "new language of revolution" in Mao-era China, including "fiery slogans, patriotic songs, and political idioms," equipped the new regime with "a potent tool with which to communicate and persuade."[45] Such a language, nevertheless, was not designed merely to communicate. Recent scholarship has indicated that the general populations of communist regimes neither blindly accepted the messages delivered through this new official language nor pretended to believe them, even "under conditions of extreme coercion."[46] This new language did not necessarily serve as a major "means of information sharing" but as a "tactic" or a "ritual of loyalty."[47] Language and reality did not need to correspond with each other. In Wang Hui's words, "What is at stake is not compliance but a willingness to comply."[48]

For all its capacity to compel individuals to swear allegiance to the authorities, propaganda in a communist regime was both repressive and productive, particularly when shaping "individuals' sense of self."[49] Xiaobing Tang shows that subscribing to the propagandistic rhetoric of the "populist identity of nation" and participating in "a collective life and national destiny" in 1960s China afforded the young generation an "artistic experience."[50] In this study, "productiveness" is given a new twist. While existing scholarship tends to view economic modernization and propaganda campaigns to "strengthen the political system" during the early years of the PRC as two competing agendas,[51] the present study seeks to unify the two by highlighting propaganda's capacity to produce something of socioeconomic usefulness—such as public works projects—on the basis of which socialist ideologies were articulated and popularized. All the projects under scrutiny here were designed to produce visible and tangible results and thereby serve the purpose of legitimating the new political system in post-Liberation China. I thus call them "propaganda-campaign projects" because, first of all, one crucial motive behind their launching was a conviction for displaying socialism's indisputable advantage over feudalist and capitalist societies. Kenneth Lieberthal finds that many campaigns mounted in the early PRC were a mere continuation of processes already underway, and the authorities purposely generated the impression that they were "more abrupt in their inception and more widespread in their impact than was actually the case." In other words, exhibiting a will to change to influence the masses' perception of the new PRC regime mattered more than what really changed at a material level.[52]

Second, local propaganda-campaign projects responded to or even prefigured political campaigns at a national level (for example, the initiative of transforming consumerist cities into productive ones, the agricultural collectivization movement, the afforestation movement, and the campaign against the "Four Olds" [sijiu 四旧]). Third, although such projects have long been dismissed for their astronomical costs, which far outweighed their benefits[53] or criticized for having led to "full-fledged disaster[s],"[54] I call attention to the fact that the benefits brought by a propaganda-campaign project were not just economic but political. Just as the political language of propaganda was not necessarily intended to convince individuals in communist regimes into blindly believing in the Party leadership but to encourage them to participate, such projects were designed not merely to accomplish economic, cultural, and ecological goals but to showcase aspects of the operation of the socialist system to the general population: the mass mobilization of labor,[55] the "labor perspective" as a means of ideological indoctrination,[56] and the state-sanctioned rhetoric of self-reliance, to name but a few. To quote Kenez again, those programs "helped to define" what socialism in China was. Hence, contrary to James Scott's observation that state-initiated projects made "the terrain, its products, and its workforce more legible" for the state,[57] propaganda-campaign projects were designed to make the Party-state's national policies legible to individuals at the local levels.

More importantly, the notion of propaganda-campaign projects sheds light on one intriguing but somewhat puzzling aspect of recent scholarship on Mao's China and beyond: the coexistence of competing narratives about the regime's accomplishments and the Party-state's failures to achieve its goals. The CCP is, on the one hand, perceived to have succeeded in establishing and sustaining a sociopolitical system via its programs of industrialization and scientific and technological advancement (even during the most tumultuous years of the Cultural Revolution [1966–1976][58]), whereas on the other hand, it is often argued that government policies were far from successfully implemented. The CCP is hailed as having organized its rank-and-file party members at the local levels to penetrate the "vast and uneven spatial expanse of China's realm" and "elicit accurate information about society beyond the centers of power."[59] Meanwhile, scholarly works have shown that local personnel tended to reinterpret, rework, deflect, and even resist the directives from above on the basis of local circumstances.[60] In the realm of the natural environment, while Jack Westboy praises the PRC for instigating the "mightiest afforestation effort the world has ever seen,"[61] other scholars emphasize the Party-state's massive destruction of forests as emblematic of its hostile attitude toward nature.[62] Likewise, Chang-tai Hung posits that the PRC created a more effective "propaganda state" than the Soviet Union.[63] Other scholars, however, offer counterexamples, indicating that the CCP fell short of building up a unified "state-created official culture"[64] or fully patronizing artists and performers in Mao's time.[65]

To reconcile those conflicting narratives, I argue that such programs were largely successful if seen through a "vertical view"—or from the angle of the upper echelons of state officials but created problems for local individuals and communities—namely those who took the "side view." In Yi-fu Tuan's analysis, the vertical view treats the landscape as "a domain" or "a work unit," available for top-down planning, but the side view "sees landscape as space in which people act."[66] Similarly, Gail Hershatter posits that post-1949 China featured two dimensions of temporality: "campaign time," from which the term "propaganda-campaign project" is partly derived, and "domestic time." While "campaign time" measured the socialist present "by state initiatives and popular participation in them,"[67] women in "domestic time" engaged in "the work of feeding, clothing, and caring for growing numbers of children." Hershatter concludes that since domestic time and campaign time were entangled in women's day-to-day life, "the official story of political change" was by no means complete.[68]

The present study conceives of the two temporalities of a given propaganda-campaign project in a slightly different light. Here, "campaign time," usually a short span of time, constituted the immediate period in which the project enacted political mobilization and secured media exposure. In the long run, however, such projects, like all infrastructure across the globe, became "flaky, falling-apart forms that constantly call[ed] out for projects of management, maintenance, and repair that challenge[d] projects of human knowledge and control."[69] This long-term, gradual, and cumbersome process—the "domestic time" of these projects experienced by local individuals—was usually not worthy of high-profile publicity and thereby slipped the propagandists' minds. It thus came as no surprise that for the planners of a propaganda-campaign project, the one-time act of construction was more appealing than the sustained efforts of upkeep that would be required thereafter, resulting in two differing readings of the same program: the propaganda apparatus boasted of the spectacular success of a project in its initiation, but the individuals living with it in their everyday lives felt more concerned about its long-term maintenance or reaped benefit from it for the "wrong" reasons. Such a disparity manifested itself more prominently in the campaigns of dredging West Lake and the afforestation initiative on its immediate shoreline. For dwellers beside the lake and in surrounding mountain forests, everyday realities were not equivalent to the state "ideology" that propaganda-campaign projects were designed to popularize.[70]

The yawning gap between the blueprints drawn up by the upper-echelon authorities and individuals' lived experiences constitutes the very essence of the present research into propaganda-campaign projects in Mao's China. On the one hand, the planning and execution of such projects not only functioned as state-led propaganda but also set up a framework within which local citizens negotiated with the state, shaped their subjectivities in socialism, and variously fell victim to or benefited from them. On the other hand, individuals at the local levels experienced and consumed the products of such projects in a different way than the political authorities had envisaged. Oftentimes, propaganda-campaign programs created a range of financial, social, and ecological problems that spelled trouble for local communities. Hence, such programs generated two different consequences or "truths": *products*—usually at high costs but with practical value—that embodied the CCP's conviction for fundamentally altering the natural and sociocultural landscape in China, and *works* or *activities,* which introduced novel experiences to local citizens but variously excited, amazed, baffled, and victimized them. In Sigrid Schmalzer's view, these two "truths"—a "rosy account" of China's socialism and a much more negative one—were mutually irreplaceable, for they stemmed from different sources and came into existence in different time periods, in the 1970s and the post-Mao era, respectively.[71] This study on propaganda-campaign projects seeks to expand upon Schmalzer's observation. I call attention to both the temporal (sources of different historical times) and the spatial (different experiences or "views"—namely, a vertical view and a side view in Yi-fu Tuan's analysis) dimensions of the production of the two "truths." In a sense, the positive evaluations of technological advancement in Mao's China conducted by American journalists, professionals, and scholars back in the 1970s themselves exemplified the efficacy of such projects as a means of propaganda that helped to legitimate this poverty-stricken and diplomatically isolated regime, both domestically and internationally.

Nature

The truth generated from the vertical "view" of the transformation of West Lake and Hangzhou was best illustrated in a 1971 news story published in the *New York Times*:

> This lovely garden city embracing the ethereal West Lake has been transformed into a major industrial complex. But Americans who visited Hangchow [Hangzhou] before the Communists took control of the China mainland in 1949 will find if they return that industrialization has not polluted what the Hangchow people call their "paradise on earth."[72]

Here, the journalist's positive assessment of the Party-state's success in both preserving West Lake as a picturesque tourist site (the "paradise on earth") and turning it into a productive industrial city, as this book shall show, was in compliance and in complicity with the CCP's propagandistic rhetoric. This idealized picture was, however, at odds with the lived experience of local cadres and residents—those taking the "side view" and having to cope with the programs over longer durations and who suffered from nagging socioeconomic and ecological issues stemming from the propaganda-campaign projects and the schema of building the city as a productive space.

By the end of the 1970s, the Hangzhou municipal government was racing to relocate over twenty heavily polluting factories from the West Lake region.[73] This dramatic turn of Party policy toward deindustrialization testifies to both the inherently contradictory agenda advanced by the municipal and provincial governments—to make the city both a productive space and a scenic destination for tourists at home and abroad—and the local government's abandonment of the Maoist rhetoric of "conquering nature." Nature in the PRC era, as numerous scholars have observed, was viewed as the foe of the socialist cause. Rhoads Murphey, for example, notes that the authorities saw nature as "an enemy" to be defied and conquered in Mao's China,[74] while Judith Shapiro argues that the PRC regime "pitted the people against the natural environment in a fierce struggle" by resorting to militarized rhetoric and through "mass mobilization in political campaigns," leading to calamitous environmental consequences.[75] Following this line of thought, recent scholarship more or less describes the human-nature relationship during Mao's time as a "war" or "conquest."[76] For Mao, the rhetoric of war was both "strategic/propagandistic" and "sociological." Its prime aim was propagandistic by nature. To be more specific, it propagated the concept of the mass mobilization of Chinese society, among other things.[77]

Mao's emphasis on the contentious human-nature relationship had its roots in the concept of the human-nature binary, which has been deeply ingrained in European thought since the Enlightenment.[78] It was during the Romantic period in Europe that the nature/humankind divide was affirmed: nature "as an external presence and power" could not shape "human destinies."[79] Such confidence gradually transmuted into a belief in the necessity of subjugating nature.[80] In this sense, Mao's war-on-nature theory was an offshoot of such conceptualization from back in the eighteenth and nineteenth centuries. Interestingly, environmental conservationists in more recent times hold a similar viewpoint. The commitment to discovering the only "correct" form of nature,[81] namely, a "naive reality"[82] or "an absolute nature" external to us, lends environmental conservationists the "moral authority."[83] For Marxists, present-day environmentalism is poised to fall short of the goal because it fails to level criticism against the capitalist mode of production, for "the degradation of the natural environment" is nothing but "a manifestation of the contradictions of capitalism."[84] Noel Castree notes that nature has been internalized in the capitalist economic system" in that "the production of nature is a continuous *process* in which nature and capital *co-constitute one another in temporally and geographically varied and contingent ways.*"[85] Hence, the rhetoric of the "conquest of nature" is thus decidedly a "specific ideology of imperialism and capitalism."[86]

Intriguingly, Karl Marx, the most outspoken critic of capitalism, has been blamed for viewing nature "as an object of labour in the production process"[87] and of taking an insufficiently critical attitude toward the destructive relationship of "industrial civilization" to the environment.[88] Marx's ambivalent attitude led to the perpetuation of the notion of "conquering nature" in socialist societies. After all, socialism, as an alternative form of modernity, shared some crucial "contradictions of modernity."[89] As Zygmunt Bauman convincingly puts it, "[W]hatever the capitalists had done to conquer nature, the socialist managers would have done or would do better" to reconfirm socialism as the ends "worthy of pursuing."[90] It is thus understandable that altering Mao-era China's natural landscape wound up being both a social movement soliciting mass participation and one of the focal points of state propaganda to publicize the advantage of socialism in post-1949 China.

Despite socialism's indebtedness to capitalism in the understanding and treatment of nature, they differ from each other in one significant aspect: while capitalism subordinates nonhuman things to the logic of the capitalist market, socialist regimes retain this approach but seek to end market-derived chaos by bringing "external" nature under complete control. Thus, the rhetoric of the "conquest of nature" in Mao-era China was an integral part of the Party-state's central planning, whose underlying assumption was the objectifiability and plannability of both disciplined human labor and docile natural elements. In reality, recent scholarship on the CCP's handling of nonhuman nature has addressed the connectedness between the PRC's planned economy and its "war on nature." For example, David Pietz coins the term "plan-*ism*"—"all projects to be approved within the structure of the five-year planning processes"—to describe the PRC authorities' management of rivers.[91] Judith Shapiro, by contrast, is more critical of the CCP's adoption of oversimplified measures without an awareness of "regional geographic variations and local practices toward nature" in her work on Mao's unsuccessful war against nature.[92]

Scholarly works that reassess the ineffectiveness of China's planned economy largely highlight the human factors: the heterogeneity of the Party members' backgrounds, motivations, and aspirations,[93] the lack of skilled personnel,[94] and the disobedience of the masses and cadres at the lower levels as I shall explain later in this chapter. What is missing here is a recognition of the role of nonhuman factors in reorienting or even derailing the central planning in Mao-era China. Rather than viewing nonhuman nature as the passive target subjected to socialist transformation, the present study underscores the role of water, microbes, silt, trees, pests, and pigs in partaking in the programs carried out by the Party-state. To rephrase Andy Bruno, nature "itself was a participant in the communist project."[95] Sometimes, those nonhuman actors were what Timothy Mitchell calls "a series of alliances" of humans.[96] On other occasions, however, they were "troublemakers"—to borrow Bruno Latour's phrase—whose recalcitrance demanded human responses and actions.[97] In other words, they possessed their own agency.

Agency

The agency of nonhuman entities has been a subject of scholarly inquiry in the past decade. Jane Bennett, for example, pledges to dispel the myth of prioritizing human agency over quasi-agency of animate and inanimate matters by highlighting "the active role of *nonhuman materials* in public life" and giving "voice to a thing-power"—that is, "the curious ability of inanimate things to animate, to act, to produce effects dramatic and subtle."[98] Bennett and her fellow scholars of the "nonhuman turn" movement blame "social constructivism for stripping the nonhuman world of agency."[99] Their critique provides an illuminating insight as I attempt to not only explore the agency of nonhuman nature but also uncover the unity in the human/nonhuman and culture/nature relationship in Mao-era China. Tina Mai Chen has pioneered exploring the melding of human and nonhuman bodies as the PRC state's strategy to "create a collective force of History."[100] My approach is quite the opposite. I examine how such unity between human and nonhuman actors posed a challenge to the state's central planning.

For this purpose, I underscore the agential power as the linkage that connects humans and nonhumans. Although Bennett has been cautious in describing the agential capacities of nonhuman things to effect sociopolitical changes by coining the term "quasi-agency," other scholars are less hesitant in articulating nonhuman agency. Bruno Latour, whose scholarship enormously inspires Bennett, has famously studied microbes' capability to "intervene and act."[101] More recently, scholars working on waters have more explicitly assigned rivers their agency. David Mosse, for example, shows how waterways elicited human response and contributed to the making of government or nongovernment institutions in South India.[102] In the context of twentieth-century China, Micah Muscolino states, "The Yellow River possessed a distinctive agency, acting unpredictably even as it was being acted upon. Humans constantly intervened to shape and reshape the river with their labor, but they never bent the river to their will."[103] A reviewer of Muscolino's book thus expresses his amazement at the author's boldness to "attribute agency to an inanimate entity," but he clearly welcomes this "new direction for historical writing."[104]

Such hesitancy necessitates further clarification of and elaboration on nonhuman agency. In his discussion of how the environment matters to politics, Nikhil Anand refuses to deem nonhumans as "a political being that is conscious and purposive."[105] One can justifiably negate nonhumans' agential power if agency is solely defined by consciousness and purposiveness. Nevertheless, Carl Knappett and Lambros Malafouris have cautioned against tying agency to "intentionality." Instead, it is vital to understand agency as "a situated process, rather than "debating what or who is or is not an agent."[106] Sean Bowden further differentiates two approaches to agency: the "voluntaristic" and the "expressive." While the former underscores intentions as primary in relation to actions, the latter refers to actions that are "primary in relation to the intentions that animate them."[107] In other words, in "expressive" agency "nonpurposive" actions predetermine, foster, and define intentions or purposes but not vice versa.[108] More often than not, the "voluntaristic" approach is more readily applicable to the descriptions of humans' agency in their defiance of, resistance to, and negotiation with power. In comparison, "expressive" best illustrates the nonhuman agency.

The voluntaristic/expressive divide should not lead to a conclusion that nonhuman agency is invariably expressive, whereas all human agency is decidedly purposive, driven by unequivocal sociopolitical agendas. The present study foregrounds expressive or nonpurposive agency as a significant way in which human and nonhuman are comparable, paralleled, and linked, and an artificial human/nonhuman binary is thereby avoided. In the context of the PRC, although studies on the peasants' and urban residents' self-activating agency to resist Party policies have been fruitful,[109] it remains problematic whether such collective or individual actions can be defined as purposive or self-conscious. As Noel Castree and Tom MacMillan cogently put it, agency is not necessarily "associated with intentionality and linguistic competence."[110] In his research into the hiding of crops, borrowing of funds, and appropriating of unregistered lands by peasant populations during the Great Leap Forward years (1958–1962), Gao Wangling 高王凌 posits that those villagers did not take action with an avowed political aim—namely, that of opposing agricultural collectivization.[111] Gao is explicit in demonstrating how the "counteractive" moves made by the peasants at the local levels led to dire political consequences—that is, the disruption of the agricultural collectivization movement in midcentury China.

The term Gao Wangling coins, *fan xingwei* 反行为 or "counteraction," is akin to the expressive approach to the Chinese villagers' agentic capacities as it does not presuppose the peasants to be a priori agents but stresses the making of their agency in the process and as a result of their actions. In Gao's analysis, those collectivized peasants tended to slack off because of their prioritization of producing sufficient grain for their own needs over that for the collectives. They did not necessarily establish their motives based on a well-thought-out agenda against the Great Leap Forward, and this tactic of survival can be dated back to the Zhou dynasty (ca. 1100 BCE–256 BCE). The peasants' ultimate goal was not to sabotage the CCP's collectivization campaign or battle the Party-state but to feed themselves without putting in extra effort. Despite this, their actions or "counteractions" proved detrimental to the very cause of the collectivization movement.[112]

While Gao Wangling's emphasis is on the expressive agency of humans, the present study underscores the agency of both humans—the dredgers of the lake, end-users of the park, pig breeders, foresters, tea growers, and pest controllers—and nonhuman entities—silt, water, microbes, aquatic vegetation, swine, tombs, pines, and insects. I argue that such expressive or nonpurposive agency is key to understanding the pitfalls that awaited the CCP's numerous propaganda-campaign projects in the West Lake region. Human actors in this book variously absconded from the worksite of the campaign to dredge West Lake, used the designed landscape to confirm their professional autonomy and find sensual pleasure, demanded private possession of pork and enlarged their privately owned plots when responding to the Party's call for breeding pigs, secretly and unlawfully expanded their tea plantations at the expense of mountain forests, stole timber and firewood from state-managed tree plantations, and worshipped beauties and heroes of imperial China. Meanwhile, the nonpurposive actions or inactions of water, microbes, trees, pests, and pigs to variously pollute the lake, infest pine plantations, and perish in collective farms constituted their "intentions," thereby attributing agency to them against human dominance.

What human and nonhuman actors did—or failed to do—simply "[got] in the way of [political] domination," to borrow Bruno Latour's words one more time.[113] They did not exercise their agency as self-conscious dissidents under socialism, but their (in)actions defined their agency as survivors, freeloaders, opportunists, and counteracting actors under this new sociopolitical system. My emphasis on such nonpurposive agency problematizes the long-held resistance-accommodation paradigm in studying the state-society relationship in the PRC, which assumes an a priori subjectivity independent of the socialist system.[114] If, as has been mentioned, the very essence of propaganda in a socialist regime was nothing but a "ritual of loyalty,"[115] in no need of responding to the realities and demanding a widespread engagement with propaganda's "constative meanings,"[116] its participants could just simply get by the sociopolitical system without taking stances as either "supporters or resisters."[117] Hence, the resistance-accommodation binary is pointless and misleading in interpreting how the propaganda-campaign projects operated at the grassroots level. In many cases, the human actors benefited from such projects. For example, the designer of the park of *Huagang guanyu* made his name known by adopting an eclectic gardening style instead of a government-sanctioned Soviet one. The visitors to the public park used the space as the locus for relaxing and poaching goldfish. Designated swine breeders received pork as rewards and opened up more private lands in the name of cultivating vegetables as pig feed. Tea growers appropriated woodlands and transformed them into tea farms. Villagers who were mobilized to catch pests on the trees focused only on moths perching on low branches but did not pursue those on the high boughs. In short, they were benefitting themselves rather than acting as opponents or resisters. Nonetheless, their personal gains decidedly hurt the Party's policies: politicizing the space of a designed landscape, the collectivization of the countryside, and the afforestation movement, respectively.

Hence, human actors' nonpurposive, self-serving actions were an outgrowth of their participation in, interaction with, and response to Party-led programs. The same thing could be said about nonhuman actors, given that the nonhuman world is notoriously chaotic and unpredictable: the levels of uncertainty increase "exponentially with elapsed time."[118] David Mosse asserts that not only are natural matters inherently uncertain, human institutions established in response to them only "contribute to or amplify this uncertainty."[119] It is thus vital to understand that the CCP's central planning was in jeopardy in no small part because of such uncertainty and unpredictability of nonhuman nature. In this book, some nonhuman actors also benefited from those propaganda-campaign projects and thereby did harm to the latter: polluting microbes proliferated because of the removal of the silt during the campaign of dredging West Lake, viruses assaulted collectivized pig farms leading to the outbreak of infectious diseases and the mass deaths of swine, and newly introduced pests multiplied quickly because of the

Party's call for expanding monoculture pine plantations in the mountains surrounding the lake. In other words, rather than viewing human and nonhuman actors as dissenters of the Party, I argue that the Party's propaganda-campaign projects were the very reason such unruly behavior became rampant and dissenting voices were generated. The Party's sociopolitical agendas wound up creating their own foes.

Hence, despite the absence of an a priori identity as the Party-state's vociferous opponents, those social and natural actors contributed to revising, reshaping, reworking, or even altering Party agendas and ruined state propaganda through their unintentional and nonpurposive "counteractions." The dredging of the lake came to a halt after six years in the mid-1950s, following the massive multiplication of algae and soaring expenses. The end product of this costly program was a body of water a few feet shallower than had been planned. The architect refused to follow the Soviet model, and the park ended up being used for sightseeing, recreation, and dating but not necessarily as a venue for political gatherings or a space to redefine work and rest in the socialist era, as the government had envisioned. Pigs languished and perished in collectivized pig farms, essentially delegitimizing the collectivization movement in the countryside; meanwhile, swine farming caused pollution and thereby ran counter to a governmental policy to make Hangzhou a tourist city. The afforestation movement not only led to the intensified struggles between foresters and tea growers but also caused the invasion of pests that proved fatal to pine trees in the West Lake region. Finally, the CCP's efforts to remove lakeside tombs and other relics were greeted with constant opposition in the 1950s and 1960s. After the Cultural Revolution, most of the burial sites were recovered.

Highlighting the nonpurposive agency of both humans and nonhumans is of special significance in conceptualizing the history of Mao's China: it helps to correct a historiographical tendency to overemphasize Mao's voluntarism (*zhuguan nengdong xing* 主观能动性, literally "subjective initiative") in transforming or subjugating inanimate parts of the world and thereby "conquering nature."[120] Liberating humankind by virtue of conquering nature had been at the heart of Mao's voluntarism—that is, social relations "were determined by the force of the individual will." As Mao emphatically pointed out, "[I]f nature has the power to determine us, we also have the power to determine nature."[121] As the entire book shall show, while human will was different from what the political authorities had expected, natural elements in West Lake proved too recalcitrant and unpredictable to be the object of subjugation.

Chapter Design

This book features five chapters. The first chapter focuses on the campaign of dredging West Lake between 1952 and 1958. This high-budget project was designed to dig the lake to a depth of two meters, with the goal of conserving water for irrigation, helping freshwater fish farming, beautifying the lake, and improving Hangzhou's weather. While the local government propagated a unilateral agenda on the benefits a deeper lake would offer and propagated the massive mobilization of labor in the midst of the campaign, the justifications of this time-consuming and costly public work proved ill-considered and pseudoscientific: the lake's water capacity was far from enough to irrigate nearby rice fields, and a still-too-shallow lake was unable to cool down its surrounding areas. More seriously, removing sediments from the lake bed released nutrients and led to the proliferation of *Dactylococcopsis*—the nonhuman beneficiary of this campaign—causing a red tide in the summer and autumn of 1958. As the recalcitrant water and rebellious microorganisms refused to cooperate, virtually all of the planners' initial justifications for dredging the lake proved untenable.

Chapter 2 investigates the first public park constructed in post-Liberation Hangzhou, *Huagang guanyu*, between 1952 and 1955. The architect, Sun Xiaoxiang 孙筱祥 (1921–2018), capitalized on the fame of *Huagang guanyu*, a long-ago perished private garden built during the Southern Song dynasty and one of the widely known "Ten Vistas of West Lake" (*Xihu shijing* 西湖十景), to proceed with this construction program. Though hailed as a masterpiece that embodied a new Soviet model, namely the "Park of Culture and Rest," the park actually diverged from this model in its style and setup. The design and construction of the park thus provide a compelling case study in which the well-entrenched professional autonomy of the architect ran counter to the planning and models of CCP cadres. Moreover, this chapter investigates how tourists and visitors benefited from the project in their diverse uses of the space, which deviated from the political/ideological motives behind its construction. Hence, this designed landscape functioned as a contested zone of differing ideologies, styles, and motivations.

The third chapter turns attention to the afforestation of the hills surrounding West Lake beginning in the early 1950s. This massive campaign served two interrelated purposes: propagandistic and ecological. In addition to "greening" the West Lake area to prevent soil erosion, the program was mounted to enact a new mode of socialist mass labor organization. The campaign bore fruit as forty square kilometers of hills were blanketed with trees by the mid-1960s but created unintended consequences: the tree plantations' vulnerability to insect infestations and the irresolvable clashes between peasant tea farmers and foresters regarding land use and ownership. Together with the project of dredging the lake, this campaign is indicative of the ironies of ecological management in post-1949 China, in which the launching of projects to resolve particular ecological problems wound up generating further and different ecological and socioeconomic impacts.

The fourth chapter continues to highlight the CCP's efforts to make West Lake a productive space, with an emphasis on pig farming in villages adjacent to West Lake in the late 1950s and early 1960s. The nationwide campaign of pig breeding was waged to both boost China's agricultural and industrial outputs and propagandistically popularize a notion of self-sufficiency in the Cold War era. Nevertheless, raising pigs, which entailed local governments reassigning private plots to pig breeders and loosening their control over the market, violated the CCP's established policy of abolishing private ownership in favor of public ownership. In addition, the high concentration of pigs in publicly owned pig pens paved the way for the outbreak of swine epidemics. In consequence, the majority of pigs in suburban Hangzhou prior to the Cultural Revolution were privately owned and reared. Hence, I argue that pigs, long trumpeted as an indispensable element of the CCP's agricultural policies, were by nature anti-socialist in the context of Mao-era China. In the West Lake region, furthermore, the campaign to encourage pig rearing was at odds with the government's agenda of preserving the city's cultural heritage because of the pollution that animal manure caused and the pig farms' usurpation of historical sites.

Chapter 5 investigates the CCP's redefinition of West Lake as a space of cultural nostalgia. Ever since the founding of the PRC, some CCP officials condemned tombs and temples beside West Lake as a reactionary feudal legacy. This controversy led to a failed attempt to move some of the graves in 1956 and culminated in the campaign to remove or relocate virtually all the ancient tombs in 1964 and 1965. Known as the "Great Cultural Cleanup," this movement retrospectively redefined the scope of "the people" in imperial China by stripping notable historical figures of their status as members of the people. The decade-long tug-of-war between radical Maoists and historical preservationists illustrated the disagreements among communist leaders on how to remember and appropriate the past and interpret its relationship with the present. More importantly, this movement revealed an inherent contradiction in a propaganda-campaign project: the difficulty in reconciling competing agendas in a single program. On the one hand, the rally for wiping out ancient burial sites foreshadowed the campaign against the "Four Olds." On the other hand, however, it was in conflict with the state's long-standing efforts to advertise the city as a location of China's enduring and splendid cultural legacy and to attach importance to West Lake as a diplomatic arena and the must-go destination for political tourism during the Cold War era. The same dilemma manifested itself in the clash between tea growers and foresters in Chapter 3, where tea cultivation and production were an integral part of the PRC's diplomatic scheme, but tree planting had long served the propaganda purpose of displaying the Party's commitment to "greening" nature.

CHAPTER ONE

Water, Labor, and Microbes
The Campaign of Dredging West Lake in the 1950s

In 1952, the Hangzhou municipal government launched an ambitious project with a whopping investment of 4,538,300 yuan to dredge West Lake. By 1958, the lake's water depth increased from about 0.55 to 1.80 meters, enhancing its water storage from three million to over ten million cubic meters. The CCP authorities hail this campaign as the most extensive dredging project in West Lake's history. Between the Tang dynasty (618–907) and the Qing dynasty, local governments carried out over twenty major dredging and hydraulic projects. Historically, the most prolonged interval between two projects was 168 years.[1] About 150 years had passed between 1800 when the Qing's provincial governor mounted a campaign to dig West Lake and the CCP's takeover of Hangzhou.[2] During the first half of the twentieth century, the lake was notoriously running dry. Japanese writer Akutagawa Ryūnosuke 芥川龍之介 (1892–1927), for example, noticed in 1921 that West Lake was so shallow that it looked more like a piece of wet field than a lake.[3] Therefore, the time was ripe for funding another large-scale project, mainly because of the state's commitment to investing heavily in Hangzhou, the "paradise on earth" and a city designed for "recreation, tourism, and cultural activities."[4]

Large-scale hydrological works in twentieth-century China have provided fertile soil for scholarly inquiries into the relationship between the state and local communities. David Pietz, for example, highlights the role of the Yellow River project in Mao-era China in constructing "a nation" and "a national identity."[5] Liu Yanwen 刘彦文 explores the state's intervention in local society through a water conservancy project in 1950s China.[6] Chris Courtney's case study on water control in 1954 shows that the Maoist state's effective response to the flood allowed it to legitimize the newly established PRC.[7] Indeed, the 1954 war against the flood, just like the dredging of West Lake, was propagandistic by nature, for the new socialist regime could claim a victory over not only water but also "history."[8] As a similar propaganda project, the dredging of West Lake in the 1950s was a combination of a success story and unintended and undesired consequences. It was a success story because the program was the first massive dredging project in

Hangzhou in over one century and a half. By 1958, this high-budget project planned and carried out by the Hangzhou municipal government attained some of its goals: a greater depth of water and enhanced water storage. Hence, the CCP authorities hailed the campaign between 1952 and 1958 as the vastest dredging project in West Lake's history, evidencing the CCP's "unprecedented capacity" to generate "acute transformations of the landscape."[9]

I consider the project of dredging West Lake as a part of state propaganda because, first of all, the motive behind its launching was to publicize a conviction of socialism's advantage over the defunct feudalist and capitalist societies (or "old China"). From the viewpoint of the project's planners, a silted and shallow lake with turbid water was a manifestation of chaotic, war-scarred China before 1949.[10] Therefore, when Yu Senwen 余森文 (1904–1992), director of the Hangzhou Bureau of Urban Construction (*Hangzhou chengshi Jianshe ju* 杭州城市建设局) and the mastermind behind this campaign, initially formulated a proposal, he gave numerous rationalizations, including bettering water quality and augmenting the lake's water storage. They all served the propaganda purpose of offering a marked contrast between West Lake (and, by extension, China) before and after the Liberation.[11] Second, running the project showcased how the socialist system operated for the general population. Yu Senwen recalled that over thirty thousand workers were mobilized to take part in this project in six years,[12] boasting a unique labor organization in socialist China. Throughout the 1950s, in actuality, news stories abounded regarding the participation of students, workers, and ordinary citizens in "voluntary labor" (*yiwu laodong* 义务劳动)—or work without pay—to make their contribution to the dredging project.[13] Such a massive mobilization of labor or "mass effort," according to Miriam Gross, functioned as a "coercive strategy" to prompt "nominal compliance."[14] In this sense, this dredging campaign was intended to not only cure the silted lake but also accomplish the goal of ideological indoctrination—that is, propaganda.

Meanwhile, the campaign of dredging this waterbody was by no means a well-planned and well-devised project. This chapter shall show that advocates of the project of dredging West Lake, mainly CCP leaders at municipal and provincial levels, imposed their will, based more on whim than thorough investigation and in-depth research. After six long years, virtually every rationale of digging the lake deeper initially proposed by planners in 1952 proved untenable. The project not only turned out to be a monster that ate up about 40 percent of the budget for landscaping in Hangzhou in the 1950s but also led to ecological consequences that kept baffling observers and researchers for many years to follow. In 1958, the same year when the dredging project finally came to a halt, the lake's water turned reddish and brownish. No consensus was reached regarding the reasons behind such an unexpected change in water quality in West Lake. A variety of biological and chemical methods were employed to purify the water, but researchers remained unknowledgeable about the causes of and the solutions to this "red tide."

The second half of this chapter thus focuses on the capacity of nonhuman things—water, mud, vegetation, and microbes—in the lake to undermine the CCP government's grand scheme of taming West Lake. The counteractions taken by nonhuman actors were decidedly "nonpurposive," a defining characteristic of the nonhuman, "expressivist" agency.[15] To put it another way, although water, silt, and microorganisms did not harbor an intention to go against the local cadres' plan to remold the lake, their very actions (turning the water reddish and brownish and the proliferation of pollutants) defined their intentions. Such action-qua-intention is close to Bruno Latour's definition of "recalcitrance": "As what suspends mastery, as what gets in the way of domination, [and] as what interrupts the closure and the composition of the collective."[16]

West Lake's recalcitrance in the 1950s was also an outgrowth of the technological modernization of the day. Although the state propaganda apparatus had attached great importance to voluntary labor as a primary means of mobilizing the masses, volunteers not only were notorious for their low efficiency and lack of work skills but also failed to constitute the majority of the labor force on the spot. The glorified story of young men's and women's voluntarism and self-sacrifice masked the fact that most workers were disgruntled salaried coolies from the countryside and forced laborers. In the final two years, it was the most up-to-date machinery that saved the day: it unearthed over 75 percent of sediments in a relatively short period. As Miriam Gross notes, it was the modern science and technology and well-trained professionals that did the work, although Maoists tended to highlight mass mobilization and mass science as the key to the success of socialism.[17]

The heavy reliance on modern machinery, according to David Pietz, testifies to the CCP's success in creating a "technological complex" that decidedly departed from the traditional hydrological patterns.[18] The most significant difference between methods of dredging West Lake in pre- and post-1949 was not necessarily machinery-enabled work efficiency but the new way of disposing of sediment. A recent study shows that in imperial times, the removed silt was usually reused to build dykes, allowing microbes originally from the lake bed—particularly those killing algae—to stay in the lake. In the dredging projects after 1949, including the 1950s one, the excavated sediment was quickly shipped to lakeside areas, leading to the extermination of microorganisms that had for centuries functioned to maintain the ecological balance in the water.[19] In this case, when the cutting-edge technology resolved existing problems, it ironically created new, unique ecological problems.

The Campaign of Dredging West Lake, 1952–1958

Trumpeting the dredging of West Lake in the 1950s as the first large-scale project in centuries was intended to provide a sharp contrast between the Republican government's inaction and the communist regime's activism in improving the environment and people's livelihood. The pre-1949 Hangzhou municipal governments, nevertheless, did make some efforts to refashion the lake. In 1928 when the Republican government made preparations for the West Lake Expo (*Xihu bolanhui* 西湖博览会, 1929), for example, lakeside embankments were constructed or repaired in numerous locations.[20] The length of such embankments amounted to 30 percent of the lake's total perimeter.[21]

Aside from repairing embankments, unfortunately, the Republican government failed to fund a full-scale project of dredging the lake. Artist Lin Fengmian 林风眠 (1900–1991) later recalled that it had been a long time without rain when the West Lake Expo opened in 1929. Therefore, the lake's water was shallow, and its lake bed became visible. In 1932, Lin, working in Hangzhou, witnessed hundreds of laborers either operating a dredging machine to dig the sediment or manually removing weeds on the lake.[22] Even such a feeble endeavor did not last long because of Japan's invasion in 1937. During postwar times, the Hangzhou government again cried for a vigorous campaign to remove the lake's silt but lamented that it lacked the necessary financial capability to fulfill the task. Between 1945 and 1949, as a result, the government managed to clear only 10,232 cubic meters of sediment from the lake bed.[23]

The Planning

The Republican government's lack of an all-out project was thus advertised as the epitome of the total failure of the "old society" (*jiu shehui* 旧社会), as opposed to the vibrant "new society" (*xin shehui* 新社会) after 1949. Therefore, the advocates of dredging West Lake had every reason to lobby for a massive campaign to display the superiority of the communist regime. It happened that the winter of 1950 was exceptionally arid, drying up most parts of West Lake. Under those circumstances, Tan Zhenlin, Party secretary of Zhejiang Province, consulted with Chen Yi 陈毅 (1901–1972), mayor of Shanghai, to explore the possibility of transforming and beautifying West Lake for tourist purposes. As Tan was unwilling to rely solely on manual labor, Chen agreed to offer financial and technological support. In early 1951, Yu Senwen accompanied Tan to visit Shanghai for the second time and struck a deal whereby Shanghai would fund and make three dredger ships.[24]

Meanwhile, the project also drew enormous funds from the central government. In 1951, Beijing allocated Hangzhou 15 billion (equivalent to 1.5 million after 1955) yuan, a big chunk of which was used to dig West Lake. One year later, the central government made a supplementary budget of 7.5 billion (equivalent to 0.75 million) for Hangzhou to purchase necessary machinery and equipment. By 1958 when the project was brought to an end, the total investment had reached 4,538,300 yuan,[25] making up about 40 percent of all funds (11,623,000 yuan) allocated by governments at both central and provincial/municipal levels for landscaping projects in Hangzhou since 1949[26] or about 2.4 percent of Zhejiang's overall infrastructure investment between 1953 and 1957 (the PRC's first Five-Year Plan).[27]

Nevertheless, the generous budgeting was not based on precise calculation. Virtually every year, the Hangzhou Bureau of Gardening Administration (*Hangzhou yuanlin guanli ju* 杭州园林管理局) attempted to divert some unused funds to other purposes. In 1956, for example, Yu Senwen was notified that 120,000 yuan from the fund for dredging West Lake was saved during that fiscal year. As a consequence, 70,000 would be transferred to a budgetary account for landscaping projects in the following year.[28] Understandably, the enormous budget of this project overwhelmed some prudent officials. A cadre from the Hangzhou Bureau of Urban Construction commented before the budget was approved, "The project of dredging West Lake entails a substantial investment. It is vital to . . . come up with a complete design and draw up [a reasonable] budget."[29] In 1955, the municipal government began to feel the pressure of exorbitant expenditure incurred by this unending dredging project and thus demanded the work teams to "diminish the scale of the project and lengthen its construction period."[30]

This project's expiration year had been set as 1957 in the proposal penned by Yu Senwen and his company back in 1952. In this document, the authors specified multiple rationalities behind funding such a time-consuming and high-cost campaign, all of which would be repeatedly cited as the justification. First, the lake had not been dredged for three centuries since the early Qing.[31] This was undoubtedly a misleading statement since the last time a large-scale project was carried out to remove silt was in 1800.[32] The longtime neglect of the lake led to the heavy deposition of sludge. The shallowest water depth of West Lake was about fifty centimeters. A deep lake and higher water quality could conceivably improve Hangzhou citizens' living conditions and restore the natural beauty of the West Lake area.[33] When the proposal's drafters were motivated to contrast the sordid lake water before 1949 with the perceived cleaner one after the dredging to glorify the communist polity, they were delusional: the lake water's turbidity would worsen because of the enhanced water depth.

Second, the lake water could be used to scour numerous waterways inside the city of Hangzhou, many of which had long been stagnant waters. Hence, a West

Lake with a larger volume of water would certainly contribute to the city's public hygiene. Third, about 100,000 *mu* (approximately 16,473.69 acres) of rice fields in counties north of Hangzhou awaited irrigation by West Lake's water. Therefore, the writers concluded that the lake was far from a mere tourist site but a productive instrument. Finally, the city dwellers would benefit from a better-regulated climate because of the lake's greater water capacity. Thus, the proposal suggested that the lake be dug two meters deeper in five years.[34]

To fulfill the goal, the planners estimated that about 6,330,000 cubic meters of sediment would be removed from the lake bed. In early 1952, when the proposal was finalized, the dredging team was equipped with nothing but one eighty-horsepower ladder dredger, with which only twenty-two thousand cubic meters of silt was dug in two months. Although the drafters emphasized that the two months was a trial period, paving the way for a campaign with a greater magnitude in the future, it goes without saying that the lack of technology was posing a major obstacle to completing the task in time. Hence, bucket chain excavators (*benni ji* 畚泥机) were particularly recommended as the most efficient machinery in places like West Lake, where the lake bed was relatively flat, and the silt was soft. Given an eighty-horsepower bucket chain excavator's capacity to remove seven hundred cubic meters of mud per day, the writers demanded five.[35]

Other thorny problems included the lakeside locations for the excavated silt and the means of transportation. The drafters proposed a number of sites (their total area amounting to 9,450 *mu* or 1,556.76 acres) within the confines of Hangzhou, big enough for over six million cubic meters of earth. Considering the mud to be excavated was soft and wet, requiring days of air drying, hardening, and

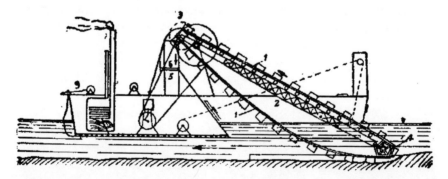

Figure 1.1. The "bucket chain excavators" or *benni ji* 畚泥机, which had been extensively used in China before 1949, were also adopted by the dredgers during the early stage of the program of dredging West Lake. *Reprinted from Wang Shoubao* 王寿宝, Shuili gongcheng 水利工程 *(Hydraulic engineering) (Shanghai: Shangwu yinshuguan, 1940), p. 49.*

piling up, it was also necessary to come up with a solution to transport the silt elsewhere. The writers reasoned that West Lake was close to the Qiangtang River (*Qiantang jiang* 钱塘江). As its water flow velocity during a severe drought season was 21.62 cubic meters per second, the river could flush ten thousand cubic meters of mud into the ocean without clogging its riverbed. Hence, steel pipes connecting the lake and the river were also requested in the proposal.[36]

The Laborers

What the 1952 document failed to mention was the organization of participants—laborers and cadres—to carry out this high-budget project. Labor was in heavy demand throughout the six years, but it was particularly the case in the first stage—between 1952 and late 1953—because only one eighty-horsepower ladder dredger was in use. It was laborers—both paid and unpaid—who manually carried silt on their shoulders from the lake to the shores. Heavy reliance on manual labor caused extremely low efficiency: only 141,900 cubic meters of sludge—or 1.7 percent of the total amount in this project—was removed in a time span of almost two years.[37] Efficiency would rise later with the arrival of a variety of mechanized equipment.

The municipal government drew labor from three chief sources: unemployed or out-of-school Hangzhou citizens, peasants from nearby counties, and prisoners. The mobilization of urban laborers has long been hailed as the new communist regime's major achievement to not only transform nature but also stabilize society in the city. It was later remembered that about eight hundred unemployed workers or students were hired initially in 1952 to jumpstart the project. Those laborers received payments not in cash but in kind. The Hangzhou government, therefore, did not view their recruitment as employment but as a way of relief—or "work in exchange for relief" (*yigong daizhen* 以工代赈).[38]

Hangzhou's local history shows that 1,150 factories, half of which were silk weaving mills, and 548 commercial enterprises in town were out of business in early 1950, leaving fifteen thousand people out of work. Three months later, when the government banned entertainment sites deemed to be "detrimental to social morals" (*youshang shehui fenghua* 有伤社会风化), more city dwellers lost their jobs. By May 1950, the population of the unemployed or semi-unemployed reached 21,000. The ensuing "Three-Anti" (*Sanfan* 三反) and "Five-Anti" (*Wufan* 五反) movements suppressed capitalists in Hangzhou, led to the closure of more businesses, and accordingly dealt a heavy blow to the already slumped job market. Consequently, another 9,686 registered themselves as jobless. In late 1952, when the project of dredging West Lake was underway, a new survey was conducted, revealing that 24,687 citizens were registered as unemployed workers, while 24,052 were out-of-school students or housewives who were hunting for jobs.[39] Looking back at the employment situation in 1949 in Hangzhou, the unemployment rate was astonishingly high: 28,000 workers in 1,786 factories and 43,189 urban dwellers involved in the business.[40]

To cope with several waves of unemployment in the opening years of the PRC, the local governments determined to develop the program of "work in exchange for relief" to keep the unemployed at work and avoid social unrest temporarily. Initially, a worker was entitled to obtain one and a half or two kilograms (kg) of rice for working eight hours a day.[41] Later, the payment was made "by the piece" (*jijian* 计件) produced by workers, who ended up acquiring up to 120 kilograms of rice and extra cash per month. The movement of "work in exchange for relief" officially kicked off in 1950. The population of its participants quickly swelled to over four thousand in a few months. By 1953, the number of participants diminished to about two thousand. With the recovery of Hangzhou's economy in 1954, "working in exchange for relief" was brought to a close after over 1,700 participants landed jobs elsewhere.[42]

In reality, the project of dredging West Lake was by no means the major employer of laborers participating in "working in exchange for relief." Most of those workers participated in projects of opening up a number of major thoroughfares in the city.[43] Aside from road constructions, the city's airport, highways, railway station, and industrial sectors also absorbed a vast number of workers who received payments in rice.[44] Although the *Gazetteer of Hangzhou* (*Hangzhou shi zhi* 杭州市志) indicates that the number of participants was only 1,100 when the work team was initially assembled,[45] the existing archival record shows that the population of those workers could well have exceeded four thousand in June 1950. Interestingly, the project of dredging the lake does not find mention in the gazetteer as an employer,[46] contradicting a long-held belief that workers in the "working in exchange for relief" program constituted the mainstay of the labor force in transforming West Lake. More importantly, Hangzhou citizens who did work for the project were by no means dependable laborers. A report filed on February 21, 1956, finds that Hangzhou's "resident-laborers" (*jumin gong* 居民工) usually soon found jobs or returned to school and thereby left the West Lake worksite.[47]

The same report was also critical of the half-hearted effort of peasants from neighboring counties. After the Spring Festival (Chinese New Year) of 1956, 2,070 peasants reportedly came back to the worksite. The leadership of the work teams felt annoyed to find that many of those peasants were reluctant to return on time after a New Year's break or pressed for unrealistic demands. The shaky morale evidently cut down work efficiency. The report concluded, "There is a wide difference between the volume of excavated earth [completed by] peasants in the suburbs and the preset target." Such low efficiency also stemmed from an insufficient workforce. The reporter discovered a wide gap between the targeted number of peasant-workers and the actual population of participants. The West Lake District Brigade (*Xihu qu dadui* 西湖区大队), for example, was demanded to dispatch eight hundred laborers in 1956, but 630 were registered. To make matters worse, only 423 were present on the worksite. Moreover, county- or village-level leaders seemed indifferent to this project. Only three lower-ranking cadres were sent to the worksite to lead and coordinate with over two thousand peasant-laborers. Even worse, some cadres from the suburbs were arrested and charged with corruption.[48]

Despite resentments and conflicts revealed in the report, the local newspaper, *Hangzhou Daily* (*Hangzhou ribao* 杭州日报), took pride in the municipal government's ability to mobilize over seven thousand laborers to restart the dredging project on January 14, 1956.[49] In this sense, the dredging project was propagandistic by nature because it was consistent with a long-standing agenda of the CCP that associated labor organization with the legitimacy of its regime.[50] Among seven thousand participants, Hangzhou citizens and peasants constituted slightly over half of the labor force, but project leaders clearly showed no confidence in them. As the February 21 report pessimistically prognosticated, students would return to school, while the majority of peasants would go back to the countryside to farm between late February and early March.[51] The most reliable source of labor supply was, ironically, about three thousand prisoners, many of whom turned out to be "counterrevolutionaries" (*fan gemin* 反革命) and other political prisoners.[52]

Though outnumbering Hangzhou's citizens as well as peasants, prisoner-laborers were notorious for their extremely low efficiency. A report filed in April 1956 found that a prisoner-laborer was able to excavate on average 0.96 cubic meters of earth per day, about 50 percent lower than a laborer of other teams.[53] In reality, this low efficiency was a marked improvement from that in February (0.47 cubic meters per person a day).[54] Such inefficiency resulted from, first of all, many prisoners' unwillingness to admit their "crimes," resulting in their uncooperativeness. Second, the working conditions were dreadful. Their lack of work experience, inadequate tools and equipment, and severely cold weather overwhelmed most prisoner-laborers. Many were convinced that they were about to "die in three ways"—namely, freezing to death, dying of overloading, and dying of starvation. Such a stifling atmosphere led many to abscond or commit suicide. A survey conducted in a work group showed that fifteen out of two hundred had attempted escape. Although the report admitted that six died or disappeared between February and April 1956, the prisoner-laborers' team downsized significantly in merely two months.[55] In the February report, the number of prisoner-laborers amounted to 2,950,[56] while the population was reduced to 2,426 in the April report.[57]

Third, prison officers were psychologically unprepared for this strenuous project. Many cadres preferred staying in detention centers to working in West Lake. In consequence, when the prisoners had already gathered, few officers showed up. Some cadres felt unsettled because of their personal issues. For example, some jailers felt shocked to find that their permanent household registry or *hukou* 户口 had been transferred—against their will—to remote provinces, such as Inner Mongolia and Heilongjiang. Most jailers were reportedly irresponsible and indifferent, allowing the prisoner-laborers to flee the worksite. They counted on the police to capture those runaway laborers. Their negligence raised the human cost of the project, as police stations nearby had to send additional police officers to supervise the laborers day in and day out. Some prison officers reportedly behaved weirdly on the worksite: some cruelly tortured the prisoners, and others were so nice that they bought the prisoner-laborers gifts and mailed letters for them. Those jailors, none of whom were strict disciplinarians, according to the report, contributed to utter confusion and sinking morale among the laborers and cadres on the worksite.[58]

To find a solution to complementing a highly unstable and poorly motivated labor force, the political authorities resorted to a familiar scheme of mass mobilization. Young workers, government functionaries, and students were asked to perform "voluntary labor" without pay. A massive campaign of "voluntary labor" was mounted on November 5, 1955, in part because of a severe drought starting in the summer of that year and the subsequent irrigation of nearby rice fields that depleted most of the lake's water. As a result, the exposed lake bed provided a favorable opportunity for earth excavation. According to *Hangzhou Daily,* young men and women in Hangzhou during this dry spell "requested the municipal committee of the Youth League [in Hangzhou to permit them to] participate in the project of dredging the lake."[59] Five days later, this daily newspaper further confirmed that over twenty-five thousand young people had applied.[60]

But only a tiny fraction of them earned the chance to attend the inaugurating ceremony of voluntary labor in West Lake on November 5, 1955. The attendees included five hundred students from a business college and thousands of representatives of schools, government offices, the army, and the police in Hangzhou. The digging work that followed the ceremony reportedly lasted for two and a half hours, removing 249.5 cubic meters of silt from the lake bed.[61] Despite the young people's avowed passion for making their contribution, their productivity was disappointingly low. Their work efficiency was equivalent to 0.8 to 1.0 cubic meters per person a day (eight to ten hours) at the maximum, equivalent to that of a poorly motivated prisoner-laborer.

The use of voluntary laborers was systemized since then. On January 29, 1956, for example, the government once again mobilized about four thousand young men and women, including government functionaries, to clean up a lakeside area and dig the lake bed. It was reported that 1,500 cubic meters of silt were excavated within one day.[62] Volunteer laborers were also recruited in many other projects. In most cases, those participants were mainly government and state-owned factory employees. A report on the filling and leveling up of two rivers in Hangzhou indicated that, thanks to the volunteers' efforts, the project was expected to be completed ahead of schedule.[63]

The use of labor during this dredging project was complex. The extensive coverage of "work in exchange for relief" and the rhetoric of voluntary labor, without a doubt, served the purpose of ideological indoctrination or state propaganda. That is, only the socialist state was willing to look after the unemployed, and only under socialism were the ordinary people filled with passion for participating in the campaign of overcoming nature. While the media coverage of "work in exchange for relief" and voluntary labor familiarized Hangzhou citizens with the mechanism of mass mobilization in a socialist society, it also covered up an untold story about the use of prisoners or "counterrevolutionaries," who actually constituted the majority of the labor force. What the Hangzhou-based newspapers refused to admit was that forced laborers, their supervisors, and peasants recruited from adjacent villages were among disgruntled participants of this major hydraulic work. They did not directly challenge the authorities but exercised their agency by adopting varied strategies: prisoner-laborers tried to abscond, the jailors took a laissez-faire approach, and villagers refused to show up. Their actions or the lack thereof led to harmful consequences for this dredging project, namely, low efficiency and a colossal waste of time and investment.

The Mechanization of the Dredging Project

An unstable and poorly coordinated labor force consisting of Hangzhou citizens, suburban peasants, prisoners, and inexperienced and incompetent volunteers proved counterproductive. In hindsight, the whole project of dredging West Lake could roughly be periodized into three stages. During the first stage, between 1952 and late 1953, the work team that counted almost exclusively on manual labor—except for a small, eighty-horsepower dredger ship—excavated only 1.7 percent of the total amount of earth. In the second period (between early 1954 and late 1955), the team was equipped with two elevator-ladder dredgers and numerous steamboats, significantly speeding up the project. By the end of 1955, 1,595,700 cubic meters (or 22.15 percent of the total amount) of sediment was unearthed.[64]

It was during the final stage (from early 1956 to late 1957) that the remaining 62.77 percent of silt was removed.[65] Undoubtedly, the addition of better machinery was a decisive factor. In a two-year plan (1956–1957) drawn up in late 1955, the authors demanded extra funding of about 1.66 million yuan for purchasing a suction dredging boat, an electric ladder dredging boat, three tugboats, eight wooden barges, an electric power station, two boost pumps, and 1,800 meters of steel pipes for discharging silt, among other things. The investment also included fees to train operators and technicians.[66] Nevertheless, the deployment of mechanized and electric equipment brought about new issues and concerns. The annual maintenance fee, it was later estimated, amounted to about 0.7 or 0.8 million yuan, a prohibitively high cost for the Hangzhou Bureau of Gardening Administration. When the municipal government decided to put an end to the dredging project in 1958, dismounting and transporting all those boats and machines was not only expensive but also time-consuming. It took about three to four months before all pieces were shipped away from West Lake. Furthermore, not only laborers but also technicians had to be dismissed or reassigned to new positions.[67] Ecologically, the mechanized dredging indiscriminately removed all microbes. As I shall show later in this chapter, some water-purifying microorganisms were lost, leading to the proliferation of water-polluting algae before this project came to an end.

The Issue of Disposing of Unearthed Earth

Despite the problems created by the mechanized and electric equipment, advanced technology proved to be the key to speeding up the dredging project. By comparison, discharging excavated earth presented an even thornier problem that entailed coordination between technology and humans and among various institutions. As noted above, the planners had envisioned two approaches to disposing of excavated earth: piling it up in open spaces or flushing it into the Qiantang River. Technologically, discharging silt required more robust suction dredging equipment, given that the designated sites for piling up earth were usually located in farther away places than the distance an ordinary suction dredger could deliver. Despite this, West Lake had two advantages: First, its water contained rich organic matter and was therefore low in density. Second, the lake was actually higher than the fields on its shores. Thus, engineers devised a plan to connect two suction dredgers to excavate silt and use boost pumps to catapult them onto the shores via enlarged steel pipes (whose perimeter was widened from three hundred millimeters to five hundred millimeters).[68]

An even more complicated issue was the sites for banking up excavated earth. The aforesaid 1952 report designated a number of locations, mostly in places north and west of the lake, to meet the needs. Its writers had absolute confidence in acquiring 9,450 *mu* or 1,556.76 acres of land within the confines of Hangzhou for that purpose.[69] In 1955, a new report was filed, admitting that the initial plan had overestimated the capacity of those designated locations. It suggested that new sites be found. At that point (1955), the work team counted heavily on lands or marshes in the Western Mountain District (*Xishan qu* 西山区)—the area west of West Lake—to dispose of excavated earth, temporarily or permanently. It was planned that 430 *mu* (or 70.83 acres) and 350 *mu* (57.66 acres) of land would be requisitioned in 1956 and 1957, respectively, for about 250 cubic meters of earth. Considering that most lands were rice fields or fishponds, the writers suggested two approaches:

> For farming lands and fishponds that are pivotal to "greening" (*lühua* 绿化) West Lake but do not significantly affect the peasants' livelihoods, they shall be requisitioned. After their lands are taken over, the peasants shall receive compensation. Those peasants who can no longer farm in the Western [Mountain] District, [the government] shall relocate them to the suburbs or other counties to [resume] their production works.
>
> [The government] shall rent most farming lands and pay [the peasants] rents. After the completion of disposing of silt, lands shall be returned to peasants.[70]

The requisitioning of arable lands became a source of bitter resentment among the peasants. In 1956, writer Chen Xuezhao 陈学昭 (1906–1991) heard the villagers complain that the lands remained unused and became waste long after they were requisitioned.[71] Another vital way was to deliver excavated earth to locations in neighboring counties. It was then widely believed that sediments dug from the bottom of West Lake were exceedingly fertile. The farms in Xiaoshan 萧山, for example, reported that jute nurtured by West Lake's silt was bigger in size and taller in height by one-third. Such a belief generated growing demands for the silt from West Lake in the mid-1950s. In light of this, a special institution—The Working Committee for Delivering Silt (*Yunni gongzuo weiyuanhui* 运泥工作委员会)—was established. The committee's report in April 1956 showed that 171,752 tons of silt had been shipped from West Lake in about five months. The primary recipients were farms in Hangxian 杭县, Xiaoshan, Jinhua 金华, Hangzhou's suburban areas, and some "reform-through-labor" farms (*laogai nongchang* 劳改农场). The recipients resorted to a wide range of means of transportation, including man-powered boats, sailing vessels, barges, steamships, trucks, and man-powered flatbed trailers.[72]

The rising demands for silt, nevertheless, also caused great confusion and an enormous waste of money and manpower. To satisfy the demands from the Xiaoshan-based farms, for example, the committee hired laborers to construct a mudflat in Changqiao 长桥 in the southeastern part of West Lake. It had been agreed that peasants from various farms would constitute the mainstay of the labor force, but, unexpectedly, those peasants were unwilling to show up before March 1956. Consequently, the committee had to meet the expenditure of 40,392 person-days (*gong* 工). By comparison, the receiving farms only contributed 4,213 person-days. By March 1956, the committee abandoned the mudflat in Changqiao to lower its operation cost. Unexpectedly, however, the farms from Xiaoshan dramatically increased their order of silt by seven times. In a rush, the committee instructed the farm leaders to obtain mud directly from West Lake.[73]

Another report penned by the same committee found that the committee and the Xiaoshan-based farms should share blame for confusion and waste. To construct the mudflat in Changqiao, for example, the committee initially expended 31,865 yuan but later approved a supplementary budget of over ten thousand yuan because of the rising demand for silt transportation and additional costs for constructing a dockyard and drainage facilities. As noted earlier, the mudflat and its dockyard were in use for only three months. Meanwhile, Xiaoshan's farms booked much more silt than previously agreed upon. This report showed that those farms had asked for only 30,000 tons in winter 1955, but the tonnage swelled to 339,000 in January 1956. Without adequate transportation and a sizable labor force in Hangzhou, the committee hastily struck a deal with those farms. When peasants from those farms were mobilized and headed for Hangzhou, they only found that the committee was totally unprepared to honor the promise.[74]

The committee later admitted that it had erred on numerous occasions within several months of its existence. First, as mentioned above, its poor planning led to a colossal waste of investment and labor. Second, laborers in Hangzhou were not fully motivated. The committee was unable to instill the idea of "constructing socialism" in them, nor could it adhere to the principle of "more pay for more work" (*duolao duode* 多劳多得). In other words, those workers received neither ideological indoctrination nor monetary incentives. Third, the committee lacked the ability to conduct scientific investigations and thereby devise feasible plans. The Xiaoshan-based farms, for example, ended up receiving over twenty-two thousand tons of silt more than they had requested, whereas the Hangxian-based farms were delivered forty thousand tons less. Ironically, the shipping cost to Hangxian was considerably lower than to Xiaoshan. The committee thereby suffered a substantial financial loss. Moreover, some plans were impractical. When various farms complained that the amount of silt (100,000 tons) delivered based on the first planning was too small, the committee promised, without proper consideration, to ship 595,000 tons in five months in the second planning. As a matter of fact, the committee soon found that transporting such an immense quantity of earth might require more than ten months. Lastly, the report lamented that the committee was understaffed and in dire need of knowledgeable specialists.[75]

The nagging issue of the unearthed silt was indicative of both the local cadres' poorly thought-out plans and the agency of mud, namely, its capacity to "impede or block the will and designs of humans" to borrow Jane Bennett's phrase.[76] Excavated earth required CCP officials to respond to its very existence and, from time to time, alter the latter's planning as necessary. The local government's plans were poorly formulated in the first place, while it soon found itself in a hard-pressed position by giving unsatisfactory responses. Hence, unexcavated earth pitted the ambitious local government against the disgruntled peasants whose lands had been requisitioned, led to the waste of monetary investments and manpower, and created managerial confusion. Ultimately, the planners and decision-makers had to constantly reformulate plans and seek new locations in line with the ever-growing amount of silt.

Recalcitrant Nature

The 1955 Drought

The issue of unexcavated earth loomed large in 1956 chiefly because the year proved to be the busiest and most productive. The municipal government both assembled a new dredger team[77] and mobilized thousands of volunteers that year. As noted above, the dried-up lake and the bare lake bed caused by a severe drought prompted Hangzhou's young workers, staff members, and students to voluntarily participate in this campaign. The existing meteorological record, however, indicates that 1955 was by no means the driest year during the 1950s. The *Gazetteer of Hangzhou* compiled in the late 1990s shows that Hangzhou underwent severe and prolonged droughts in 1953 and 1957–1958.[78] In Hangzhou's neighboring counties, such as Lin'an 临安, Yuhang 余杭, and Fuyang 富阳, the lack of rainfall reportedly dealt a blow to agricultural production in 1955. But there was no record of drought in Hangzhou proper.[79]

Although arid weather was not the deciding factor behind the lake's substantial loss of water, the drought experienced by the peasants in counties surrounding Hangzhou did contribute to the depletion of the lake's water. The archival record reveals that the authorities in Hangzhou had consistently come under pressure to release the water from West Lake to irrigate about 100,000 *mu* (16,473.69 acres) of rice fields across the outskirts of the city and in Hangxian. In the relatively dry summer and autumn of 1955, a resounding call for using West Lake's water to ensure a harvest—one of the justifications for launching the dredging project proposed in 1952—finally compelled the municipal government to draw off the lake water. It quickly proved a terrible blunder. In the autumn and winter of 1955, as mentioned above, the lake temporarily lost a considerable portion of its water storage, and most of its lake bed was thus exposed.[80]

Watering rice fields turned out not to be the only reason behind the lake's sudden water shortage in 1955. In the same year, alkalinization occurred in various Hangzhou waterworks. It was later remembered that dry weather lowered the freshwater level, allowing saltwater from the ocean to flow backward. In consequence, West Lake also served as a source of water for the waterworks. In hindsight, it was confirmed that the demand from the waterworks, the need to irrigate rice fields, and the loss of water amid the dredging project collectively contributed to West Lake's embarrassing drying up.[81] The incident of 1955 was a wake-up call for the planners and authorities of the dredging movement. Never again would West Lake's water be used for irrigation in decades to follow. In other words, a water source for irrigation to support agricultural production—one of the well-advertised functions of the lake promised by the planners in 1952 to rationalize such a time-consuming and costly project—proved mere wishful thinking, if not an outright hoax. On this occasion, the water exercised its agency with its uncooperativeness, which disavowed the rationale of this project and decidedly altered the agenda pursued by local cadres.

The "Red Tide" in 1958

The dry weather in 1955, according to the meteorological record, paled in comparison with that in 1958. The 1958 drought hit Hangzhou proper and its nearby counties hard in late May and lasted for over fifty days. In some areas, the rain did not fall for ninety-seven consecutive days.[82] Also, starting in May 1958—just a few months after the dredging project was finalized—the water of West Lake turned reddish and brownish. The red tide spread fast and eventually affected 5,000 *mu* or 823.68 acres—about two-thirds—of the entire lake.[83] After the summer, Hangzhou's residents were shocked to find that West Lake had transformed itself into a "red lake." While the lake's abrupt and dramatic change of color worried foreign and Chinese visitors and tourists, the city's dwellers and local authorities felt ashamed.[84] The pollution worried the CCP's top leadership, too. Liu Shaoqi 刘少奇 (1898–1969), the PRC's vice chairman, was astounded to see the lake's degraded water quality. As late as November 1958, the concerned Liu continued to make inquiries into the updated information about the reddened lake after returning to Beijing from Hangzhou.[85] Given the 1953 blueprint to make Hangzhou a "city for recreation, tourism, and cultural activities" laid out by the Soviet expert, therefore, a brownish, polluted lake was undoubtedly blasphemy against the city's reputation as the "paradise on earth" and the mecca for tourism and cultural activities.

As a matter of fact, the decade since the CCP's seizure of Hangzhou saw a speedy deterioration of water quality in West Lake, despite the government's endeavor to purify its water. Since 1950, political authorities at both municipal and provincial levels launched afforestation campaigns in the hills surrounding West Lake, intending to avoid soil erosion and subsequent contamination of the lake's water (See Chapter 3). Such an effort to militate against water pollution, however, was offset or dwarfed by the uncontrolled construction of a galaxy of hotels, restaurants, sanatoriums, and hospitals on the lake's shoreline. Unrestrained by any regulation, those facilities unscrupulously pumped sanitary wastewater into the lake, significantly reducing the lake's self-purification capacity.[86]

Investigations and research conducted during the 1950s and beyond have helped to quantify water pollution in West Lake. Immediately after the Liberation, the lake's water depth was merely 0.5 meters, but water quality was excellent, with water transparency being 0.5 meters.[87] In other words, the lake was then wholly transparent. Such perfect water quality resulted, in part, from the proliferation of aquatic plants and aquatic snails. During the 1950s, water transparency dipped below 0.4 meters most of the time. Meanwhile, ammoniacal nitrogen, nitric nitrogen, and nitrite nitrogen all increased steadily, leading to the massive multiplication of microorganisms. The proliferation of microbes further caused the loss of oxygen in the lake. Tests of water quality found that oxygen consumption in a designated location in West Lake was fifteen milligrams/liters in 1954 but swelled to 18 mg/l in two years after an explosion of microorganism multiplication. In reality, the water had already turned yellowish and greenish in 1956.[88]

The growing turbidity of the lake's water actually delegitimized a claim advanced by propagandists that the pre-1949 West Lake had been a muddy and sordid pond dotted with floating green clumps and infested with mosquitoes, incarnating an impoverished and decaying China.[89] After all, West Lake does not have a considerable self-cleaning capacity because of the limited water inflow from creeks nearby. As a relatively small lake, West Lake has its water replenished with the water inflow from three streams originating from nearby hills, Jingshajian 金沙涧, Longhongjian 龙泓涧, and Changqiaoxi 长桥溪, making up a tiny catchment area of about 27.25 square kilometers.[90] In summers and autumns, when the temperature is high and rainfall is scarce, water flow in those small waterways frequently discontinues, reducing the water storage in West Lake to such a degree that it would become a "stagnant water lake" (*sishui hu* 死水湖).[91]

Higher temperatures and less water created the precondition for the massive proliferation of microorganisms and water contamination in 1958. However, the central questions are which microbes caused the "red tide" and how to resolve it. As the lake seemed to refuse to purify itself, and the PRC's tenth anniversary was approaching, the municipal government of Hangzhou finally decided to work out a solution. On October 21, 1958, experts from twelve institutions, including the Zhejiang Medical School (*Zhejiang yixue yuan* 浙江医学院) and the Hangzhou Water Works (*Hangzhou zilaishui chang* 杭州自来水厂), and seasoned fishermen on West Lake convened to discuss the current situation. After the meeting, a research team was assembled. Several days later, a report was submitted, averring that the red tide resulted from overconcentration of a type of green algae, *Ankistrodesmus*, and possibly other species.[92]

More experiments were performed on killing such microbes, and a conclusion was quickly reached in a few days. The research team applied copper sulfate solution (0.75 grams/liters) to water samples from West Lake and discovered that the water could be repurified in twenty-four hours. Hence, the report asserted that pumping a millionth solution of copper sulfate into the lake could eliminate most unwanted microforms and clean the water. Thus, the research team requested funds for eight tons of copper sulfate and other instruments. The report further indicated that the dredging project in the past six years should also be held accountable because not only sediment but also hornwort, a plant known for its usefulness in purifying water, had been removed. Moreover, the research made other suggestions to avoid water pollution in the future:

> First, digging West Lake one meter deeper to eradicate the ecological condition for the growth of various microorganisms. Meanwhile, a deeper lake is highly beneficial to regulating the "micro-climate" (*xiao qihou* 小气候) in the lakeside area.
> Second, transplanting a large number of (aquatic) species, such as hornwort and bladderwort.
> Third, reinforcing the management of West Lake . . . by tightening control over wastewater discharge to the lake.
> Fourth, reducing the population density of fish.[93]

The four measures, however, were proposed not necessarily on the basis of careful investigation and planning. First of all, a deeper West Lake was the very cause of, rather than the solution to, fast self-reproduction of microbes. A study conducted in West Lake in the early 1980s reveals that light intensity is reduced to zero in any given spot 1.4 meters under the surface of the water. Without sunlight, consequently, subaquatic plants could not survive, optimizing the condition for the proliferation of microorganisms.[94] More seriously, the velocity of water flow decreases, and the water temperature rises accordingly when the lake becomes deeper.[95] Thus digging the lake one meter deeper could well be counterproductive by further slowing down water flow and raising the temperature inside the lake, and thereby providing microorganisms with a more favorable ecological condition.

Second, imposing a limit on fish farming not only ran counter to the political authorities' policy of making the "West Lake a big fish pond"[96] but also proved generally irrelevant to water pollution. A survey on the production of fish in West Lake between the 1960s and 1980s shows that water quality in the early 1980s was inferior to the early 1960s, even though fish production in the 1980s was merely 39 percent of that in the 1960s. Researchers thus concluded that the fish population was far from the principal factor of water pollution in the first four decades of the PRC.[97] Lastly, the comment on "tightening control over wastewater discharge to the lake" was of vital importance in maintaining high water quality. However, considering that most builders, owners, and occupants of the lakeside facilities were the PRC's leading officers (such as Mao Zedong), government institutions, or the military personnel, disciplining those facilities went beyond the Hangzhou municipal government's jurisdiction.

Hence, the report filed on October 30, 1958, was too sketchy to explain the cause of the red tide and failed to provide feasible solutions. Two months later, the Zhejiang Medical School submitted a much more detailed report that synthesized the opinions of not only academicians but also laypersons. The authors started the report with an understanding that beautifying West Lake was "a scientific research of international political significance" and a commitment to purifying the lake before October 1, 1959, the tenth anniversary of the PRC. The report was drafted after completing a series of experiments that lasted for over one month. During this period, aquatic plants, aquatic snails, and varieties of freshwater fish were raised to help to arrive at effective solutions.[98]

The report pointed out that a combination of the dredging project and fish farming in West Lake since the early 1950s had contributed to the severe disruption of ecological equilibrium in the lake. Digging the bottom of the lake led to the release of enormous amounts of nutrients that had long been locked up in the sediments. Meanwhile, fish preyed on aquatic snails and plants, both of which feasted on or absorbed algae. Fish also eliminated a large quantity of plankton, which consumed algae, too. Consequently, a specific type of reddish and robust algae—*Dactylococcopsis*—took advantage of the opportunity to dominate the lake. Such a conclusion was drawn also because additional tests were conducted, reaffirming that incoming water from various creeks was perfectly clean, and water turned red and brown inside West Lake.[99]

The researchers further discovered that in two ponds beside West Lake, their water looked limpid and turbid, respectively, depending on the existence of aquatic weeds or not. Furthermore, veteran fishermen recalled that the lake's water was clear partly because of the prevalence of marine snails in the lake. Such observations strengthened a conviction that the red tide could be controlled in a natural way. To uphold their belief, the researchers conducted several tests. The first one was on aquatic weeds. In a water tank filled with water from West Lake, aquatic weeds—especially snapdragons and *Alternanthera philoxeroides* (also known as the "revolutionary weed" [*gemin Cao* 革命草])—could effectively remove algae within seven to ten days. Another test on aquatic snails showed that ten snails could purify four thousand cubic centimeters of West Lake water in twenty-four hours. Other anatomy demonstrated that a snail's digestive system was full of *Dactylococcopsis*. Another test on a type of clam produced the same result.[100]

The research unit further tested bighead harps and silver carps. Seven to fifteen days after eight or nine harps were raised in a water tank filled with West Lake water, no major change could be spotted, proving those fish's inability to consume algae. The final test was a comprehensive one that included all the abovementioned means. In a tank full of brownish water from West Lake, eight or nine harps, fifteen aquatic snails, fifteen clams, and waterweeds (including snapdragons, "revolutionary weeds," and water hyacinth [*fengyan cao* 凤眼草]) were cultivated. In five days, the water turned clear, and it stayed uncontaminated for one month. The researchers thus jumped to the conclusion that such a synthetic way could most effectively control the red tide. At some senior fishermen's recommendation, the writers also suggested putting in a large quantity of freshwater mussels in the ensuing anti–red tide campaign.[101]

Considering the solution proposed by the fishermen was not corroborated by any experiments or tests, the emphasis on peasants' role in a scientific study testified to the pervasion of "Maoist grassroots science" that "encouraged rural leaders to conduct field investigations and process their data to find solutions for pragmatic problems."[102] As Sigrid Schmalzer posits that the widespread use of "grassroots science" during Mao's time was intended to attack "intellectual elitism and [seek] to overthrow the division between mental and manual labor,"[103] the inclusion of the fishermen's opinion spoke volumes for a well-publicized notion that the laboring people had been this new republic's backbone. Therefore, the decision served propagandistic—rather than practical—purposes. "Maoist grassroots science" would remain valid in post-Mao times. In 1981 when water in West Lake turned brownish again, it was "old workers" (*lao gongren* 老工人) but not any researchers with specialized expertise who convened to recollect the 1958–1959 campaign against the red tide and make analyses of the changed color of the lake at present.[104]

It, nevertheless, remained a problem whether such a synthetic solution that combined laboratory research and past work experiences proposed by the Zhejiang Medical School would take effect in a real-life scenario. Not only was the fishermen's suggestion unsupported by any scientific studies but the tests done in the laboratories were an oversimplified version of the actual ecological condition of West Lake. In all those tests, the samples were small, and the time periods were short (between twenty-four hours and a few weeks). Therefore, it was impossible to ascertain the long-term effect. Take aquatic snails as an example. Although it was clear that snails did consume algae, one question stayed unanswered, namely, whether algae could be fully assimilated or would be discharged to repollute the water in the long run. Obviously, the test in the laboratorial environment only showed that the algae remained in the snails' digestive system.[105]

The municipal government was impatient to collect more data before making a decision. The authorities waged a massive campaign by resorting to all conceivable measures to cure the ailing lake. In spring 1959, more than 550,000 *jin* (275,000 kilograms) of aquatic snails and over 500 kilograms of river mussels were put into the lake. Meanwhile, ten tons of copper sulfate were prepared. After the summer of 1959, the red tide visibly receded, and the lake's water turned more limpid. While many attributed its disappearance to the implementation of a biological approach, researchers had never actually identified the reasons behind the rise of the red tide, nor could they arrive at a full understanding of whether snails and mussels had rescued the lake. Some observers of the day even refused to acknowledge that the red and brown water was a crimson tide. Instead, they believed that the water was reddened because of the release of ferrous elements after sediments on the bottom of the lake were removed. The reddish water vanished not because of the effects of snails or mussels but because heavy rains in the summer of 1959 thoroughly flushed the lake.[106]

A test on aquatic snails was reconducted in the mid-1980s, whose result seemed to corroborate the theory that the biological method did not really take effect. In a 0.5-acre pond close to the *Huagang guanyu* park, 200 kg of aquatic snails were put in. No visible change of color took place after ten days. Hence, it is highly questionable that results gained from small-scale tests conducted in the laboratorial environment were applicable in a situation of much greater magnitude. Furthermore, some researchers commented that snails and mussels could not consume algae. On the contrary, they could be killed by algae. Dissection of dead clams in 1959 revealed that they contained a high concentration of reddish matter, indicating that algae had actually poisoned them. With so many mysteries surrounding the water in West Lake during and following the dredging movement, scientists and academicians in Hangzhou failed to conduct further studies. In hindsight, some investigators of water quality in West Lake during the first thirty-five years after the founding of the PRC regretted that frequent political movements consistently disrupted research on water and precluded the acquisition of meaningful data. Consequently, water quality continued to degrade in the following decades.[107]

The End of the Dredging Project

The 1955 drought and the explosion and disappearance of the "red tide" in 1958 and 1959 were telling examples of elusiveness, incomprehensibility, and even mystique of a body of water that went beyond the expectation and understanding of its planners and administrators. Such unpredictability constituted the lake's agency, as not only did it demand the local cadres' prompt response and action and turned the project in a different direction, but human interventions only intensified—rather than mitigated—the degree of unpredictability. Yu Senwen, director of the Hangzhou Bureau of Urban Construction between 1949 and 1956 and director of the Hangzhou Bureau of Gardening Administration since 1956, had staunchly advocated for the project and had proposed to dig the lake two meters deeper back in 1952.[108] At the start of 1957, the last year of the original plan, the work team completed only two-thirds of the planned work as the lake was dug 1.3 meters deeper, and over seven million cubic meters of silt was removed. It was clear that the initial goal was not quite attained. Under those circumstances, the municipal government was pondering whether to launch a renewed campaign by committing another three million yuan in the following three years to dig another fifty centimeters, further elevating the lake's water storage from twelve million cubic meters to seventeen million cubic meters.[109]

Even the most ardent supporters of a new project were concerned that several seemingly insurmountable problems they faced might sway the decision of the general public. First, a deeper lake meant it would produce greater waves. Therefore, all sightseeing boats had to be retrofitted, and the cost could be considerable. Second, the requisitioning of lands for excavated earth was viewed as detrimental to agricultural production and had therefore long been a focal point of conflict between the government and the local villagers. Third, the whole nation was short of steel, making it harder to purchase steel pipes for discharging unearthed silt. To consult with various institutions and experts, the Hangzhou Bureau of Urban Construction held a meeting on August 9, 1957, to discuss the necessity and feasibility of extending the project's duration for another three years. During the meeting, only a minority of attendees voted for the new project for reasons similar to what Yu Senwen had proposed in 1952: to make lake water more limpid, to flush waterways in Hangzhou, particularly the Huansha River (*Huansha he* 浣纱河), to irrigate rice fields nearby, to provide the city with fresh water if necessary, to improve the city's microclimate, and to use unearthed silt as fertilizer.[110]

Those rationalities met with clause-to-clause rebuttal from the opponents of the project, who constituted the vast majority in the meeting. First, the bottom of the Huansha River was, in reality, higher than West Lake, essentially precluding West Lake's water from flowing into the river. Second, the past experiences indicated that West Lake had not contributed to watering the fields and flushing waterways in Hangzhou. Here, although the opponents did not explicitly cite the example of the 1955 drought, the debacle that led to drying up the lake was still a fresh memory. Third, sunlight could be fully absorbed only when the depth of water was six meters, and the air of its surrounding area would be cooled down accordingly. A West Lake with a water depth of two or three meters would not help to lower the temperature in Hangzhou in the summertime. The key factors that affected the city's microclimate were, according to those opponents, afforestation, water flow, and wind. Fourth, it was true that silt could be used as fertilizer, but the prohibitively high cost was unfeasible for the villagers. Fifth, locations designated to dispose of excavated earth had been increasingly hard to find. Requisitioning more lands would certainly reignite clashes with peasants in suburban Hangzhou.[111]

Indeed, such comments completely overturned the arguments put forward by Yu Senwen and his like-minded proponents in 1952. The goals set by the planners looked more like delusions than well-devised plans at this point. After putting in enormous effort and splurging millions of yuan in the past five years, most CCP cadres decided to wrap up the project without increasing the budget any further. Well before the meeting was held, Yu Senwen might have foreseen that the project would not last long. In a report filed in June 1957, Yu discussed dismounting the large equipment and dismissing laborers and cadres in preparation for the end of the project. However, Yu was unwilling to see the project, which he had planned and wholeheartedly promoted, to be brought to a close unceremoniously.

Therefore, he suggested that a monument to celebrate the "completion of a project of historical significance" be erected, possibly at the lake's center.[112] Obviously, the proposal of constructing such a monument did not win approval as desired. Given the magnitude of this dredging project, it would take the entire year of 1958 to tie up all the loose ends. In a location between the Liu Estate and *Huagang guanyu*, about 230,000 cubic meters of silt—the proof of the unreliability of manual labor in mechanized times, as the area had initially been assigned to laborers in 1956—was in urgent need of removal.[113]

The 1950s campaign, arguably the largest dredging project in West Lake's history, typified a propaganda-campaign project in post-1949 China. On the one hand, it attained some goals, such as enhancing the lake's water storage and using excavated silt as fertilizer and fuel, a common practice in PRC times.[114] On the other hand, because of its enormous expenditure, the dredging of West Lake could be considered a typical project in Mao's time that seemed to "be of little or no benefit, or to be accomplished at a cost, including an opportunity cost, which outweigh[ed] their value."[115] Aside from its astronomical monetary cost (4,538,300 yuan), the human cost was also immense. The local governments mobilized vast masses of city dwellers, peasants, and prisoners. It is tempting to argue that the PRC governments displayed a commitment to continuing and expanding the "traditional ways of building waterworks" and an outstanding ability to make laborers "converge on the sites and toil without the benefit of any machinery."[116] This chapter, nevertheless, shows that the rhetoric of "self-sufficiency" or intensifying labor input to overcome the insufficient mechanized and electric equipment was a mere myth: this dredging project could not have been completed without advanced technologies.

Despite this, the media continued to cite the campaign of dredging West Lake as a "showroom" to highlight socialism's superiority when a supposedly cleaner and deeper waterbody was produced and, meanwhile, to popularize the concepts and practices of mass movement and voluntarism. Peter Kenez notes that propaganda was essential to communist regimes not necessarily because "it convinced people to do what they did not want to do," but because it defined what the novel political system was.[117] This explained why a high-profile propaganda-campaign project could afford to waste money and labor excessively. Hence, the crux of the dredging program as a propaganda-campaign project was to familiarize Hangzhou citizens with some aspects of the operation of the new socialist system and the latter's seeming allegiance to the Party-state by participating in or heaping praise upon this movement.

This said, the agency of both human and nonhuman actors diminished the efficacy of this propaganda-campaign project. This chapter has portrayed a group of participants: careless planners who lacked expertise and work experience; workers under the program who "work in exchange for relief" and were prepared to quit the work as soon as they landed new jobs elsewhere; mindless and unmotivated jailors who felt unimpressed by the significance of the project; disgruntled prisoner-laborers who sought the opportunity to abscond; and unprepared villagers who refused to show up. Their notorious low efficiency was the manifestation of their capacity—or agency—to affect the project. For most of them, however, their actions or inactions did not signal their intention to resist this new sociopolitical system. More often than not, their motivations were purely personal: jobs with better pay, chances to vindicate their counterrevolutionary "crimes," prioritizing their own agricultural work over dredging the lake, and striving to keep their residential registry in the cities.

The human agency was comparable with the nonhuman one in this story of dredging West Lake, as both were "expressivist" or "nonpurposive" by nature. Silt, water, microbes, and aquatic vegetation displayed their agency by slipping the leash of human plans and executions and thereby undercutting and reshaping the government agendas. Hence, such a high-budget project purported to clean West Lake's water ironically led to worsened water quality, and the issue of water quality remains a nagging concern until today.[118] It merits mentioning that such nonhuman agency was activated because of the human efforts to dig the lake bed: some polluting microbes long deposited at the bottom of this lake were freed, while water-purifying ones were taken away along with silt because of this campaign.

The deployment of up-to-date technology was both productive and destructive—from the perspective of humankind. The new, mechanized way of removing sediment instituted during the campaign both expedited the project's completion and exterminated clams, snails, and aquatic plants that could have absorbed polluting microorganisms. Indeed, the more efficient the machinery, the greater the deterioration in water quality. Between 1999 and 2002, the Hangzhou government funded another campaign of dredging the lake. By 2003, the depth of the water reached 2.27 meters. Despite this, the chief target of this project—that is, improving West Lake's water quality—was not realized. The lake was still a eutrophic body of water rich in nitrogen and phosphorus. A 2008 study showed that the faster and vaster removal of silt at the turn of the twentieth-first century caused the massive loss of some water-purifying microorganisms, such as magnetotactic bacteria, that had existed in the lake for centuries and thereby considerably diminished the lake's self-cleaning capacity.[119]

In this sense, this campaign, which was purported to tame nature, wound up creating its own enemies, and the nonhuman agency was actuated because of strenuous human efforts. After all, nature is a notoriously "chaotic system" with a high degree of unpredictability and randomness.[120] Not only do its inner workings—coordination and interaction of its different parts—remain incomprehensible and unpredictable to the administrators and planners, but human activities in their response exacerbate the situation by "contribut[ing] to or amplify[ing] this uncertainty."[121] Hence, in the case of the program of dredging West Lake, it was not just seemingly docile citizens under the communist regime but nonhuman agency that posed a more serious challenge to the legitimacy of this propaganda-campaign project.

CHAPTER TWO

"Watching Fish at the Flower Harbor"
Landscape, Space, and the Everydayness in Mao's China

Beginning in 1952, the same year when the project of dredging West Lake kicked off, the Hangzhou municipal government set out to construct a lakeside park, later known as *Huagang guanyu gongyuan* 花港观鱼公园 or the public park of "Watching Fish at the Flower Harbor." The first phase of the project ended in 1955, but the park underwent continual expansion, modification, and maintenance for several years to follow. As the first phase came to a close, the park was advertised as the most spacious and finest public garden in Hangzhou.[1] By 1964, the park covered an area of over twenty-one hectares, and the CCP thereby boasted about it as the largest and the most picturesque public park designed and constructed during PRC times in this city.[2] Between the 1950s and the 1970s, the park—as the arena to display a peaceful and prosperous socialist China—was chosen to be a sightseeing spot for not only domestic tourists but also most foreign leaders who paid visits to China. It thus carried political ramifications as it served as a window through which foreigners could glance into post-1949 China, a relatively closed and isolated country during Cold War times. Aside from its political usefulness, the park has been hailed as a genuine masterpiece of landscape design, as its models were later put on display in expos in the Soviet Union and Britain.[3] Designed landscape—a park or a garden—has long been viewed as "imitated nature,"[4] but it is by no means a freestanding artifact.[5] It articulates human beings' relationship with specific places and, therefore, with themselves.[6] In other words, the landscape is intimately tied to ideology.

As a landscape project produced in PRC times, *Huagang guanyu* served two ideological or propagandistic purposes. First, it was intended to instill into the public ideas of labor and rest in socialism. The emphasis on the new relationship between work and leisure was most saliently embodied in the Soviet concept of the "park of culture and rest."[7] A "park of culture and rest" is characterized by a combination of "rest in picturesque surroundings" and "wholesome, rational recreation."[8] As the "park of culture and rest" carries ideological weight as a reorganization of labor and everyday life in communist regimes, it was introduced in China as a guiding principle of landscape design throughout the 1950s.

47

Second, the park was designated as a site for public gatherings to carry on activities of "participatory propaganda," to borrow Denise Ho's phrase,[9] and for showcasing peace-loving and affluent "New China" for visitors and tourists from both China and abroad. More specifically, it played an indispensable role in political tourism—a key component of the PRC's foreign affairs—as the very location to host high-profile visitors, such as President Richard Nixon. Although tourism has long assumed salience in foreign relations in different contexts across the globe,[10] the one in socialist regimes, China included, took on special significance. The park of *Huagang guanyu* was precisely the locus where Chinese diplomats proffered their guests what Paul Hollander calls "techniques of hospitality" so that foreign visitors could be immersed in "selective" realities during Mao's China in "highly organized and planned" tours.[11] Hence, the making of *Huagang guanyu*—both a new-style public park and the newest iteration of the time-honored "Ten Vistas of West Lake"—testifies to Chang-tai Hung's observation that the CCP's reconfiguration of urban space is parallel with its program of ideologically rebuilding China and establishing a "propaganda state."[12]

Scholars have recently cited the campaign to refashion Beijing in the early PRC years as the prime example of the CCP's politicization of urban space—namely, lending specific places political meanings—for the purpose of state propaganda,[13] but the spatial dimension in Hangzhou's reconstruction in the 1950s and 1960s seemed more ambivalent. The municipal government was constantly torn between making the city a productive space and developing it into a space for foreign affairs—a center for international conferences known as "the Geneva of the East."[14] Given such uncertain and contradictory visions of the city's space, Hangzhou had at the outset posed a challenge to the CCP's program of spatially reconstructing China as a part of a grander scheme of ideological inculcation and state propaganda.

More importantly, cityscape and landscape, such as the park known as *Huagang guanyu,* are never a mere political space imposed upon local communities. They have, more often than not, been a lived space. Michel de Certeau notes that spatial practices, namely "the ensemble of movements deployed within" a given place by residents, users, and walkers in everyday situations, are able to produce spaces different from those of planners.[15] Following de Certeau's line of thought, Jeremy Brown posits that it was in the realm of everyday life that individuals in the Mao era "behaved in ways contrary to what policy-makers, planners, and propagandists intended."[16] Brown's argument, however, presupposes an a priori everyday life separate from and impervious to external forces—namely the PRC state's intervention. Similarly, James Gao explores the capacity of Hangzhou's urban culture to bring about a "countervailing change in the communist mentality" in his pioneering book on the CCP's takeover of the city, presuming a preexisting "traditional" culture that interacted with the southbound cadres.[17]

In contrast, this chapter emphasizes that Hangzhou's urban culture and its citizens' everyday lives in Mao-era China were in constant flux. Thus, I argue, first, that the CCP's efforts to politicize space as a means of state propaganda were derailed because different parties carved out their own spaces—the political, the discursive/mnemonic, and the experiential/everyday spaces. In other words, making the park a political space of ideological inculcation had never been the only way to conceptualize and use it. Second, although the park did not always perform its function as the political authorities had envisaged, its making and very existence exerted a profound impact on the everyday lives of the urbanites and visitors, for this public garden provided a locus where they variously participated in political activities, came up with and expressed artistic sensibilities, and reaped (sometimes unlawful) profits. Rather than assuming that such a high-profile public project made inroads into an "innocent" everyday life in Chinese society, I contend that it was a constitutive element in the making of a new type of everydayness—an amalgamation of the political, the discursive, and the personal—in Mao-era China.

As has been analyzed, the political authorities had planned this public garden as a political space, which, according to Hung Wu, functioned as both "an architectonic embodiment of political ideology and as an architectural site activating political action and expression."[18] This said, however, the planners could hardly dictate the professional architect's approaches. As the concept of the "park of culture and rest" increasingly carried ideological weight and became a canon in landscape architecture in 1950s China, it did not resonate well with Sun Xiaoxiang, the architect of *Huagang guanyu*. On the contrary, Sun purposely avoided following such a formula but borrowed gardening skills and the philosophies of modern England, Japan, and late imperial China. The architect's self-activating agency to select proper styles and approaches attests to Craig Clunas's observation that imaginations, representations, and interpretations of a designed landscape create a "site of contested meanings."[19] Sun's well-entrenched professional autonomy was made possible, in part, because of the communist cadres' lack of expertise in landscape design.[20] Sun was capable of resorting to gardening techniques and concepts of imperial China also because of the CCP's long-standing practice of "defining cultural relics as national patrimony."[21] Such a practice created an unintended consequence: *Huagang guanyu* grew into a site of cultural nostalgia. As Sun was eager to draw inspiration from a poem composed by Emperor Qianlong 乾隆 (1711–1799) to highlight the flower and the fish as the park's central components,[22] this public garden evoked artistic and poetic sensibilities and sentiments among a vast number of scholars, writers, and poets in Mao's time, and it thereby became what Pierre Nora called a *lieu de mémoire*—a site or realm of memory.[23] Various strands of "sited memory," according to Peter Carroll, were key to modernizing and reconstructing a city with a rich history in modern China.[24]

However, this raises the question regarding who was entitled to the memory of the flower and the fish in the scenic spot of *Huagang guanyu*. In other words, the park delivered a "sited memory," but not for all. Just like the designer and scholars/poets who prioritized cultural nostalgia over the Party-state's agenda of transforming the public park into a political space, ordinary citizens in this region did not necessarily share the memory with cultural elites but "used" this park in a widely diverse way. For them, the public garden was the location for trysts, casual walks, tea consumption, or poaching aquatic creatures. My emphasis on the "uses" of the garden is inspired by Perry Link's analysis of novels produced and circulated in the Mao years. Link posits that the Mao-era literature that performed multiple functions was "used" differently by different readers.[25] Here, literary works are comparable to landscape precisely for their polysemic nature, open to myriad understandings and interpretations. As Robert Rotenberg argued, the landscape is a "conversation" of many "voices" and "visions."[26]

It is the comparability between text and landscape that impels Michel de Certeau to draw a parallel between reading a text and walking on a street—both are spatial practices.[27] Such practices, which lend a given landscape multiple meanings, call into question the assertion that landscape plays a role as "an instrument of cultural power"[28] because of its capacity to give "physicality to abstract notions of ideology."[29] In the case of *Huagang guanyu* in Mao's China, different actors harbored different intentions and made different movements within this public garden, creating political, discursive/mnemonic, and lived spaces of their own. If de Certeau's observation that spatial practices are "everyday tactics" still holds true in the context of post-1949 China,[30] the story of how Hangzhou citizens and visitors appropriated the *Huagang guanyu* park was thus one about the making and refashioning of individuals' everyday lives in Mao's China because of, and not in spite of, the state-initiated projects for ideological and propaganda purposes.

Huagang guanyu: Its Origin and Transformations

Huagang guanyu and the Landscape Painting

The earliest iteration of *Huagang guanyu* was the Lu Garden (*Luyuan*), a villa built between 1225 and 1239 by Lu Yunsheng 卢允升, an influential and powerful eunuch in the Southern Song dynasty.[31] The garden was soon in decline but was remembered for its high reputation of having raised scores of types of exotic fish and its geographical location at a harbor at the foot of the Hua Family Mountains (*Huajia shan* 花家山).[32] Therefore, the location's name, "Hua's Harbor" (*Huagang* 花港), did not carry the connotation of "the flower harbor," as painters, poets, designers, and tourists would choose to believe in the following centuries. During Southern Song times, this garden consistently evoked artistic and poetic sentiments despite its decline shortly after Lu's death. The artist Chen Qingbo 陈清波 under Emperor Lizong 理宗 (r. 1224–1264) set a precedent by giving his paintings about West Lake four-character titles, such as *duan qiao can xue* 断桥残雪 (melting snow at the broken bridge) and *Su di chun xiao* 苏堤春晓 (spring dawn at Su causeway). After that, the Ten Vistas, all of which were known for their four-character names, took on enhanced importance as the representative scenic spots in the lakeside area.[33]

Those literati-artists' keen interest in such scenic spots did not necessarily translate into their ability or willingness to portray those locations with precision. Art historians find that artists took the liberty to alter the geographical locations of certain scenic spots to fit the overall layouts of paintings.[34] The scene in Ye Xiaoyan's 叶肖岩 painting about *Huagang guanyu* bore a striking resemblance to that in another painting of his.[35] Hui-shu Lee (Li Huishu 李慧漱) reasons that those paintings did not have to reflect the realities of West Lake because they were nothing but a "memory site."[36] Anyhow, a conspicuous lack of accuracy hinted at the fact that artists might have worked on their paintings based upon not necessarily actual scenes but their memories, speculations, and imaginations. Namely, the ten vistas were, in reality, imaginative, pictorial, and discursive constructs of elite artists as early as Song times. Commentators in later generations did not fail to understand that the completion of landscape paintings preceded the making of the Ten Vistas.[37]

The Qing's Reconstruction Projects

With the Southern Song's demise, *Huagang guanyu* inevitably underwent ruination because of political disorder.[38] During the Qing, the government and local elites set out to reconstruct the garden twice, in 1699 and 1869, for political reasons: the Manchu emperor's effort to win over the local elites in Jiangnan and a commitment to restoring the war-scarred Qing Empire in the wake of the Taiping Rebellion (1851–1864), respectively. To restore a site only existing in artists' and poets' memory for centuries, the Qing officials based in Zhejiang arbitrarily selected a lakeside location—formerly the site of Dingxiang Temple (*Dingxiang si* 定香寺)—1.5 kilometers south of the original location of the Lu Garden, to rebuild it in 1699 in preparation for Emperor Kangxi's 康熙 (1654–1722) visit.[39] Designers of *Huagang guanyu* in 1699 were evidently unaware of the fact that the first character of its name, *hua* 花, originally referred to a surname but took it for granted that the name of this scenic spot was an indication of the two most important elements of the garden: the fish and the flower. *Gazetteer of West Lake* (*Xihu zhi* 西湖志), compiled in 1731, vividly portrayed a scene inside the newly constructed rectangular pond: fish "are alternately diving into the bottom (of the pond) and launching themselves out of the water to swim," while "thousands of falling flowers are lighting on the water surface, contrasting finely with red waterweeds and green planktons." Such a view lent a sensibility of "holding oneself aloof [from the world and others]" that the great Daoist Zhuangzi 庄子 (369?–286 BCE) once articulated in his works.[40] Citing Zhuangzi's unbound freedom and eternal bliss had long been a cliché in virtually all poems about *Huagang guanyu*. Li E 厉鹗 (1692–1752), a celebrated *ci* 词-poet during the high Qing, for example, ended his *ci*-poem with "The fish are swallowing or spitting out flowers; Flowers appear or vanish when chasing the fish; Human's life is not as joyful as that of the fish."[41] Emperor Qianlong's poem similarly mentioned the flower, the fish, and the Zhuangzi-style freedom.[42]

The Public Park of *Huagang gongyuan*

Fish that Qianlong and other poets had loved with a passion gradually disappeared from *Huagang guanyu* with the closing years of the Qing dynasty. As China entered the first half of the twentieth century, this scenic spot grew hopelessly old and forlorn. As numerous private villas mushroomed on nearby lots, this scenic spot shrank in size and, therefore, gradually slipped into obscurity. Not only did it cover only a tiny area of merely 0.2 hectares,[43] but its reputation as an exhibition center for exotic goldfish also waned as an increasingly large number of tourists preferred to enjoy the view of goldfish in Yuquan 玉泉. Shortly before 1949, it seemed that Yuquan was poised to overtake *Huagang guanyu* to become one of the Ten Vistas of West Lake, known as "Watching Fist at Yuquan" (*Yuquan guanyu* 玉泉观鱼).[44]

Under these circumstances, a plan of reviving and expanding *Huagang guanyu* was set in motion in 1952, one year before the Soviet specialist A. C. Maxim published his proposal to make Hangzhou "a public space for recreation."[45] The planned public park was primarily intended to serve not Hangzhou's citizens but rather the occupants of newly built rehabilitation facilities. In so doing, the CCP advanced a political agenda of privileging some social and political groups, such as the workers and the soldiers, over others. Despite this, its planners continued to resort to the rhetoric of serving the Chinese people to rationalize the restoration of this time-honored garden. Its chief planner, Yu Senwen, for example, boasted of *Huagang guanyu* as the first new-style park constructed after West Lake "returned to the embrace of the people." To this end, the park's planners and promoters had to rewrite the history of this scenic spot, transforming it from an emblem of the ruling class's political and monetary powers, lifestyles, and aesthetic values in imperial China into a cultural heritage "long liked by the people" (*jiuwei renmin xiai* 久为人民喜爱).[46] By absorbing the eunuch, emperors, and local officials of imperial China into the category of the "people," CCP cadres and the architect evaluated *Huagang guanyu* as a "familiar and pleasing" (*xiwen lejian* 喜闻乐见) site "easily comprehensible to the masses in order to win their support"[47] and thereby to display socialism's advantage over the "old society," the typical propaganda rhetoric in Mao's China.

The CCP's Planning

The supremacy of socialism manifested itself in the park's unprecedented vastness. By 1964, when the final phase of its construction ended, the park occupied a large swath of territory, about forty-two times as big as the one before 1949.[48] The site's size and the lack thereof in pre-1949 China carried political and ideological ramifications. A 1956 report filed by a cadre in Hangzhou indicated that the city lacked spacious public parks before 1949 because of capitalist private ownership, under which capitalists, landlords, and bureaucrats willfully sliced up and shamelessly usurped the lakeshore area. It was the public ownership of land during the PRC era that enabled "general planning and designing" (*zongti guihua sheji* 总体规划设计).[49] In other words, the enlargement of *Huagang guanyu* itself served a propaganda purpose, making the program of restoring this time-honored scenic spot a propaganda-campaign project. The CCP's claim about the advantage of the public ownership of land—an indispensable component of the PRC's social system—seemed to be well-justified in this case because, with the abolition of private ownership, CCP authorities were entitled to requisition the lands of nearby private villas and other spaces to expand the park considerably. Conducting "general planning and designing," however, proved more complicated than CCP officials had presumed.

The plan initially devised in 1952 suggested that *Huagang guanyu* would be enlarged from about 0.2 to 1.7 hectares by incorporating the lands of neighboring private residential complexes, notably the Jiang Estate (*Jiangzhuang* 蒋庄). The plan emphatically included a meadow of 1,800 square meters—known as the Great

Lawn (*Da caoping* 大草坪) or the Great Cedar Lawn (*Xuesong da caoping* 雪松大草坪)—dotted with ornamental plants.[50] In the same year, however, the CCP's municipal committee in Hangzhou tabled another proposal of a far greater magnitude not only to renovate *Huagang guanyu* but also to connect it to the vast tract of land on the western shore of West Lake:

> On the lakeside area in the south, [the areas] of the former Jiang Estate, *Huagang guanyu*, Liu Estate, and Ding Family Mountain (*Dingjia shan* 丁家山) shall be integrated into a park in a recreational district centering on Chairman Mao's bronze statue.... [An area] of 5,000 *mu* (333.33 ha) shall be designated as the recreational district.[51]

This overly ambitious plan, which could have turned the southwestern shore of West Lake—known as the Western Mountain (*Xishan* 西山) area—into a mammoth public park, bore no fruit principally because Liu Estate and Ding Family Mountain would soon be taken over to build Mao Zedong's villa.

Despite its failure to materialize, this plan happened to conform to the 1953 urban plan drafted by A. C. Maxim. The 1953 plan designated West Lake's western shore, a relatively remote and isolated place, as the "convalescence zone" (*xiuyang qu* 修养区), as opposed to the densely populated administrative district on the lake's northeastern shore and the college town in the north. Despite the Soviet expert's supreme authority, the 1953 plan did not come to fruition, either. Throughout the 1950s, the Western Mountain area's geographical isolation and serenity attracted various governmental and military institutions nationwide to build hospitals, sanatoriums, and guesthouses, undermining Hangzhou's overall urban planning as proposed by Maxim. In hindsight, the mushrooming of all such facilities, along with Mao's villa, none of which was open to the public, unintentionally precluded the Western Mountain area from undergoing overexploitation and overdevelopment. Scholars and urban planners in later generations thus felt lucky that the landscape in this region did not undergo drastic changes.[52]

The Construction and the Design

As the ambitious plan became stillborn, *Huagang guanyu* grew into a sizable public park in its own right. Throughout the 1950s and 1960s, the park's construction proceeded in three separate phases. In the first phase between 1952 and 1955, the government cleared 14.6 hectares of land west of the Qing-era *Huagang guanyu* by dismantling an old villa and requisitioning farmlands, vegetable gardens, farmhouses, and ponds. The project officially started in the winter of 1952. In 1953, the soil was prepared, some paths were paved, and work began on digging the Red

Figure 2.1. Film footage showed that the stone had been restored, but a pavilion designed to protect the stone had yet to be built by 1958. *Screenshot from* Xihu 西湖 *(West Lake),* Shanghai kexue jiaoyu dianying zhipian chang 上海科学教育电影制片厂 *(Shanghai scientific education film studio), 1958.*

Fish Pond (*Hongyu chi* 红鱼池)—the park's largest body of water. By late 1954, the 1.1-hectare Peony Garden (*Mudan yuan* 牡丹亭) was completed. Thus, the two most significant components of this time-honored site, the fish and the flower, were officially ushered in. In front of the Great Lawn in the northern part of the park, a wooden and bamboo structure named the Green Rain Hall (*Cuiyu ting* 翠雨厅) was built as a principal resting place beside the lake. The second phase, starting in 1959, was focused on restoring the relics of the Qing-era *Huagang guanyu*. Consequently, a pavilion was rebuilt to house the stone stele erected by Emperor Qianlong for *Huagang guanyu*. During the third phase, which started in 1964, the park was further enlarged to occupy an area of 21.3 hectares after annexing the adjacent locations previously designated as the space for the excavated earth in the project of dredging West Lake, as discussed in the preceding chapter.[53]

It merits mentioning that the completion of the three phases did not follow a well-laid-out blueprint. Rather, this public park's design and construction were continually subject to revision and reprogramming for over a decade. Its planned size, for example, changed three times. The first proposal filed in the autumn of 1952 suggested that the park cover an area of fewer than two hectares. The municipal government soon made the decision to requisition 14.6 hectares of land, and, as shown above, by 1964, the park's size had further increased by one-third.[54] The name of the park seemed to stay undetermined for a while. Yu Senwen, the leading CCP official in charge of the project, for example, chose to call it the Western Mountain Park (*Xishan gongyuan* 西山公园) when the first phase was completed in 1955, signaling his reluctance to subscribe to the name it had borne in imperial times. As late as 1979, one writer continued to call it Western Mountain Park.[55] As a matter of fact, the controversy surrounding the need to preserve and recover the Qing site raged for almost a decade, hinting at a pervasive unwillingness among CCP cadres to appropriate the long-held reputation of *Huagang guanyu,* given the name's connectedness to China's feudal past.[56]

More intriguingly, a design for the park by the professional landscape architect Sun Xiaoxiang went forward as late as October 1954 and was not completed until September 1955, at the tail end of the first phase. In hindsight, researchers concluded that only a few bridges, the Green Rain Hall, the Great Lawn in the north, and some plants in the area of the Red Fish Pond had been installed strictly in line with Sun's design drawings. The clearance of the land, the arrangement of the rockeries, the vegetation planting, and the building of the Peony Garden took place mostly on the basis of a "generalized master plan." Here, a "generalized master plan" meant a sketchy plan with a few guiding principles but lacking necessary details. In this sense, the park's first phase was completed through compromise and collaboration between the architect and the builders. In one writer's words, the construction and the design occurred simultaneously in an "abnormal state" (*bu zhengchang zhuangkuang* 不正常状态) beyond the architect's control.[57] More seriously, the park's vast expansion during the third phase of construction wholly altered *Huagang guanyu*'s well-publicized design drawing presented by its architect, Sun Xiaoxiang, to a national audience in 1959, as I shall discuss in greater detail later.

The Architect and the Planner

The architect Sun Xiaoxiang was then a professor of landscape design at the Zhejiang Agriculture University (*Zhejiang nongye daxue* 浙江农业大学) in Hangzhou. He accepted Yu Senwen's invitation to carry out the task of designing the park in the early 1950s.[58] Sun, who had earned a degree in landscape architecture in 1946, felt deeply impressed by European-style gardens, particularly those in the International Settlement and the French Concession in Shanghai. Heavily influenced by the style of those parks, Sun once proclaimed that public gardens in Shanghai, such as Jessfield Park (*Zhaofeng gongyuan* 兆丰公园, established in 1914), were his de facto mentors that had taught him about the use of contour lines in landscape design. Hence, despite all the chaos arising from the process of design and construction, Sun was given credit as the park's chief architect, and *Huagang guanyu* was hailed as the first garden designed with elevation planning and contour lines. These features had never existed previously in garden design in China.[59]

It would do him an injustice, however, to presume that Sun Xiaoxiang employed nothing but techniques of Euro-American landscape architecture when designing the park of *Huagang guanyu*. In reality, Sun could be best described as an eclectic who was willing to absorb experiences, skills, and styles from varying sources. First of all, Sun embraced elements of the imperial gardens of the Qing. Between September 1953 and July 1954, when he was teaching landscape architecture classes in Beijing as a visiting lecturer, he closely observed the buildings and the fish pools at the Summer Palace (*Yihe yuan* 颐和园), on the basis of which he would later design the Green Rain Hall and the garden for goldfish. Second, Sun gained inspiration from Japanese gardens to rearrange the stonework in the Red Fish Pond by displaying large-sized, Japanese-style rocks. Third, Sun pledged to emulate such European gardens as the Royal Botanic Garden in Edinburgh to place emphasis on plant ecology when designing the Peony Garden.[60] Such an eclectic approach prompted one writer to complain that the park looked overly new and exotic and, therefore, lacked the allure of Chinese tradition.[61]

Thus, it is fair to argue that Sun Xiaoxiang enjoyed full professional autonomy when selecting the most appropriate styles for the park and jettisoning the Soviet model—namely, the "park of culture and rest." Although Sun later acknowledged that he purposely avoided the Soviet style, he did not mean to play a role as a dissenting intellectual in socialism. Instead, Sun openly sang high praises of the Soviet style when necessary. In books and essays he later authored during Mao's time, for example, chapters that promoted the styles and techniques of China's late imperial garden designs were usually prefaced by Sun's complimentary remarks on the "park of culture and rest."[62] For Sun and his contemporaries in China, such rhetoric as the "park of culture and rest" was undoubtedly novel and alien. Scholars have argued that figuring out the socialist system was akin to learning a "foreign language," and propaganda lent the masses the new and foreign syntax.[63] Speaking this new language, figuratively and literally, without a full understanding of it constituted a ritual of loyalty to socialism. Here, it did not matter whether Sun's utilization of the new language resulted from his genuine belief or mere dissimulation. He carved out his autonomous space of professionalism by parroting this new "language." As landscape architecture was outside the ken of most CCP officials, including Yu Senwen, Sun was able to exercise the

Figure 2.2. Architect Sun Xiaoxiang adopted a Euro-American way of designing the park. *Reprinted from Sun Xiaoxiang and Hu Xuwei, "Hangzhou Huagang guanyu gongyuan guihua sheji" (The Planning of "Hua Gang Guan Yu" Park, Hangchow), Jianzhu xuebao (Architectural Journal) 5 (1959): p. 22.*

privilege of free choice and expression by either heartily endorsing or generally ignoring the Soviet model at this point.[64]

Although he harbored no intention of following the Soviet model, the urban dwellers' rights to rest, rehabilitation, and sightseeing were foregrounded as the justification for building this park in a 1959 article coauthored by Sun Xiaoxiang and his colleague, which offered full details of the designing and planning of *Huagang guanyu*. Sun and his colleague made it clear that *Huagang guanyu* was not a "park of culture and rest" in the Soviet sense. It did not feature athletic facilities because of its "relatively small size." Nor were there recreational services and playgrounds for children due to the considerable distance between it and downtown Hangzhou and the lack of public transportation.[65] In 2006, Sun proffered another explanation for why he intentionally avoided building a Soviet-style "park of culture and rest": he had to take Hangzhou's local culture and West Lake's scenery into account.[66]

Both explanations for not making a "park of culture and rest" are marked with the stamp of the times. The 2006 answer revealed both Sun Xiaoxiang's eagerness to highlight his professionalism as a designer independent of party officials' interventions and a politico-cultural necessity to emphasize the city's profound cultural heritage. In the late 1950s, in comparison, the Soviet "park of culture and rest" remained an authoritative landscaping practice from which Sun did not desire to deviate. Therefore, Sun necessarily cited the lack of space as an excuse for *Huagang guanyu* failing to conform to the Soviet model. Furthermore, the late 1950s proved an apt time to revive China's "tradition," as the Soviet Union's withdrawal of experts from China led to a shift from a communist cosmopolitanism to the pursuit of "a self-confidence that could come only from a deep sense of tradition" in China.[67]

In order to display "a deep sense of tradition," Sun Xiaoxiang's 1959 article, which summarized the design of *Huagang guanyu,* addressed the architect's indebtedness to the canonized late-Ming work of Ji Cheng 计成 (1582–1642) on garden construction, *The Craft of Gardens* (*Yuanye* 园冶). To be more specific, Sun and his company highlighted a few concepts and techniques that they learned from the book, particularly "borrowing" (借 *jie*).[68] To reach the goal of "borrowing," namely, using views from outside, Sun was devoted to taking advantage of West Lake's scenery beyond *Huagang guanyu*. Visitors to the Great Lawn in the northern part of the park, for example, could "borrow" the views of picturesque Su Causeway (*Sudi* 苏堤), Qixia Ridge (*Qixia ling* 栖霞岭), and Liu Estate.[69]

Although Sun Xiaoxiang traced his philosophy and techniques of landscape architecture back to the Ming dynasty for his design of the Great Lawn, Yu Senwen,

Figure 2.3. The Great Lawn at *Huagang guanyu* that embodies the landscape designing skill of "borrowing": views of lakeside hills and Su Causeway could be "borrowed" from the open space. *Photo taken in April 2020.*

the mastermind behind the revival of *Huagang guanyu* and Sun's political patron, later recalled that his insistence on installing a sizable grassland stemmed from his experiences in European countries in the 1930s. In 1934, Yu grasped an opportunity to stay in Europe as a representative of a government-affiliated institution. Over the following two years, Yu toured various countries, including Britain, Italy, and France, during which time it was the large lawns in England that most profoundly impressed him.[70] In post-1949 China, Yu's preference for the vast, British-style meadows gained a renewed political legitimacy since the lawn in a public park had long been considered an institution that encouraged the public's participation in political and communal affairs in European countries,[71] akin to the notion of mass mobilization endorsed by the CCP. It was thus crystal clear that when Yu sought to build up a large lawn in this park, what inspired him were his memories and photos of parks in Europe but by no means his reverence for the technique of "borrowing" as proposed by Ming gardening specialists.

Spaces and Their Uses

Political Space

The various perspectives of the same Great Lawn were a telling example of differing spatial practices in this garden. For upper-echelon CCP officials and local planners, this public park functioned as a political space serving propaganda purposes in two senses. Domestically, it was a part of a lakeside zone of "recuperation" (*xiuyang* 休养)—with a host of newly constructed sanatoriums, guesthouses, hospitals, and recreational facilities—that was purported to display class distinctions and redefine work and leisure, that is, the "laboring people's" inalienable right of rest in a socialist society.[72] In other words, while "leisure activities" were considered the ruling class's exclusive privileges, in Mao-era China, they were subject to politicized reinterpretation.[73] A tour guidebook published in 1956 cited the region west of the lake as an example of marked contrast between pre- and post-1949 China. Before the communist takeover, the author emphasized, this area had been sliced into pieces by landlords and capitalists, and the Japanese invaders ruthlessly ate up all the fish in the pond. After the Liberation, this region had developed into a district of all sorts of sanatoriums for the working class, the leader in New China. The brand-new *Huagang guanyu* park had been fully integrated into this district.[74]

The working-class members' right to rest in the scenic sanatoriums had long served as propaganda to display the socialist system's unquestionable advantage over the "old China." A 1960 report contrasted the hellish lives of the working people before 1949 and their new access to a "heaven"—namely West Lake and the sanatoriums on its shoreline.⁷⁵ The park of *Huagang guanyu* was the centerpiece of this heaven, for workers were portrayed wearing pajamas and casually taking walks in it.⁷⁶ This image of the new, harmonious everyday life in the post-1949 era served the purpose of not only legitimating this new political system domestically but also of exhibiting a prosperous and egalitarian communist China internationally as a diplomatic scheme. In August 1961, for example, a delegation led by the Brazilian vice president was guided on a visit to a lakeside sanatorium designed and constructed for workers from Shanghai.⁷⁷

More often than not, the *Huagang guanyu* park was designated as a destination for a galaxy of high-profile visitors from abroad, such as President Nixon, President Sukarno of Indonesia, and Prince Norodom Sihanouk of Cambodia. This park provided a window through which the outsiders could take up a rare opportunity to peep into a relatively closed, isolated, and hence mysterious Maoist China because the park, in Paul Hollander's words, "had something for everybody," both metaphorizing "a hard-working, simple, [and] efficient modernizing country" and embodying "thousands of years of Chinese culture." Hence, those scripted and carefully programmed tours were designed to demonstrate the CCP's "attainment of equality and social justice," something the Soviet Union had failed to achieve.⁷⁸ Touring new socialist China thus allowed the visitors to find ideas in China to "solve their own problems," such as violence, social injustice, and social inequality.⁷⁹ The existing archival records corroborate Hollander's observation. In the early 1950s, for example, Sha Wenhan (沙文汉 1908–1964), then governor of Zhejiang Province, urged his subordinate cadres in Zhejiang to offer better accommodation and reception services to foreign visitors to augment their understanding of "the greatness of China" and to debunk stories about impoverished China by displaying an "affluent and peace-loving" country.⁸⁰ To this end, the CCP authorities usually stage-managed some "unexpected encounters" for those foreign visitors. On September 28, 1962, for example, the first lady of Indonesia, who was walking in the *Huagang guanyu* park, "happened" to bump into a few "tourists" with various connections with Indonesia, including a Chinese-Indonesian student who was going to school in China and a Chinese-Indonesian woman who was visiting her family in Hangzhou.⁸¹

In most cases, the flower, the fish, and the tea were indispensable props for the pre-scripted political tours. In April 1957, for example, Kliment Voroshilov, chairman of the Soviet Union, was guided on a tour of the *Huagang guanyu* park, where he enjoyed the views of exotic goldfish and drank Chinese tea inside the Hall of Green Rain.⁸² Displaying New China in a traditional, if not explicitly self-Orientalized, way, however, had long been a matter of bitter controversy.

Yao Wenyuan 姚文元 (1931–2005), the future member of the Gang of Four, commented in 1962 that displaying traditional architectural structures and arranging rare and precious vegetation in public gardens across the country were a manifestation of the revival of the gentry class's tastes in a feudal society.[83] The radical intellectuals' antitraditionalist bent was bolstered by a long-standing political agenda of transforming China's consumerist cities, Hangzhou included, into productive ones.[84] Under those circumstances, radical Maoists finally proceeded to wipe off the "feudal legacy" of *Huagang guanyu* in the late 1960s.[85] Hence, halfway into the Cultural Revolution, the park almost collapsed under the weight of the inherent contradiction in the CCP's policies—that is, the competing practices of making the park a political space for foreign affairs and transforming it into a site of cash crop production.

The decay and vandalism this park underwent coincided with a series of setbacks in foreign affairs the PRC suffered in the late 1960s, when numerous countries severed ties with Beijing. Beginning in the early 1970s, as the PRC government was poised to normalize its relationship with the United States and other Western bloc countries,[86] the *Huagang guanyu* park was once again restored as a chief locus for the orchestration of political tourism. As early as 1971, for example, the Hangzhou municipal government began to make preparations for reopening this park to prospective foreign visitors by erecting a new signboard for the park with new, less politically radical texts.[87] The renewed utilization of the park as a political space in the closing years of the Mao era culminated in President Nixon's visit to this park in February 1972 and the planting of the American president's gift, three redwood seedlings, inside it as the symbol of the newfound US-China friendship.[88]

Discursive/Mnemonic Space

Despite the CCP authorities' intention to make the park a political space, as I have shown, landscape architect Sun Xiaoxiang took the liberty of proclaiming that he harbored the intention of giving China's cultural tradition a new lease on life. In the early 1950s, when his design was underway, his "revivalism" was well-justified because of the Soviet experts' emphasis on the socialist cosmopolitanism that "denotes the convergence of formerly isolated traditions" across the socialist world.[89] In the late 1950s, when Sun provided the audience across the country with a rundown of the design and construction of the park, the necessity to illustrate a "severe difference with the Soviet Union" (thanks to the ongoing Sino-Soviet disputes)[90] prompted Sun to unashamedly highlight the "traditional" components of the park—namely, the flower and the fish—that had been remembered and repeatedly represented for centuries. For writers, scholars, and poets who were conversant with countless literary works in association with *Huagang guanyu*, this newly constructed public park was the very site of their refreshed memories of allusions, such as flower and fish. Goldfish continued to be an indispensable component part for composers of traditional poetry after 1949—such as Liu Beiye 柳北野[91] and Wang Tuizhai 王退斋[92]—to reiterate a time-honored theme that associated the fish's joy with a desire to pursue the unfettered, Zhuangzi-style individual freedom. Zhou Shoujuan 周瘦鹃 (1895–1968), a renowned novelist of popular fiction, similarly voiced his aspiration for absolute freedom when he visited the park in 1956.[93] Even Guo Moruo 郭沫若 (1892–1978), widely known for his embrace of socialist culture and collaboration with the PRC regime, penned a classical poem in this park in 1959. It illustrated his empathetic feeling for the carefree fish.[94]

The flower was also a much sought-after topic in various literary works of the cultural elites. One of Liu Beiye's poems, for example, articulated the poet's fascination with the peony (*mudan* 牡丹; specifically, the tree peony), arguably the king of all flowers. Liu cited an essay authored by Su Shi 苏轼 (1037–1101) to highlight his passionate love of peonies.[95] Another old-style poetry master, Zhang Houxuan 张厚绚, was fond of lotuses in the pond.[96] By comparison, Shen Congwen 沈从文 (1902–1988), a preeminent writer in twentieth-century China, was a fan of the park's chrysanthemums.[97] By introducing precious breeds of flowers, landscape architect Sun Xiaoxiang came under criticism for ignoring the needs of the masses.[98] Under these circumstances, Sun apologized in 1959 for falling short of meeting the demands of the masses and having pursued the sole aim of "restoring the historical site of *Huagang guanyu*"—that is, designing a site of memory for his like-minded scholars, writers, and artists.[99] Sun's goal could not have been reached without the endorsement of Yu Senwen, the CCP leader and supervisor in Hangzhou. At the height of the Cultural Revolution, Yu was censured as an advocate for cultivating expensive and exotic flowers in all Hangzhou-based gardens.[100]

Lived/Experiential Space

Although the rare species of flowers and fish constituted what Peter Carroll calls "sited memory" for the cultural elites,[101] they took on different significance in the everyday lives of Hangzhou citizens and tourists. Take the peony, the subject of many a poem about this park, as an example. Peonies could thrive in the park, with its location in warmer and more humid South China, because of the existence of shading trees.[102] Hence, it was the shaded areas in this park, notably the

Peony Pavilion, but not the peonies per se, that appealed to the park's visitors who were intent on taking walks and resting in a cooler environment. A contributor to the *People's Daily* (*Renmin ribao* 人民日报) recalled that strolling in those shady zones became a routine when he stayed in a rehabilitation facility nearby.[103] For Hangzhou denizens, the shaded areas were more popular than the Great Lawn, a scenic spot both Yu Senwen and Sun Xiaoxiang felt compelled to build because of the intolerable sunburn caused by excessive exposure to sunlight that the visitors suffered in the open space of the lawn. Hence, the tourists jokingly gave the park—alternatively known as the Western Mountain Park or *Xishan gongyuan* 西山公园—an epithet as the "Park with a Western Exposure" (*Xishai gongyuan* 西晒公园).[104] For them, the allure of the Great Lawn did not reside in the grass or the technique of "borrowing" that Sun had attempted to popularize but in the nearby Green Rain Hall, a wooden structure for resting and tea consumption. When this teahouse was dismantled in 1960 to ensure the safety and security of the nearby Liu Estate, Chairman Mao's villa in Hangzhou, the lawn's popularity plummeted immediately.[105]

Aside from being a location for avoiding excessive sunshine, the quiet and secluded shaded areas also functioned as places for dating for the young generation. The renowned female writer Chen Xuezhao once expressed her amazement when she found that some of those young men and women making their secretive rendezvous late at night in the park were in their early teens. Her fellow travelers explained that the political campaigns against feudal arranged marriage were inspiring the younger generation to choose their partners at an early age.[106] Considering that the promotion of free-choice love and marriage had been a state-initiated movement to display the progressiveness of the socialist system, the youths' appropriation of this state-sponsored rhetoric and the space of the park—initially planned as a political space in which to perform propaganda functions—to serve their own interests provided an arresting example of how the younger generation's spatial practice deviated from what the political authorities had envisaged. In a similar fashion, other teenagers utilized this park to gather shrimp-like plankton or even to steal goldfish directly from the waters.[107] In this sense, rather than presuming that the state-initiated projects encroached upon individuals' everyday lives, I argue that those projects, though they played a constitutive role in the PRC's state propaganda apparatus, allowed for the making of a new type of everyday life under socialism, one in which individuals negotiated with and appropriated the official rhetoric and practices to reap their own benefits. Indeed, even in highly politicized cities, such as Beijing, public spaces, which were built to serve specific political and ideological purposes, would be easily turned into the loci of "people's leisure activities."[108]

The Great Lawn as Three Spaces

This everyday life differed from the imaginary world of CCP cadres in which the young men and women were by no means pleasure-seekers and loafers but active participants in group/political activities in the park. In a 1955 news story, children's strolling about in the park was endowed with political significance: the younger generation in China could "happily grow up in a worry-free and peaceful environment" in this new regime.[109] In a similar fashion, in a 1959 essay purporting to establish a national reputation for the *Huagang guanyu* park, Zhejiang's

Figure 2.4. The CCP authorities had long imagined that West Lake was in possession of the new generation. The cover of the June 1952 issue of *People's Pictorial (Renmin huabao* 人民画报) illustrates children's group activity beside West Lake. "Children and West Lake." *Reprinted from cover, Renmin huabao* 人民画报 *(People's pictorial) 6 (March 1952).*

provincial governor presented to the national audience an image of boys and girls either sitting together to sing songs or gleefully frolicking on the lawn.[110] This was visually represented in a cartoon published in a Hangzhou-based newspaper in 1964. In this cartoon, children, some of whom were guided by a People's Liberation Army (PLA) soldier, were portrayed as participants in collective activities and political rallies inside the *Huagang guanyu* park.[111] Hence, the youth were conceived of as the embodiment of the PRC, a young and vibrant republic. In many prearranged visits to the park by foreign visitors, children were indispensable actors who symbolized the Chinese people's character: working hard and loving their lives. During Prince Norodom Sihanouk's visit to this park in December 1960, for example, he was greeted by a group of children who "happened" to bring musical instruments to hold a gathering on the Great Lawn. The amused Cambodian prince thus performed dances amid the children's laughter and applause.[112]

The CCP leaders' use of the Great Lawn as a political space notwithstanding, its designer, Sun Xiaoxiang, harbored a different intention, as I have shown. Although the lawn in a park as a landscape architectural practice—essentially a Victorian gardening style in England—initially emerged in China in public gardens designed and owned by foreigners,[113] Sun managed to Sinicize it, as the vast open space of the Great Lawn afforded him the opportunity to practice "borrowing," a time-honored gardening technique of imperial China. Hence, the lawn functioned as a discursive space with which Sun made a firm connection between the discourses on gardening of late imperial times and the political situation in Mao's China. Deep down in his mind, however, Sun was intent on advancing an agenda of restoring the ancient relic of *Huagang guanyu* rather than of offering public services of indoctrinating and mobilizing the masses, as envisioned by the political authorities.[114] Given Sun's training in Chinese-style fine arts, such an understanding was consistent with his awareness of the capacity of beasts, birds, fish, and vegetation in Chinese paintings to inform and inspire landscape design in China.[115] As shown above, Sun's priority afforded the intellectuals, writers, and poets the luxury of revisiting the allusions to flowers and fish that had been repeatedly cited for millennia.

The spatial practice of the ordinary citizens of Hangzhou and visitors in their day-to-day lives differed from those of the CCP leaders and the architect. To them, the Great Lawn was a space for strolling, drinking tea, enjoying the lake view, and engaging in various outdoor activities. Their spatial practice also included their deliberate avoidance of this space to keep themselves away from direct sun or to seek a place for a tryst in the shade. It was the disparity among the spatial practices of the political authorities, the cultural elites (including the architect), and the everyday visitors/tourists that during the Cultural Revolution prompted radical Maoists to hurl charges against the "revisionists" (*xiuzheng zhuyi zhe* 修正主义者) who had transformed Hangzhou-based parks into nothing but a locus of "taking a rest for seniors, dating for the youngsters, and playing for children" and had turned a blind eye to those parks' "considerable political significance."[116]

Throughout this chapter, I have shown how a politicized location burgeoned into political, mnemonic, and experiential space. The construction of the park exemplified what György Enyedi calls "the built environment" created by "planned urbanization" in socialist countries. Such central planning of urbanization was intended to alter "the social structures and relations," but was not necessarily successful.[117] This chapter has underscored a complex relationship between the park as the built environment and its users, who benefited from this new public space by taking the liberty to make use of the park in their own ways. The three spaces were by no means mutually exclusive. As I have shown, the fish, the vital element of the *Huaguang guanyu* park, allowed writers, scholars, and poets to express a yearning for freedom à la Zhuangzi; whereas the same fish were the trophy from poaching for children from nearby neighborhoods in their day-to-day lives. The fish assumed a role as a vital prop in the political realm, for their exoticness continually fascinated foreign visitors to the park, including President Nixon, who made the world-famous statement: "I never saw goldfish that large."[118] The fish became a nodal point where the three spaces intersected with one another. It is thus fair to argue that the CCP-initiated and -led political and propaganda programs gave rise to novel aesthetic and lived experiences and were thereby conducive to making a new type of everyday life in socialism.

My emphasis on the intertwining of the political/propaganda and the experiential/everyday uses of the park constitutes an attempt to wrestle with two trends in the study of everyday life in the socialist world. On the one hand, everyday life took on special significance because it was the very locus at which the party's ideological power was "naturalized" and thereby became legible to the general population.[119] On the other hand, it provided an arena where individuals at the grassroots level staged their resistance to state domination.[120] In contrast, this chapter downplays the opposition between the interventionist party-state and a resistant population. Hence, I contend that the political, the discursive, and the personal could be mutually constitutive, and their intermingling, interaction, and intertwining were the very essence of the day-to-day in Mao-era China.

CHAPTER THREE

Forests, Propaganda, and Agency
The Afforestation Movement in Hangzhou, 1950–1976

The public park of *Huagang guanyu* received renewed national attention in the late 1950s due to the publication of Sun Xiaoxiang's 1959 essay, as mentioned in the preceding chapter. This article's release and circulation coincided with the CCP's call for a nationwide campaign of the "garden-ization of the earth" (*dadi yuanlin hua* 大地园林化) at the height of the Great Leap Forward movement. In "The Resolution Regarding Several Issues on the People's Commune" (*Guanyu renmin gongshe ruogan wenti de jueyi* 关于人民公社若干问题的决议), enacted in December 1958, the "garden-ization of the earth" was construed as a measure of improving the people's living and working conditions and minimizing the urban-rural differences in China when agricultural productivity was believed to have grown exponentially. According to this resolution, given a massive hike in grain production, one-third of the land across the country could be transformed into fields specifically for cash crops and ornamental plants to meet the goal of the "garden-ization of the earth."[1]

Propagating the idea of "garden" or *yuanlin* 园林 in the 1958 resolution signaled the CCP's commitment to learning from China's gardening tradition and its decision to depart from the Soviet conception of the "park of culture and rest" in light of the acrimonious China-Soviet dispute.[2] More relevant to this chapter, this political campaign was the continuation and upgrading of the ongoing movement of "making green the motherland" (*Lühua zuguo* 绿化祖国)— that is, the Party's long-term afforestation effort in China. For radical Maoists as well as laypersons, the movement of "making green the motherland" and its late-1950s transmutation, the "garden-ization of the earth," were nothing but planting trees. In an editorial published in the *People's Daily* on March 27, 1959, for example, the editorialist explicitly equated the "garden-ization of the earth" with establishing "timber forests" (*yongcai lin* 用材林), "economic forests" (*jingji lin* 经济林), and "shelter forests" (*fanghu lin* 防护林).[3] The heavy emphasis on afforestation thus illustrated an irony in this political movement: the "garden-ization of the earth" was indeed intended to reject the very idea of traditional (spectacle) gardening in China, despite the rhetoric of keeping China's cultural tradition alive.[4]

This chapter is devoted to documenting the afforestation—another propaganda-campaign project with a mixed blessing—in the West Lake area during Mao's time. Scholars recently find that afforestation in different historical contexts was key to the government's centralized state-making initiatives to "rehabilitate state authority."[5] Along a similar vein, the decades-long afforestation campaign in the hills surrounding West Lake has been propagated as a success story to serve state-building purposes: mountains had been stripped bare because of the substantial loss of trees in this region caused by bloody wars, and the disappearance of trees led to severe soil erosion before 1949. In the three decades following the CCP's takeover of Hangzhou, by comparison, over three million trees have been planted and nurtured, and approximately four thousand hectares of bare hills were thereby blanketed with green vegetation.[6]

This well-publicized afforestation campaign in the West Lake area constituted a part of the nationwide movement of "making green the motherland." Initially, the campaign was hailed in 1956 as both a political affair that helped the Party preach the conception of agricultural collectivization and an economic mission purported to supply timber and other forest products.[7] Developing monoculture tree plantations—namely scientific forestry—had long been cherished by planners and foresters all over the world as a method of maximizing timber production. James Scott posits that scientific forestry was a simplification and thereby manipulation of "an otherwise far more complex and unwieldy reality" engineered by the state. Under such well-calculated management of trees, "the actual tree with its vast number of possible uses was replaced by an abstract tree representing a volume of lumber or firewood."[8] Ravi Rajan further points out that modern forestry as a "bureaucratic-scientific approach to resource management" was quintessentially a "contract" or a "quid pro quo"—that is, "conservation, in exchange for sustained, long-term yield."[9]

Both Scott and Rajan put emphasis on the supply of timber to meet economic goals and the state's central role in the rational management of trees and other plants. Nevertheless, the case of the afforestation of the West Lake area during Mao's years tells a different story. Timber production had hardly been at the heart of afforestation endeavors. In the early 1950s, local cadres drew up an afforestation agenda for lessening soil erosion and thereby boosting agricultural production. In other words, the planners were, in reality, coping with the issue of "desiccationism"—that is, making a "connection between the depletion of tree cover and phenomena like drought or soil erosion."[10] Such an agenda was a testimony to the unparalleled intimacy of the relationship between forestry and agriculture" in China.[11] Moreover, the planners in Hangzhou were also intent on stopping soil erosion to keep West Lake's water pure, given the lake's irreplaceable role in political tourism, as the preceding chapter has shown.

While the local cadres boasted of the benefits brought about by the afforestation in the West Lake region to Hangzhou's agriculture and tourism, it is vital to understand that the state was far from a rational planner and calculator, as in the case of the project of dredging the lake. Party policies on planting trees and other plants underwent frequent revision and alteration, creating a high degree of confusion and misunderstanding at the local levels. Hence, the effectiveness of this campaign, just like that of the afforestation efforts in other parts of the country and during different historical ages, was conditioned by a plethora of local factors: cultural, institutional, and economic.[12] The success or failure of an afforestation movement thus went beyond the planners' expectations and calculations.

This chapter documents both the accomplishments in the afforestation campaigns in the hills in Hangzhou and the predicaments and difficulties that foresters and CCP cadres faced. The coexistence of a success story of the decades-long afforestation movement and a heartbreaking account of deforestation was not unique to Hangzhou. The juxtaposition between the two competing narratives is the defining characteristic of the existing scholarship on forestry in post-1949 China. While Jack Westboy praises the PRC for instigating the "mightiest afforestation effort the world has ever seen,"[13] other scholars emphasize the Party-state's massive destruction of forests as emblematic of its hostile attitude toward nature.[14] As Geoffrey Murray and Ian Cook nicely put it, the CCP's successes on the environmental front and severe ecological problems existed side by side in Mao's China.[15] The gulf between the two narratives attests to the operation of "two different *kinds* of truths" in post-1949 China, namely, "much optimism about socialism" and the disillusionment "by the distortions of Mao's regime and the failures of socialism to live up to its many promises."[16]

Throughout the book, I have argued that this disparity stemmed, in no small part, from two different angles—the vertical view and the side view—from which a propaganda-campaign project was viewed, experienced, and assessed. Thus, the gap between the blueprints drawn up by the higher authorities and individuals' lived experiences constitutes the very essence of the present research on propaganda-campaign projects in Mao-era China. On the one hand, the planning and execution of such projects not only functioned as state-led propaganda but also set up a framework within which local citizens negotiated with the state, shaped their subjectivities in socialism, and reaped the benefits from them. On the other hand, individuals at the local level experienced and utilized the products of such projects in different ways than the political authorities had envisioned. It is true that the afforestation project at issue was a "form of participatory propaganda" that demanded local inhabitants take their part.[17] However, it raises the question of how individuals at the local level participated in and received it. As this chapter shall show, this project fostered its own nonconformists: local villagers who harbored an intention to protect their own private properties vis-à-vis the collectivizing and interventionist state, poachers who illegally felled trees for firewood and timber, and, most importantly, tea growers who were keen on expanding their tea plantations at the cost of mountain forests.

The account of the confrontation and interaction between state propaganda and the villagers leaves out a significant actor in the story of Hangzhou's afforestation movement: nonhumans—trees and pests. As Anne Whiston Spirn cogently

Figure 3.1. The map of the West Lake area with an emphasis on locations mentioned in this chapter.

puts it, "humans are not the sole authors of landscape." Other living creatures also contribute to the making of landscape and respond to its changes.[18] In the case of Hangzhou's afforestation movement, nonhuman entities exercised their agency and cast a long shadow over the CCP's decades-long afforestation efforts: the lower-than-expected density of pines caused concerns, and pest infestation proved particularly catastrophic. It thus came as no surprise that local officials drew a parallel between damages inflicted by humans and havoc wreaked by bugs, labeling them as the two archenemies.[19]

The Afforestation Movement in the Early 1950s

To rationalize the launching of the afforestation movement in the West Lake region immediately after the CCP's takeover of Hangzhou, the Party's propagandists depicted the mountains surrounding West Lake as wastelands and thereby painted a bleak picture of forestry in the Hangzhou area before 1949: the scarcity of woodlands was exacerbated by the Anti-Japanese War (1937–1945), when the Japanese occupiers and poverty-stricken local inhabitants ruthlessly cut down all trees, especially pines, in the nearby hills.[20] A striking contrast between an ecologically degraded China before the Liberation and a greener China during PRC times thus symbolized the temporal gap between "old China" and "new China." In Nicolai Volland's words, socialism "became present as much as future," whereas its "other (the West, capitalism) became the past, both their own past, now left behind, and that of global history."[21] It was thus no surprise that news stories about deforestation in Taiwan—the PRC's "other"—in the 1950s bore a resemblance to the description of the massive disappearances of forests in pre-1949 Hangzhou, paralleling pre-Liberation China with present-day Taiwan as the PRC's past.[22]

Nevertheless, blaming pre-1949 governments in Hangzhou for purposely damaging forests or not putting in any afforestation effort was an unfounded accusation. Shortly after the war against Japan had ended, for example, the government of the Nationalist Party (Guomindang 国民党 or GMD) instituted a ten-year afforestation program in Hangzhou. A government report shows that the Hangzhou authorities had planned to afforest about 15,000 *mu* (1,000 hectares) or over 20 percent of the land surrounding West Lake in 1949 alone. With the GMD's defeat in the civil war, the plan never came to fruition. Like its CCP counterpart, the GMD's municipal government in Hangzhou also issued injunctions against unauthorized woodcutting, quarrying, and tomb building in the lakeside hills to protect mountainous woodlands.[23]

In the opening years of the 1950s, CCP authorities adopted a similar protective approach known as "closing hillsides to facilitate afforestation" (*fengshan yulin*

封山育林), a conservancy policy deployed by the PRC government across the nation in the early 1950s. This method entailed sealing hilly areas to preclude livestock and humans from grazing and gathering fuel to allow saplings to grow. With additional human efforts to nurture trees, semi-artificial woodlands could thus be created.[24] In the case of Hangzhou, a government institution known as the Committee of Protecting Forests in Hilly Area of West Lake (*Xihu shanqu hulin weiyuanhui* 西湖山区护林委员会) was established in late 1949.[25] It aimed at mobilizing the masses to reverse a trend of wanton felling of trees in this region. A report filed in 1950 pointed the finger at not just the local inhabitants who sneaked into the hills to gather firewood and steal saplings. More seriously, PLA soldiers in Hangzhou shipped truckloads of timber or firewood from the mountains to save their operational and living costs and support their productive work. The committee thus created 102 protection teams with 1,866 members to guard against woodcutters, gatherers, and poachers. The same report confirmed that by the end of 1950, 13,373 *mu* (891.53 hectares) of hilly areas had been shut off.[26]

The committee could not have reached its goals without the full support of the municipal and provincial governments. Tan Zhenlin, Zhejiang's supreme leader, gave an order on April 19, 1950, instructing government institutions, schools, and the PLA in Hangzhou to cease felling trees to reclaim woodlands in both mountainous areas and scenic spots close to West Lake.[27] Between 1950 and 1953, the ban on entering the mountains was lifted between early April and late December on an annual basis, permitting the locals and tea growers to gather firewood as fuel in their day-to-day lives and for tea production.[28] By contrast, constructing burial sites in the mountains was specifically prohibited practically from day one of the PRC.[29] Throughout the Mao era, three surveys were conducted to assess the effectiveness of the program of "closing hillsides to facilitate afforestation" in 1950, 1959, and 1975. In Mount Jade Emperor (*Yuhuang shan* 玉皇山) area, the examiners saw mostly stumps, weeds, and eroded soil in 1950. By 1959, buds had reportedly begun to appear on the stumps, while newly planted saplings were growing fast and had begun the canopy closure process. Sixteen years later, the same area was found to have been a grove with a certain degree of biodiversity consisting of white oaks, sawtooth oaks, camphor, *Schima superba*, pines, and other trees whose average diameters measured between eight and sixteen centimeters and canopy density amounted to 0.6 to 0.8.[30]

Within 65,000 *mu* (4,333.33 hectares) of hillside areas in the mountains surrounding West Lake, 10,000 *mu* (666.67 hectares) turned out to be forests created under the program of "closing hillsides to facilitate afforestation." The majority of the land (51,000 *mu* or 3,400 hectares) was covered with human-made forests developed ever since the opening years of the PRC.[31] Woodlands grown out of the plan of "closing hillsides to facilitate afforestation" differ considerably from monoculture tree plantations in that the former are semi-artificial with limited human intervention, whereas the latter are single-crop cultivation requiring maximal labor input.

It was the outlook for developing monoculture tree plantations that boosted the Hangzhou municipal government's confidence in drawing up a plan in 1950 to complete greening 65,000 *mu* of mountainous woodlands in five years,[32] but the campaign proved far more time-consuming. Calling for the participation of soldiers, cadres, students, and ordinary citizens of Hangzhou was a standard way to initiate, sustain, and accelerate the afforestation movement, as its mobilization enabled them to arrive at a complete understanding of what mass movements were. Among them, students from various schools in Hangzhou were usually subject to mass mobilization. Their service to the movement of greening the West Lake area was occasionally rewarded with naming rights. A woodland near Yellow Dragon Cave (*Huanglong dong* 黄龙洞), for example, was named "Juniors' Grove" (*Shaonian lin* 少年林) on Children's Day in 1955.[33] Galvanized by young men's and women's unbridled enthusiasm about planting trees across the city, a Buddhist priest rallied his fellow monks to partake in the 1955 forestation campaign.[34] In all fairness, such a mass mobilization succeeded in organizing the general population and instilling the notion of voluntarism. In a six-year period between 1956 and 1961, the number of volunteer enrolled laborers from Hangzhou amounted to 808,000.[35]

The afforestation campaign was thus the embodiment of a unique mode of production in the early years of the PRC—what Miriam Gross calls "mass effort"[36]—that entailed intensifying labor input to overcome the scarcity of material resources without incurring a high cost. Jack Westboy attributes the PRC's success in afforesting China to the part-time engagement of "tens of millions of Chinese" in "forestry activities."[37] Just like in the campaign of dredging West Lake, voluntary laborers were not expected to achieve high efficiency, but the way of organizing them served as the "showroom" of mass mobilization of labor and the spirit of self-sacrifice under socialism.

In reality, the best solution to the accelerated afforestation was to select fast-growing tree species, particularly *maweisong* 马尾松 or the horsetail pine (*Pinus massoniana*). The choice was not made randomly. Hailed as the "most ecologically and economically significant tree genus" across the globe and a plantation tree that grows "in harsh environments that are cold and/or dry,"[38] the pine is widely distributed in regions south of the Yellow River in China.[39] The abovementioned ten-year afforestation plan carried out by the GMD government in the late 1940s also placed a premium on cultivating the horsetail pine.[40] Not surprisingly, it soon topped the list of designated tree species for speedy afforestation recommended by CCP officials after the Liberation.[41] A study conducted in the 1960s highlighted the advantages of all types of pines, especially horsetail pines, such as supplying sturdy timber with high resilience and producing rosin, an important industrial material. The same study emphasized the horsetail pine's remarkable speed of growth: it could reach over one meter in one year and three meters in five or six years.[42] As a matter of fact, as early as the 1930s, foresters in China had been impressed by the horsetail pine's ability to grow more swiftly than any other tree species.[43] Among all its advantages, it was the knowledge of this pine's exceedingly high growth rate and ability to endure harsh surroundings that prompted local officials in Hangzhou to choose it as the mainstay tree for the afforestation movement in the early years of the PRC.[44]

A second factor behind the CCP government's consideration of pines as the mainstay tree genus was a longtime cultural tradition in Hangzhou. A report filed by a botanist in 1964 reminded its readers that poets in the Tang dynasty, such as Bai Juyi 白居易 (777–846), composed poems in praise of pines. Some scenic spots had long been defined by the existence of pine groves ever since the Tang and Song dynasties.[45] Pine was a favorite theme in paintings, poems, and prose in imperial China because the imagery of rugged pines symbolized the gentry's special temperament: an agonistic ethos and an uncompromising attitude.[46] Beyond China, praising the pine's unique qualities and exploring its rich symbolism—namely, "longevity, loyalty, virtue, and even masculinity"—was a transcultural tradition in East Asia.[47] In actuality, the Hangzhou authorities were keenly aware of the necessity of cultivating specific species to fit the cultural heritage of certain regions. In Yunqi 云栖, for example, a large stretch of bamboo groves was created, while osmanthus trees were reintroduced to Manjuelong 满觉陇.[48] Historically, bamboos at Yunqi and sweet-scented osmanthus at Manjuelong had inspired poetic sentiments and long appealed to tourists and visitors. The recuperation of China's cultural tradition—the selection of trees in this case—carried particular politico-cultural ramifications within the socialist bloc in this period: a sense of nationalist particularism was generated "outside the evolving nations" in the context of political universalism, namely, the international communist movement.[49]

Given the economic, cultural, and political significance of pine cultivation in the West Lake area, pine forests—mainly those of the horsetail pine—dominated Hangzhou. By 1964, two-thirds of hillside lands in the West Lake area were blanketed with horsetail pines.[50] In 1977, the percentage dipped after other species were introduced in the ensuing afforestation movement. A survey indicated that pine woodlands constituted 49.3 percent of all arboreal forests.[51] Despite such notable success, pine plantations in the West Lake area were not without their problems. Other than pest infestations, which I shall discuss at length later in this chapter, horsetail pines were notoriously known for their low survival rate in this region. A 1950 survey revealed that its average survival rate was 60 percent, 10 to 30 percent lower than that of other trees.[52] As a matter of fact, 60 percent might be an overblown number to begin with. Vaclav Smil, for example, estimates that the success rate of afforestation across China was a mere 30 percent.[53] Even though it was very likely that the survival rate in Hangzhou was far higher than that of the entire country, the fact remains that Hangzhou-based foresters found it hard to keep horsetail pines alive.

Given the afforestation movement's role in propaganda, the low survival rate of trees was understandable, or even foreseeable, as the initial massive labor mobilization was more "visible," or a better fit, for media coverage than the slow and continuous process of upkeep. In 1957, local cadres began to express their concerns over the poor forest form of horsetail pine groves. Given the pressing need for accelerated afforestation in the early 1950s, most, if not all, pines were hastily planted. Necessary silvicultural work, such as thinning, was largely ignored. In consequence, trees were throwing out branches rampantly, and the spacing among them was uncomfortably small.[54] Eight years later, local officials confirmed that thinning projects had been carried out in the past several years, effectively improving the forest form and enhancing the spacing.[55] Nevertheless, a separate study conducted in 1964 identified a new problem: the inability of saplings to grow up. The researcher explained that pine trees at the age of fifteen or so could theoretically be mature enough to shed seeds, and accordingly, new trees would grow. Unfortunately, his observation of several sections of woodland kept disappointing him. In the space of sixteen square meters, for example, he saw twelve saplings in May 1964. Upon returning in September, he was upset that those saplings had either died or vanished—none had survived. The researcher thus attributed the grove's lack of reproductive ability to a number of factors, including the undesired high canopy density, bad landform, poaching by nearby villagers, and animals' activities.[56]

Hence, this report revealed a chilling fact about afforestation in this region—the lack of well-thought-out planning and proper management of mountain forests/plantations. In this sense, most horsetail pine plantations could hardly fall into the category of modern scientific forestry in the strictest sense, which is characterized by "clean-weeded, even-aged, and regimented rows of export corps."[57] The absence of efficient management also manifested itself in the fact that those groves slipped from excessively high density to relatively low density within a decade. The 1964 report discovered that, on average, each hectare of woodland featured 2,096 pine trees less than ten years old.[58] As a comparison, the CCP administrators in Beijing set a goal nationwide to plant ten thousand to twelve thousand saplings with a survival rate of 90 percent.[59] The real-life scenario, however, is that the density of a ten-year-old pine forest is between 3,900 and 4,500 per hectare during the PRC era.[60] Such a low density in the West Lake area once again hinted at an underwhelming survival rate. An unintended but positive consequence of mismanaging those woodlands was slightly higher biodiversity than in a proper monoculture plantation. The 1964 report found that Hangzhou's horsetail pine forests consisted of an abundance of largely green vegetation. In all horsetail pine forests, there existed 182 species of ferns and vascular plants under sixty-two families. In a sample woodland (one hundred square meters), the researcher spotted over twenty plants, including white oaks and sawtooth oaks.[61]

The Afforestation Movement in Hangzhou since the Late 1950s

In 1956, a CCP-led, countrywide movement of "making green the motherland" officially kicked off with the publication of an editorial in the *People's Daily* on February 17, 1956. Entitled "Making Green the Motherland" (*Lühua zuguo* 绿化祖国), the essay conveyed some important messages. First, seven years into the PRC era, overall forest acreage stagnated across the country, despite some local endeavors to plant trees in the mountains or on wastelands, especially in northern and northwestern China.[62] Second, a bountiful supply of timber and other forestry products took precedence in this campaign. In other words, the necessity to industrialize China rather than conserve and expand forests per se was the top priority. In reality, the CCP leadership, particularly Mao, had already called for afforesting China for the sake of augmenting timber supply in the early 1950s.[63] In a sense, it was the enormous demand for wood that offset the afforestation efforts across the country. Third, the afforestation movement constituted a vital part of the ongoing collectivizing campaign that was sweeping the entire nation. It is thus no surprise that the editorialist called for rural collective organizations' activism in this movement. Finally, the campaign played a vital role in ideologically indoctrinating "190 million youngsters" in China, urging them to participate in the mass effort of labor nationwide.[64] Hence, the movement of "making green the motherland" typified a propaganda-campaign project that sought to simultaneously reap economic profits and attain political/ideological purposes.

In October 1957, the call for making China green was officially instituted as a national policy. The document that was circulated in 1957, "An Outline of National Agricultural Development, 1956–1967" (*Yijiu wuliu nian dao yijiu liuqi nian quanguo nongye fazhan gangyao* 一九五六年到一九六七年全国农业发展纲要),

adopted all the comments made in the editorial described above in the *People's Daily* but added that the aim of planting trees should never be accomplished at the cost of arable lands.[65] On December 10, 1958, the Party leadership, seized by a whim that China had to tackle a new problem of overproducing grains across the country, offered a more detailed directive, demanding peasants to "reduce the cultivated area of fields for agricultural products by, say, about one-third [of what is now]." Hence, according to the directive, the portion of the land saved by the peasants would serve multiple purposes, including conserving water, planting trees, and developing cash crops.[66] Although the directive was generated on a false presumption of soaring agricultural production nationwide, the rhetoric of expanding cash crop production—namely, the "garden-ization of the earth"—as an integral part of the movement of "making green the motherland" continued to ring true until Mao's last years.

In line with the upper-echelon leadership's vision that one-third of the land in China could be transformed into spaces for woodlands, ornamental gardens, and suppliers of cash crops, the Hangzhou-based cadres filed a report on April 27, 1959, suggesting that one-third of the lands in the West Lake area be reserved for planting trees, digging artificial lakes, and growing varieties of ornamental plants. Hence, the "garden-ization of the earth" movement steered afforestation in the West Lake area toward a new direction: beginning in the late 1950s, local authorities began to lay emphasis on cultivating cash crops in addition to pines and other trees. To maximize the use of those lands as a productive space, furthermore, this report's drafter(s) called for cultivating a greater number of oil plants, medicinal plants, and fruit trees.[67] By 1965, Hangzhou's lakeside hills were reportedly dotted with not only pines but also camphor, sweet-scented osmanthus trees, horse chestnuts, and other trees of economic importance.[68] Furthermore, local officials devised a detailed plan that had fundamentally refashioned public parks in Hangzhou in the final years of the Mao era. Hangzhou Botanical Garden (*Hangzhou zhiwu yuan* 杭州植物园), for example, was rebuilt as a nursery garden specifically for medicinal herbs.[69]

The public park of *Huagang guanyu* was undoubtedly another main target. According to a report published in 1976, a large number of cash crops—including osmanthus, persimmon, *Citrus medica*, apple, crimson glory (*mohong* 墨红), orange, palm, and walnut—had been introduced to the park. Among them, osmanthus and crimson glory, which had been extensively grown as early as 1958, were critical sources of perfume. In 1958, the West Lake Perfumery Plant (*Xihu xiangliao chang* 西湖香料厂) and other factories were established to process the local produce in a timely fashion.[70] Nevertheless, the local authorities soon felt dismayed to discover a major issue related to the movement of the "garden-ization of the earth": severe pollution caused by those newly established factories threatened not only the beauty of scenic spots nearby but also lakeside residents' livelihoods.[71] By 1979, the Hangzhou government was finally scheduled to relocate the perfumery plant within three years.[72] Pollution, however, was not the lone problem that this afforestation movement generated. In the remaining part of the chapter, I shall discuss at length some other issues associated with the movement of "making green the motherland" in the West Lake area that could well jeopardize the very cause of afforestation.

The Issues

For the local authorities, the most pressing issue was the low survival rate of trees planted in the lakeside hills. It resulted, in part, from human activities, namely the mismanagement of local villagers and cadres. However, nonhuman factors could hardly be negligible. Throughout the Mao era, both human and nonhuman actors competed with planners and foresters and kept undercutting the afforestation efforts in the West Lake area.

Ownership Rights

From day one of the PRC era, the CCP's cadres in the West Lake area faced the grave problem of poorly defined land ownership in the mountains adjacent to the lake. Although land reform was conducted immediately following the Liberation in an attempt to give inhabitants in the hills land for planting trees, land ownership was complicated and confusing, in no small part because of the landholdings of religious institutions (chiefly Buddhist temples). As the CCP had abolished the ownership rights of monasteries in other parts of China as early as 1947,[73] those of hillside lands formerly under the control of Buddhist temples had become a gray zone after the majority of monks had disrobed and fled Hangzhou for fear of religious persecution, leaving large chunks of land unattended. The occupation of some temples by government and military institutions also precluded local officials from adequately managing their affiliated lands.[74] Under these circumstances, the CCP government classified the mountain land into three categories for afforestation. First, the owners of privately owned hillside lands were responsible for planting trees. Second, in lands originally possessed by monasteries, individual foresters partnered with the government to engage in afforestation. Third, local PLA soldiers, government clerks, schoolteachers, and students undertook tree planting in areas inaccessible to local dwellers.[75]

The local government also promulgated a regulation as early as 1949 to further encourage the first category, namely owners of private lands, and the second category, namely participants of joint afforestation, to plant more trees. This regulation mandated that the Bureau of Gardening Administration supervise those privately owned plots and share revenue if trees were cultivated cooperatively by the government and individual foresters.[76] The 1949 regulation, however, failed to appease the disgruntled villagers who continued to claim their rights in the mountains. The local authorities soon ran into more problems related to the afforestation movement and land or tree ownership. For example, the 1949 regulation did not take into account woodcutters' and herders' usufruct rights, stirring up bitter animosity between tree planters and woodcutters/herders. Moreover, the proprietorship of some hills was far from clear, allowing multiple parties to wrestle with one another for the rights to a single mountain. Under those circumstances, a new regulation was enacted in 1952, which attempted to draw clear-cut lines between the three categories mentioned above.[77]

The agricultural collectivization movement that began in the mid-1950s further complicated the ownership rights and thereby demoralized foresters in the West Lake area as well as in other parts of Zhejiang. As the collectivization campaign prevailed, the ownership of trees that local inhabitants had been cultivating for years became a sticking point. A report filed in 1956 indicated that trees were indiscriminately felled in some areas because they, just like the land, had been labeled public property. Hence, local villagers obtained inadequate—or even no—compensation for handing over land and trees to join the cooperatives.[78] In consequence, a contributor to a journal in mid-1956 reemphasized a ruling that it was unnecessary to confiscate the villagers' scattered trees in the process of collectivizing the countryside. Rather, allowing the villagers to own a small number of trees would certainly strengthen their motivation to participate in the collectivizing movement.[79] The ruling, nonetheless, fell on deaf ears. By the summer of 1957, a Zhejiang-based agriculture official reported that 70 percent of woodlands remained unincorporated into the newly established communes in the countryside because local CCP leaders tended to make low appraisals of trees initially possessed by foresters. In response, the villagers began to cut down trees on a massive scale before the communes could seize them at unfair prices.[80]

Groves originally possessed by Buddhist temples, which constituted the majority of hillside woodlands, posed a different problem. By rule, the state appropriated and managed all such lands, but various cooperatives proclaimed that their members kept tending ancient trees therein for years, and they were therefore entitled to receive the revenue from those lands. The clash between local governments and collectives thus intensified and remained unresolved by the mid-1960s.[81] Occasionally, such controversies escalated into armed conflicts.[82] As late as 1974, an archival record shows that the People's Commune of West Lake (*Xihu renmin gongshe* 西湖人民公社), the administrative unit of the West Lake region for most of the Mao era, constantly vied with various production brigades under its control for land ownership of woods in lakeside hills.[83]

Such ill-defined and contested rights to land and trees led to the illegal felling of trees, which was usually interpreted as poaching by local authorities. As shown above, some of this tree cutting could be understood as the individual villagers' defiance of the state's imposition of collectivization. Toward the end of the Great Leap Forward movement, abject poverty impelled some local inhabitants to secretly cut down "publicly owned" trees in mountains and exchange timber for cash. Finally, the provincial leadership in Zhejiang decided to severely punish a few offenders as a stern warning in 1961. In a public trial with five hundred attendees, the four poachers, one of whom was found to be a Party committee member of a production brigade, were sentenced to one to three years in prison.[84] During the early years of the Cultural Revolution, the mismanagement of mountain forests worsened because of the dysfunction of government and judiciary institutions. A report filed in 1968 revealed that hundreds of jobless young men and women in their twenties organized themselves to raid woodlands in the mountains beside West Lake. They attacked whoever tried to stop them, including local villagers, rangers, and cadres, and became violent and burned down peasants' houses. Cherry blossom trees and bamboos in Mount Jade Emperor had been wiped out, and timber and firewood were illegally sold. The reporter estimated that 10 percent of trees had disappeared.[85] In sum, forests in the Hangzhou area endured three major waves of sabotage: 1958, when timber and fuel were in enormous demand for smelting steel; 1960–1962, when the national and local economy collapsed; and the early Cultural Revolution period, when local governments were in paralysis.[86]

The Rivalry between Tea Growers and Foresters

The stories about violence against rangers and cadres were a testimony to the unabated tension between afforestation and agriculture in post-1949 China. Across the entire country, the high-profile afforestation movement, which compelled national or even international attention and thereby served an explicit propaganda purpose, could not mask the less publicized story of the massive loss of forests for the sake of providing fuel and supplying farmlands by the end of Mao's rule.[87] Across China, the alternating afforestation and deforestation led to the expansion of cropland from about eighty million hectares to 120–130 million by 1980.[88]

In the West Lake area, it was not necessarily farmers, but tea growers, who clashed with foresters and rangers competing for space. In actuality, developing tea production in the Hangzhou region was not a lesser program for propaganda.

First of all, Hangzhou-made tea was the favorite beverage of the CCP's top-echelon leaders, such as Zhou Enlai 周恩来 (1898–1976) and Liu Shaoqi.[89] Second, demands for Hangzhou-made tea as gifts for international exchange soared, especially after the normalization of the diplomatic relationship between China and countries of the Western bloc in Mao's final years. Lastly, some lakeside tea-producing villages, especially Meijiawu 梅家坞, gained Premier Zhou Enlai's favor as model collectivized tea farms, allowing Chinese diplomats to show foreign visitors the astounding success of the PRC's agricultural collectivization movement.[90] Therefore, tea production continued to gain enormous importance in the productive space in the hills surrounding West Lake.

Interestingly, tea did not usually count as a cash crop in the "garden-ization of the earth" movement in Hangzhou. On the contrary, tea-producing villages or brigades were made to engage in planting trees of economic value besides fulfilling the task of supplying "gifts tea" (*lipin cha* 礼品茶) to the state.[91] In consequence, the dual mission of afforestation and tea cultivation, understandably, gave rise to conflicts over land use between foresters and tea peasants. Such clashes lingered throughout the Mao years in the hillside areas along West Lake. In the opening years of the PRC, the importance of tea production in Hangzhou gained little recognition. Considering the limited space in the West Lake area, in December 1951, the municipal planners allocated a modest amount of land (up to twenty hectares) to build up tea plantations.[92] Such conservative planning demonstrated the local authorities' priority in the early 1950s, namely, dredging West Lake and constructing sanatoriums on the lakeshore. It is thus no wonder that tea peasants complained in the mid-1950s that their lands had been encroached upon for three reasons. First, some lands were requisitioned to store silt from the lake, as I have shown in Chapter 1. Second, amid the afforestation movement, tea growers further lost their lands. Third, constructing sanatoriums, hotels, and hospitals by various government and military organs had proved a colossal waste of land, most of which initially belonged to tea peasants. The president of Beijing Agriculture University (*Beijing nongye daxue* 北京农业大学) conducted an investigation in Hangzhou in 1957 and concluded that tea plantations had lost enormous lands for the ongoing project of "making green the motherland."[93] Hangzhou's deputy mayor similarly admitted in 1957 that tea growers' interests had been infringed upon over the years, but he found it impossible to deforest some afforested areas as compensation to those tea farmers.[94]

Among the three, tea peasants were particularly upset by local officials' ill-planned programs of requisitioning their tea farms without taking into account tea growers' livelihoods. Since avoiding soil erosion had been deemed the main motive behind the afforestation movements in the West Lake area, some peasants retorted that soil erosion posed a threat to the lakeside regions, but not necessarily the hills. Therefore, it was pointless to wipe out their tea plantations to grow trees. In the hillside space in the City God Hill (*Chenghuang shan* 城隍山), for example, the government took over the lands of twenty tea-growing households, many of whom had not received any compensation.[95] During a meeting attended by Party officials, tea peasants, and representatives from the Hangzhou Bureau of Gardening Administration in May 1957, a consensus was reached to reclaim more "wastelands" for tea cultivation as a response to tea peasants' bitter complaints.[96]

Several years into the PRC era, tea's importance loomed large as a beverage and as a gift in the political arena, and tea cultivation in the Hangzhou area accordingly gained greater leverage. Statistics show that the size of tea plantations across Hangzhou increased by six times between 1949 and 1976.[97] Although I do not have the numbers about tea fields in the West Lake area during Mao's time, it was clear that they also underwent remarkable growth. The acreage of tea plantations in Longjin 龙井, one of the dozens of villages/production brigades under the People's Commune of West Lake's control, amounted to 267 hectares in 1959, as opposed to the planned 200 hectares in the entire West Lake region estimated by the local authorities in 1951.[98] Similarly, the acreage of tea plantations in Meijiawu was scheduled to increase by 30 percent in 1964.[99] Not all newfound tea fields grew from reclaimed wastelands as the CCP officials had envisioned in 1957. In Longjin, for example, six hectares of paddy fields were transformed into tea fields under the authorization of the Hangzhou government in 1961.[100] In other parts of Hangzhou, the local governments appeared quite generous, allowing villages or production brigades to expand their tea plantations. In 1954, for example, a distant village under Hangxian County reportedly converted 133 hectares of land into tea fields.[101]

Besides schemes to garner new space for tea production endorsed by the local authorities, plans to steal land without official authorization were afoot in various villages throughout Mao's time. A local cadre observed that tea growers' keenness on acquiring more land to cultivate tea stemmed from the high population density in the West Lake area: the acreage of arable lands per capita was 0.04 hectares in the 1970s, compelling tea producers to carve out more space, legally or illegally, from woodlands.[102] Between 1960 and 1962, for example, about 133 hectares of forest were erased. On most occasions, tea peasants, without the approval of their superiors, did not grab lands with great fanfare but resorted to the approach of "nibbling up" (*canshi* 蚕食) woodlands—that is, occupying them piece by piece.[103] Well into the 1970s, the tea peasants' nibbling up of forests had still not ended, despite the injunction issued by local governments. A report filed in

1979, for example, confirmed that 50.6 hectares of groves in the West Lake region had been removed by local tea farmers, with the disappearance of over twenty thousand trees.[104]

Pest Infestation: Pine Moth

Conflicts between the customary usufruct rights to grazing and pasture (in Hangzhou's case, tea growers' rights) and modern, scientific forestry are universal in various cultural and social contexts;[105] in much the same way, pest infestation has also been a commonplace predicament in monoculture forests.[106] Given the almost exclusive cultivation of horsetail pines in the West Lake area, pine moths posed the most severe menace in this region in the first three decades of the PRC. As early as 1936, the Nationalist government had faced severe pine moth infestation in Zhejiang, Fujian, and other provinces and had already promulgated a pest control regulation.[107] In the early 1950s, pine moths were discovered only sporadically. As the afforestation movement gained greater momentum, the pine moth infestation grew exponentially in Hangzhou as well as in other parts of Zhejiang. Across Zhejiang, for example, pine moths assaulted around 16,133 hectares of pine forests each year between 1951 and 1955. The acreages affected skyrocketed to 93,800 hectares per annum between 1971 and 1975 and 231,467 in the 1980s.[108] Generally speaking, pine moth infestation constituted about 80 percent of pest infestation in Hangzhou as well as in other parts of Zhejiang.[109]

For rangers and ordinary villagers, the outbreaks of pine moth infestation cast off a bloodcurdling memory. Research conducted in 1956 found that an adult pine moth was capable of devouring over twenty pine needles in a single day. Pine trees were decimated in woodlands attacked by pine moths. Even trees that were fortunate enough to survive pine moths could not grow normally.[110] A report filed in 1968 vividly portrayed the outbreak of pine moth infestation that haunted the West Lake area:

> Pine forests have generally fallen prey to pine moths. The area hit [by the infestation] amounts to 3,000 *mu* (200 hectares). In some extreme cases, [one can see] over 1,400 moths crawling in one single tree.... In those infestation-affected areas, pine needles have been eaten up, as if [the trees] were burnt down.
>
> [When] the next generation [of pine moths] are hatched, [they] have spread to the entire mountain forest in West Lake, of which horsetail pine woodlands constitute seventy percent. Once [those horsetail pine trees] fall victim, not only will the decade-long afforestation effort come to naught, but the landscape of West Lake will also be affected.

Forty-two thousand *mu* (2,800 hectares) of horsetail pine forests have, to varying degrees, been damaged [by pine moths] at present.[111]

More often than not, the lack of insecticide and other pesticidal technologies exacerbated pine moth infestation. Under those circumstances, local governments in Zhejiang usually intensified labor input to overcome such deficiencies in technology throughout the 1950s, the 1960s, and even the 1970s. The author of the abovementioned 1968 report, for example, proposed mobilizing local inhabitants to "manually catch bugs" (*rengong buchong* 人工捕虫) in the woodlands near West Lake.[112] To provide participants with incentives, local cadres in some counties in Zhejiang devised a plan of exchanging moths with cash. Despite combining a political approach of massive labor mobilization and a monetary incentive, this pest control campaign not only failed to motivate the half-hearted villagers but also provided a means for them to earn profits. A witness report confirmed the following:

> This said village mobilized its villagers three times last year. . . . [The villagers] were paid by the amounts [of the pine moth]. . . . In consequence, in the process of pest control, [villagers] displayed a tendency of catching big bugs but not small ones, catching [moths perching on] low branches but not [those inhabiting] higher boughs, and catching [those] easy [to catch] but not [those] difficult [to catch]. Pest infestation has, therefore, not come to an end.[113]

This account constitutes a counternarrative to the efficacy of "mass effort," a defining character of socialist labor organization, attesting to the gap between the pronounced intention of state propaganda and the everyday realities of participants in those propaganda-campaign projects. The villagers' participation in the movement but seeking to serve their own interests corroborates Timothy Johnston's observation that citizens in communist regimes neither supported nor resisted the political system imposed upon them. They "simply got by."[114] In other cases, the exacerbation of pest infestation resulted from the villagers' ignorance: they presumed that all infested pine trees must be destroyed, causing unnecessary death of savable trees.[115] To minimize pine moth infestation, Soviet experts advised that mixed forests be developed to replace the monoculture pine forests, but the suggestion fell on deaf ears principally because of the local villagers' lack of knowledge and material resources for planting trees other than pines.[116]

Figure 3.2. Pine moths remain a major threat to pine trees in the West Lake area at present. The photo, taken in September 2019, shows dying pine moth-infested trees on a lakeside hill. The infestation is highlighted in this photo.

Pest Infestation: the Japanese Pine Bast Scale (*Matsucoccus matsumurae [Kuwana]*)

Compared with the pine moth, the Japanese pine bast scale (*Riben songganjie* 日本松干蚧, *Matsucoccus matsumurae [Kuwana]*) was a relatively new pest but presented equally, if not more, severe problems for Hangzhou's horsetail pine trees since the 1960s. Originated in Japan, this invasive pest was said to be discovered first in Shandong and then in some other Chinese provinces, including Zhejiang, as early as the 1950s.[117] Around 1966, the Japanese pine bast scale finally descended upon mountain forests beside West Lake.[118] By 1972, confirmation came that it was the very cause of massive damages to horsetail pine forests in the West Lake area.[119] That year, about 4.66 million pine trees were reportedly affected by the Japanese pine bast scale, half of which had been proclaimed dead, with the remaining trees in a critical condition. In other words, about 388 hectares of pine woodlands (namely, one-third of those in the West Lake Scenic Zone) had been destroyed by this tiny bug. Beyond the West Lake area, the Japanese pine bast scale was held responsible for the demise of 63.9 percent of horsetail pines in other parts of Hangzhou in 1972. The author of a report filed in 1980 recalled that local cadres were concerned with not only the massive death of trees but also the changed look of the scenic zone because of the apparent disappearance of pine trees. In his/her words, the loss of trees had "caused a negative effect upon [China's] foreign affairs," given West Lake's unparalleled significance as a site for political tourism and foreign visitors in the 1970s.[120] By the end of 1973, this uncontrolled pest infestation ruined about two thousand hectares of pine groves and brought down around three hundred thousand trees, posing a deadly threat to all the horsetail forests in the West Lake area.[121]

To cope with the worsening situation, officials and entomologists from various provinces made a concerted effort to understand the mechanism of the destruction wreaked by the Japanese pine bast scale in the wake of the outbreak of this pest infestation. Studies that proliferated in the early and mid-1970s found that it is, in reality, a type of scale insect with a size as big as a grain of sesame. It parasitizes the gaps of trunks or branches of pine trees to suck up tree sap, thereby dehydrating the branches. It can reproduce two or three generations a year, spreading its eggs via wind, water, and human activities.[122] Researchers, meanwhile, came up with various solutions to the infestation. During a meeting on the Japanese pine bast scale held in December 1973, delegations from Liaoning, Shandong, Jiangsu, and Zhejiang suggested that this pest could be killed with the application of the fluoroacetamide solvent. Furthermore, insects, such as *Harmonia axyridis* and *Brumus mongol*, were natural enemies.[123] As time went by, more natural enemies were identified. More importantly, studies on different variants of the Japanese pine bast scale were conducted throughout the 1970s, allowing for a thorough understanding of this hitherto unknown pest.[124] Nonetheless, despite progress made by scientific researchers, villagers at the local level remained ignorant of the basics of pest control techniques. An observer was disturbed to witness villagers selling firewood cut from the Japanese pine bast scale–infested pine trees in 1976 without proper knowledge of the risk of spreading this pernicious bug.[125]

Deadly pest infestations that altered the landscape of mountain forests and poachers who wiped out woodlands in the West Lake area have been juxtaposed in government archives as the two formidable foes of the afforestation movement during the Mao years in Hangzhou.[126] Throughout the chapter, I have shown that the grand program of afforesting the hilly areas surrounding West Lake had been conditioned by a host of local factors, both human and nonhuman. If modern scientific forestry invariably causes tension between the state—the presumed center of calculation—and local conditions,[127] this chapter shows that such a tension mounted because of not only the activism of (or lack thereof) local inhabitants (villagers, cadres, rangers, religious priests, and tea growers) but also the responses of a range of nonhuman things, such as trees and bugs.

Throughout the book, I have underscored the nonpurposive agency that both humans and nonhuman entities possess to affect and even alter the state's central planning. In the case of the afforestation movement in the West Lake area, villagers residing in lakeside hills did not harbor an antigovernment intention but acted to protect their interests and maximize their profits, if possible. Therefore, foresters disputed with local cadres surrounding the issues of rights to lands and trees, particularly because the Hangzhou government vacillated irresolutely between tree cultivation and the expansion of tea plantations. The municipal government's self-contradictory policy tacitly allowed, if not encouraged, tea growers to steal land from forests. The gulf between the state-initiated rhetoric of a nationwide afforestation movement and villagers' private behavior attests to what Vladimir Shlapentokh calls the "privatization" of the socialist society. The "privatization" theory, which presumes that "everyone—from minister and first regional secretary to the orderly in a hospital or a sales clerk in a rural shop—will exploit their position for their own personal interests against the interests of the state and official policy," finally contributed to the erosion of the socialist system.[128]

It is not my intention to overstate those villagers' behavior as a self-conscious challenge to the movements of rural collectivization and afforestation in Mao-era China, but their actions—felling trees as a response to the collectivizing movement, vying with local political authorities for land and tree rights, poaching, nibbling up forested spaces, and catching easy moths in exchange for cash—made a profound impact on the execution of Party policies. So did the bugs. Pests discussed in this chapter benefited from the severe consequences of human ignorance (for example, the lack of knowledge about the production of pine moths and shortage of necessary pesticide equipment and technologies) and inaction (for example, failure to develop mixed forests) impelled humans to respond to their presence and actions. In consequence, the afforestation policies and techniques underwent constant adjustment in accordance with the bugs' fatal assaults.

Despite the twists and turns this afforestation project underwent in Mao's time, the very core of the plan, namely, building up greener mountains surrounding West Lake to pose a contrast between pre- and post-1949 China, remained largely unchanged for several decades. In this sense, afforesting the West Lake area as a propaganda-campaign project was partially successful in that millions of trees were planted, albeit at immense financial and labor costs. In the process, the general population was given an opportunity to understand and participate in voluntary labor, a defining feature of the socialist labor organization. As an integral part of state propaganda, the nationwide afforestation campaign fascinated some foreign tourists in China. In 1954, a British visitor, for example, witnessed and felt deeply impressed by "the greening of New China" movement that dwarfed anything he "would later see in India" and thus optimistically prophesied, "floods and silt-laden waters [would] exist only in literature and memory" in China thanks to this mass movement.[129]

It is apparent that what Sigrid Schmalzer calls "two different *kinds* of truths" held true in post-1949 China in this case.[130] The disparity between the "two truths" stemmed from a gulf between upper-echelon authorities and inhabitants of the local communities. From the political leaders' perspective, the campaign attained at least some of its goals and was fit for state propaganda. From the standpoint of local villagers, for whom such a campaign constituted parts of their everyday life, this decades-long program allowed them to variously subscribe to the Party's agenda, go by it, or reap their own benefits. Here, humans and nonhuman entities were interconnected with each other, for they both possessed nonpurposive agency. This agency was an outgrowth of their interaction with, response to, and internalization of the Party's policies but was capable of profoundly affecting planners and executors of such a propaganda-campaign project. In other words, the afforestation movement in the Hangzhou area, just like the campaign of dredging West Lake in the 1950s, ended up creating its human opponents and nonhuman foes and, thereby, fell victim to its own success.

CHAPTER FOUR

Socialist Pigs
Fertilizer, Collectivization, and Cultural Heritage in Mao-Era Hangzhou

The agenda advanced by the Zhejiang and Hangzhou governments was to make West Lake a productive space for motivated foresters to plant trees and harvest various forest products in the hilly areas surrounding the lake. For the same reason, the peasants in the lakeside villages were mobilized to rear pigs. This chapter centers around pig farming in the West Lake region to explore the agency of both humans and nonhumans (mainly pigs in this case) to respond to the political authorities' call for a nationwide campaign of pig rearing in Mao-era China. The swine has long taken on social, political, and economic significance in the history of humanity. For example, J. L. Anderson notes that pig breeding has been the epitome of production-consumption relations in a global capitalist economy.[1] Indeed, the title of the present chapter is derived from his book-length study on pig farming in the United States in the past two centuries, *Capitalist Pigs: Pigs, Pork, and Power in America*. Along a similar vein, Tiago Saraiva's study on pigs in fascist countries shows "how new forms of life intervened in the formation and the expansion of fascist regimes." Saraiva posits that "technoscientific organisms"—namely, "modern products of scientific breeding operations"—were "constitutive of fascism." Under fascism in Nazi Germany, pigs proved vital in whipping up an anti-Semitic nationalistic feeling.[2]

In the context of socialist China, pigs similarly carried special political and ideological ramifications. In a letter penned by Chairman Mao in October 1959, he heaped praise upon CCP cadres' and farmers' will to raise pigs as a manifestation of the "lofty aims and noble ambitions" of Marxists and Leninists. Mao further reasoned, "The pig takes the leading role among six domestic animals (pig, horse, ox, goat, chicken, and dog)" (*zhu wei liuchu zhishou* 猪为六畜之首) because each pig was "a miniature factory of organic fertilizer" as well as a source of meat and industrial raw materials.[3] In this letter, Mao addressed a rumbling tension between a desire for China's modernization and the absence of necessary conditions (in this case, chemical fertilizer). Given China's long history of pig breeding and using animal manure as fertilizer,[4] therefore, the peasant's practices and knowledge—such as breeding pigs and collecting animal wastes—were underscored as the prerequisite to the realization of agricultural modernization.

Indeed, the significance of pig breeding went beyond the mere supply of hog meat and organic fertilizer in Mao's China. This government-sponsored movement of raising pigs was a typical propaganda-campaign project nationwide, namely a program to display China's will and ability to modernize its agriculture and industry in a mass-mobilizing and self-sufficient manner. As Mao's letter indicated, in spite of the Party-state's leading role in promoting pig rearing, this mass movement proceeded under the pretense of a grassroots campaign that peasants possessed the necessary knowledge and took the initiative. By promoting such ideas as "farmers' fertilizer" (*nongjia fei* 农家肥, that is, manure) and boasting of the transmutation of illiterate peasants into skillful veterinarians, the CCP recognized, in Sigrid Schmalzer's words, "a body of knowledge possessed by farmers" to advance an agenda to challenge "the privileged position of intellectual elites."[5] Moreover, the production and use of pig manure, which required more labor but entailed lower cost,[6] typified "mass work" in Mao-era China, namely, to increase intensive labor input to compensate "for the lack of records and quality control" and to achieve the goal of self-sufficiency.[7]

Given the putative connectedness between swine and the socialist mode of production in Mao's China, pig rearing had become a mass movement that swept the whole nation years before Mao wrote the letter. Not only peasants but also city dwellers were urged to raise pigs, if possible. A directive published by the State Council in 1955 called government institutions and schools on the outskirts of towns to rear hogs to allay market pressure for the supply of pork products.[8] It thus came as no surprise that clashes would arise when swine breeders vied with not only their fellow peasants but also urban residents for space. In the West Lake area, such a scramble for land received media exposure in April 1957, when a contributor to *Wenhui Daily* (*Wenhui bao* 文汇报), a Shanghai-based newspaper, openly protested pigs' occupation of a renowned 1911 Revolution martyr's graveyard at Solitary Hill, a peninsula in West Lake. This satirical article, which the author expressly entitled "Ducks and Socialism, Historical Relics and Superstition, Pigs and Xu Xilin" (*Yazi he shehui zhuyi, lishi wenwu he mixin, zhu he Xu Xilin* 鸭子和社会主义，历史文物和迷信，猪和徐锡麟) to make an explicit connection between pigs and socialism in China, is another source of inspiration for the title of this chapter:

> Everyone knows: pigs won't eat up socialism. On the contrary, [people in] socialism must eat pigs. Who doesn't support socialism? What on earth is Xu Xilin [for]? [He] can be used neither as food nor as nutrition! For the

sake of [constructing] socialism, [let's allow] adorable pigs to hold the limelight! Look! How plump and bright they are! We are materialists (?). [We] prefer the "materialistic" (*weiwu de* 唯物的) pigs over the "idealistic" (*weixin de* 唯心的) tombs of a [revolutionary] martyr![9]

This article was written based on the disgruntled author's observation that the grave of Xu Xilin 徐锡麟 (1873–1907), a late-Qing anti-Manchu hero, grew undiscernible after some government officials refashioned it into a showroom for pigs during an agricultural expo. As hogs were visible to visitors, the tomb was completely sealed off by newly installed structures.[10] This essay conveyed some important messages. First, the agenda of building Hangzhou into a productive city went against the blueprint of making it a city of cultural heritage and tourism. Second, deep down in the hearts of CCP cadres, Xu Xilin and other 1911 Revolution martyrs did not fall into the category of the "people" in Chinese history and, therefore, their tombs were undeserving of preservation. Lastly, local CCP cadres shared a deep-seated bias: pigs were a constitutive element of socialism, whereas the city's historical relics were dispensable.

This chapter addresses the connection between swine and the socialist mode of production in the countryside by taking Hangzhou's suburb in the West Lake area as an example to highlight the role of pig breeding during the agricultural collectivization movement. Contrary to Andrew Walder's assertion that "household sidelines," including hogs, were "effectively banned" between the 1950s and 1970s amid the collectivization movement,[11] the case of Hangzhou's suburb shows that swine breeding in individual families was preferable to collectivized pig farming for technological and economic reasons. Using pig farming in the Nanshan Agriculture Cooperative (*Nanshan nongye hezuoshe* 南山农业合作社, later known as the Nanshan Brigade), a village under the People's Commune of West Lake (formerly known as the West Lake District [*Xihu qu* 西湖区]), as a case study, this chapter's central argument is that pigs were anticollectivistic: pig breeding usually gave priority to an individualized mode of production over a collectivized one in Mao-era China. This preference, therefore, ran counter to one of the avowed goals of the propaganda-campaign project of swine rearing, that is, to legitimize the PRC's rural collectivization movement. While scholars have emphasized Chinese peasants' agency to resist[12]—such as not attending meetings and refusing to work[13] or hiding crops, borrowing funds, and appropriating unregistered lands[14]—the Party's collectivizing program, this chapter also foregrounds the nonhuman factor, namely swine, which contributed to undermining local cadres' collectivizing endeavors. Pig's anticollectivism, as I shall show in detail, stemmed from a peculiar difficulty in centralized pig farming in Mao's time: pigs were subject to the onset of epidemics as the population density was high in large-scale collectively or state-owned pig farms, considering a pervasive insufficiency of vaccines. Furthermore, individual peasant households had long been motivated to rear pigs because they were entitled to retain and even expand their private plots (*ziliu di* 自留地) in the name of growing crops as pig feed. As Gao Wangling discovers, struggles to keep private plots were central to the peasants' activism to battle local cadres during the Great Leap Forward period.[15]

Given pigs' pivotal role in shaping the PRC's agricultural policies, the existing research into pig breeding's sociopolitical implications is inadequate. More often than not, pig raising does not constitute a central theme or is merely mentioned in passing in scholarly works. For example, Wing-hoi Chan's investigation into young married women's role in rearing pigs to make up for the shortage in paddy land in the densely populated New Territories of Hong Kong reveals a gendered division of labor in the countryside in southern China.[16] E. C. Ellis and S. M. Wang confirm that growth in the human population could lead to the rise of the pig population, but not necessarily for the sake of enhancing the supply of pork, but for producing more manure fertilizer to feed nutrient-demanding crops, such as vegetables.[17] Vegetable cultivation and pig breeding, according to G. William Skinner, were mutually bolstered in the countryside in Mao-era China. Skinner attempts to assess the political ramification of vegetables and pigs by suggesting that self-sufficiency brought by the production of sideline products, including pork and vegetables, simplified the process of planning in socialist China.[18] By comparison, Kenneth Walker[19] and Erika Platte[20] are more explicit in explaining the relationship between pig breeding and the retention of private plots in rural China. However, a firmer connection between the swine/private plot and the state policy of collectivizing the countryside has yet to be made.

Meanwhile, scholars have not forgotten pigs' integral role in society and politics in Chinese history. A recent study asserts that applying pig manure to fields was the decisive factor behind the unbroken line of Chinese civilization for several millennia.[21] Sigrid Schmalzer calls our attention to the pig's sociopolitical significance, namely, its "unique relationships with the families, communities, and societies that have lived and written our history."[22] While her main concern is the tension between the universalistic mode of science and China's local conditions in the nation's quest for modernity, the present chapter is intended to position pigs at the center of the historical inquiry in order to explore this domestic animal's capacity to undermine the CCP's endeavor of reorganizing labor and peasants' day-to-day life in the countryside. The potential threat swine posed to the collectivizing effort stemmed from, on the one hand, its indispensability, that is, a compelling need for both pig meat to serve principally city dwellers and manure as fertilizer. On the other hand, as Anita Chan and Jonathan Unger posit, pork was categorized as a "Class II" commodity that the PRC state did not have to enforce a rigid quota system for, as it did for "Class I" commodities (for example, grain).[23] Therefore, the governments both in Beijing and at the local levels were willing to devise and implement more flexible policies in pig rearers' favor from time to time.

Pig Breeding as a State Policy

The CCP began to urge peasants to redouble their effort to breed pigs as soon as the First Five-Year Plan was instituted. On account of a growing need for pork products, especially in large cities during the opening years of the PRC, the central government expressly published a directive in April 1954, calling for raising more hogs. This directive listed three rationales for pig breeding, namely, meeting the ever-growing demands for pork, enhancing the supply of fertilizer, and raising peasants' revenue. It was thus clear that using manure as fertilizer, whose looming importance would be well-publicized a few years later, constituted only one aspect of the massive campaign of pig breeding at this point. To attain the goal of quickly increasing the swine population, the author(s) of the directive clamored for encouraging peasants in areas without a pig-breeding tradition to participate in the movement. Furthermore, the directive requested local governments to ensure a plentiful supply of fodder, such as the beancake, and caution against the outbreak of swine-related diseases.[24]

The 1954 directive was issued against the background of the stagnation of pig farming across China between 1952 and 1953, following an extraordinary surge in the first four years of the PRC. The existing data show that the pig population more than doubled between 1949 (73.773 million) and 1952 (155.22 million), but the growth rate was merely 6.6 percent between 1952 and 1953 (165.69 million).[25] As the demand for pork products soared, it was thus understandable that the central government was keen on pushing for a nationwide program of raising pigs. The 1954 directive, however, had little effect. Premier Zhou Enlai acknowledged in late 1955 that the goal for that year was missed.[26] On the contrary, the swine population slumped by 12.5 percent from 1954 (175.87 million) to 1955 (153.97 million).[27] This decline in pig numbers was a marked contrast to the growing significance of pork products in the PRC's national economy and self-defense by the mid-1950s. In 1955, a Hangzhou-based CCP official openly admitted that China-produced pork was one of the few commodities accepted in the international market in exchange for steel.[28] Under those circumstances, Zhou reiterated the cardinal significance of pigs in an instruction he issued in December 1955.[29]

What Zhou did not mention was the peasants' intentional killing of animals or contributory negligence for not avoiding the massive death of pigs amid a nationwide movement of collectivizing the countryside. Kenneth Walker notes, "The serious decline in pig numbers between 1954 and mid 1956 was associated with the socialisation drive in agriculture and the Government's policy towards the private plot." The private plot or *ziliu di* made up a large portion of peasants' private properties and was usually retained for the sake of cultivating fodder for swine. As overzealous local cadres set out to reduce or even abolish private plots in the mid-1950s, peasants "responded by continuing to kill pigs and poultry, while allowing their draught animals to die through neglect, so exacerbating the decline which had begun during 1954 in anticipation of the co-operativisation campaign and the uncertainty it brought regarding ownership."[30] By 1955, over one million pigs were slaughtered across China due to the ongoing agricultural collectivization movement.[31]

To tackle the issue, the central government continued to call peasants to put in extra effort to raise pigs. The editorial in the *People's Daily* on February 25, 1956, for example, attempted to reassure peasants that pigs did not excessively consume grain. The editorialist pointed out that swine ate not only grain but also "coarse fodder" (*cu siliao* 粗饲料), namely, miscellaneous melons and "green manure crops" (*lüfei zuowu* 绿肥作物) or beancakes, among other things. To fulfill the goal of growing more coarse fodder, local cadres were urged to meet peasants' demands for more private plots. Ironically, while acknowledging peasants' ownership rights to private properties and possessing private plots amid collectivization of the countryside, the editorial continued to sing high praise of public ownership of pigs to propagate the advantage of the commune system. To dispel a doubt that raising a large quantity of "publicly owned pigs" (*gongyou zhu* 公有猪) would lead to the outbreak of swine diseases, the editorialist insisted that rural cooperatives be inclined to adopt new technologies and to pool funds to implement preventive measures.[32] As I shall show later in this chapter, this assertion would prove mere wishful thinking.

Moreover, the government resorted to market mechanisms to entice peasants to engage in swine breeding, despite a call for furthering the collectivization movement across China. In July 1956, Premier Zhou Enlai emphatically pointed out that the procurement price of swine was not commensurate with the rising cost of grain, decidedly sapping peasants' enthusiasm for raising pigs.[33] Two months later, Zhou announced the reopening of the free market to stimulate local trade and private sideline production. The decision was made in the context of a pervasive resentment at radical cadres' abolition of private properties as well as unsuccessful experiments with rearing pigs by local collectives.[34] As a matter of fact,

Premier Zhou had already realized the weaknesses of public ownership of pigs and proposed an adjustment to existing policies and measures. Zhou suggested that pigs be reassigned to individual pig-rearing households, and cooperatives across China carry out flexible policies in favor of those individual pig breeders. The CCP was willing to loosen its tight control over the market partly because of a reduced swine population, which affected not only consumers' everyday life but also agriculture in China. Given that swine manure was a critical source of fertilizer, the instruction issued in July 1956 was the first government document that foregrounded the vital significance of the production of and the demand for pig manure to rationalize pig breeding in the PRC.[35]

In February 1957, Vice Premier Deng Zihui 邓子恢 (1896–1972), whom Mao had compared to a "foot-bound woman" (*xiaojiao nüren* 小脚女人) and condemned for his conservativeness and prudence amid the collectivization movement in 1955,[36] published an article to establish a firmer connection between China's agricultural development and pig rearing. As an upper-echelon official in charge of agriculture, Deng reasoned, "A key issue of improving agriculture is to meet the demands for fertilizer." Given China's limited capacity to produce the desired amount of chemical fertilizer, "farmers' fertilizer" (manure) is in great need."[37] Deng optimistically anticipated that in the final year of the Second Five-Year Plan (1958–1962), Chinese peasants would be raising 250 million pigs and therefore produce about 15.75 to 26 billion kilograms of manure.

To respond to the central government's call, the *Hangzhou Daily* published its editorial on March 29, 1957, reconfirming the state's determination to reward pig breeders more tangibly. The article stressed that the government had raised the purchase price of hogs by 10.9 percent.[38] While Deng Zihui, an advocate of "the household contract system" and "individual pig-breeding,"[39] felt pleased to find that over 90 percent of pigs in China were privately raised and owned,[40] the *Hangzhou Daily*'s editorialist echoed high praise of the policy of "private ownership, private rearing, and state assistance" (*siyou, siyang, gongzhu* 私有, 私养, 公助).[41] Initially set forth by the State Council in July 1956 to reverse the national trend of a shrinking swine population,[42] such a policy ran counter to the public ownership of the means of production, the cornerstone of the ongoing collectivization campaign in the countryside. The editorial cited the Nanshan Agriculture Cooperative, a village on West Lake's southern shore and the protagonist of this chapter, as an example to publicize the unrivaled advantages of "private ownership, private rearing, and state assistance": cost was low because of the use of the existing hog rings and tools; farm work would not be disrupted because pigs could be tended during the villagers' off-hours; and the dispersion of pigs minimized the peril of swine epidemics. In the meantime, Nanshan's farmers also excelled in gathering course fodder to feed pigs to save grains and beancakes.[43]

The emphasis on private ownership of hogs could be interpreted as the Hangzhou government's tactic to cope with increasing discontent over collectivization, followed by a citywide movement of decollectivization in 1957. Existing records show that shortly after 99 percent of rural households were incorporated into cooperatives in the early months of 1957, cries for withdrawing from collectives resounded in Hangzhou throughout 1957.[44] The district- or commune-level governments in Hangzhou, nevertheless, turned a deaf ear to peasants' requests and continued to scrap the policy of "private ownership, private rearing, and state assistance" in the late 1950s. Between 1959 and 1961, in consequence, the percentage of pigs raised by collectives in Hangzhou reached 80. Accordingly, the year-end hog inventories plummeted by 37.09 percent between 1957 and 1961.[45] The variation curve of the swine population in Hangzhou was consistent with that of the whole nation. During the same period, the national year-end pig inventories decreased by 48 percent.[46] It is thus fair to argue that the swine population was inversely proportional to the degree of collectivization and the expansion of public ownership in rural China prior to the Cultural Revolution.

Manure

The swine population nationwide rebounded in 1962, the closing year of the second Five-Year Plan, but the number (108.52 million) was only 57.19 percent of what Deng Zihui had predicted in the mid-1950s.[47] To undo the harm inflicted by public ownership on agricultural production, including pig breeding, the governments at various levels were racing to decollectivize in 1962. In the Hangzhou area, for example, the People's Commune of West Lake disbanded in October 1962.[48] In the same year, the Hangzhou municipal government instituted a number of policies, such as "exchanging manure for grain" (*yifei huanliang* 以肥换粮), to provide incentives to pig breeders. Consequently, Hangzhou's year-end pig inventories grew by 62.75 percent between 1962 (776,900) and 1966 (1,264,400).[49] Once again, the growth curve in Hangzhou was consistent with that of the entire country in the same period: The year-end inventories climbed by 93.42 percent.[50] The countrywide pork production rose by 38.27 percent from 1957 (3.985 million tons) to 1965 (5.551 million tons).[51]

It was thus clear that the governments' adjustment in policies to allow peasants to sell not only hog meat but also manure was key to the remarkable growth of the swine population and a hike in pork production. Sigrid Schmalzer has noted that the Party highlighted the benefits that pig manure brought to the fields to convince hesitant peasants to engage in pig rearing, a relatively costly husbandry business.[52] The abovementioned article written by Deng Zihui in 1957 explicitly cited the term "farmers' fertilizer" to define fertilizers made of swine excrement. According to Schmalzer, the government's use of such terms exemplified the CCP's recognition of "a body of knowledge possessed by farmers" or the politicization of knowledge.[53] The Party's unreserved promotion of "farmers' fertilizer," nevertheless, was both a political action and economic expediency. As Robert Marks has shown, virtually all cultivated lands in China were "deficient in nitrogen" by 1949. As China lacked the capacity to produce sufficient chemical fertilizer, pig manure was obviously a realistic option.[54] The significance of pig manure loomed large, especially because of the CCP's intensified effort to boost agricultural production under the rubric of "taking food grain as the key policy" (*yiliang weigang* 以粮为纲) since the mid- and late 1950s. As shown above, Premier Zhou Enlai began to cite pig manure as the principal reason to justify the central government's policy of encouraging pig raising across China starting from July 1956.[55] Hence, the use of pig waste to fertilize arable lands functioned as state propaganda to popularize the Party's commitment to achieving self-reliance. Throughout the Mao era, similar statements were made repeatedly. Even foreign visitors in China were imbued with the idea of pig manure's irreplaceable importance. American writer Orville Schell (b. 1940), for example, records in his memoir Mao's famous assertion: "Each pig is a fertilizer factory."[56]

By the time Schell visited China (1974), chemical fertilizer had begun to surpass animal manure in agriculture. Take Hangzhou as an example. One *mu* (0.067 hectares) of the field was, on average, applied the amount of animal waste equivalent to 8.1 kilograms of nitrogen (7.38 kilograms of pig manure and 0.72 of ox manure), but 39.96 kilograms of nitrogenous chemical fertilizers in 1974.[57] Prior to the early 1960s, however, animal manure was undoubtedly predominant in the countryside, particularly considering that China had only two chemical fertilizer factories in 1949.[58] Among all animal excrement, pig manure took precedence over that of other livestock because of the former's high volume of nutrients. Research conducted and publicized by the *People's Daily* in 1959 indicated that pig manure contained 1.56 percent to 2.96 percent nitrogen, several times higher than that of horse or ox manure. Although the nitrogen content in goat and pig manure were similar, pig manure had a clear advantage for its ability to release nitrogen more speedily. Therefore, a researcher affiliated with the Chinese Academy of Sciences (*Zhongguo kexueyuan* 中国科学院) in an essay published in 1959 in the *People's Daily* confirmed pig manure's capacity to considerably improve soil quality in all fields, particularly saline and alkaline land.[59]

This 1959 essay typified the wide circulation of popular scientific knowledge about transforming pig manure into a biological fertilizer during Mao's time. What such writing did not mention were the potential perils of accumulating, storing, composting, and applying pig waste. Recent studies have shown that storing an excessive amount of swine manure poses an ecological threat to rural residents. It, for example, causes and exacerbates illness through waterborne transmissions, such as enteric disease.[60] The disposal of hog manure is presently becoming a universal environmental problem across the globe. Taiwan, a region with the highest density of pig farms in the world, has to adopt a highly expensive waste treatment system "similar to the municipal sewage engineered system which includes aerobic treatment" in the new millennium.[61] In addition, composted manure or organic fertilizer applied to fields could pollute water because of the runoff of animal wastes into waterways.[62]

In mainland China, studies on the environmental concerns brought about by large-scale pig farms did not start until recently. Research conducted in 2011 reveals that the systematic way of disposing of pig manure has been nonexistent even in farms with over ten thousand pigs in Mao's China. Traditionally, solid manure was given away at meager prices, and liquid manure was used to generate marsh gas. However, a byproduct of producing marsh gas was wastewater that tended to be a source of water pollution.[63] Based on the existing data, it is not difficult to estimate the percentage of hog manure applied to fields in rural Hangzhou in any given year. Take 1963 as an example. That year, Hangzhou possessed 205,727 hectares or 3,085,905 *mu* of arable land.[64] The number of pigs raised was 1.603 million.[65] Research done in the mid-1970s showed that a pig could generate more than two thousand kilograms of manure.[66] As mentioned above, pig manure contains 1.56 percent to 2.96 percent nitrogen (let's take 1.56 percent for this study). If all manure were to be used to make fertilizer, the minimal amount of nitrogen applied to each *mu* of land would be 16.207 kilograms, more than five times the actual amount in 1963 (3.55 kilograms) recorded in the annals.[67] In other words, at least 80 percent of the pig manure stayed unused. As manure was not in short supply in other provinces or regions considering a gradually balanced pig rearing in all Chinese provinces at this point of the Mao era,[68] shipping manure to other counties or provinces was not only costly but also unnecessary. It is thus conceivable that the vast majority of pig manure remained unshipped and was left to pollute water resources in the Hangzhou area.

If ecological problems were not a cause for concern for peasants and CCP officials, they certainly were concerned when there was an outbreak of a pig epidemic. The high population density of pigs in collectively or state-owned farms was particularly vulnerable to all sorts of infectious pig diseases. Even before the agricultural collectivization campaign set in in the mid-1950s, such diseases had wreaked havoc for pig breeders. In Zhejiang, for example, hog cholera in 1954 affected about 10 percent of all pig farms across the province and contributed to the death of thousands of pigs. In hindsight, researchers blamed the peasants for failing to raise awareness of epidemic prevention and refusing to implement necessary measures. Some stubborn peasants turned a deaf ear to the advice of veterinarians.[69] It is worth mentioning that veterinarians were glaringly lacking in this period, even in the economically developed areas with superb education infrastructure and training facilities, such as Shanghai.[70]

Thus, the absence of a proper understanding of the prevention of swine-related infectious diseases plagued the countryside across China. The existing data show that only 2.51 percent of the pigs raised in China were vaccinated in 1954. Throughout Mao's time, over half of the pigs received vaccinations in only six years (1965, 1970, and 1973–1976).[71] To make matters worse, peasants were reluctant to slaughter, burn, and bury sick pigs but chose to eat the meat, further enabling the spread of the diseases.[72] It was thus no surprise that the Party and its organ newspapers repeatedly cautioned peasants against the potential dangers of swine diseases and called for training peasants to become veterinarians throughout the 1950s and 1960s. On November 6, 1959, for example, the *People's Daily* published a front-page news story to laud the pig-breeding accomplishments of the People's Commune of West Lake of Hangzhou. The writer emphatically pointed out that Nanshan, a cooperative under the commune, had trained eleven of its villagers into veterinarians, who contributed to eradicating such diseases as hog cholera, swine erysipelas, and swine plague.[73]

The People's Commune of West Lake

Located in an area surrounding West Lake and west of downtown Hangzhou, the People's Commune of West Lake fell into the category of the city's "nearby suburb," to borrow G. William Skinner's term. Skinner observed in the 1970s that the nearby suburbs in Mao's China were permitted to focus on "side-line production"—such as vegetable cultivation—despite the CCP's rhetoric of "taking grain as the leading factor."[74] Throughout the PRC era, this region earned a national reputation as a tourist site and a world-famous *Longjin* tea production base. As an administrative unit, it underwent frequent changes in its name and scope during Mao's time. In May 1950, immediately after the CCP seized Hangzhou, it was named the "West Lake District," one of Hangzhou's administrative zones.[75] At the height of the Great Leap Forward movement, in late 1958, the West Lake District was officially renamed the People's Commune of West Lake.[76] In

April 1960, it was given a new name, the City People's Commune of West Lake (*Xihu chengshi renmin gongshe* 西湖城市人民公社).[77] After the tide of communization ebbed, its name switched back to the West Lake District in 1962. By the spring of 1969, its name became literally the "Suburb" (*Jiaoqu* 郊区) of Hangzhou.[78] The brief history of its name changes sheds light on this region's ambiguous nature: it was the borderline area between the urban and the rural throughout Mao's time.

The collectivization movement set in in the West Lake District quite early. In January 1952, the district government had already published a directive to urge peasants to join the mutual-aid groups or cooperatives. By December 1955, 82 percent of rural households had been collectivized. A month later, the percentage jumped to 95, paving the way for the creation of a people's commune two years later.[79] It is, however, one thing to form a nominal cooperative or commune, but it is another to actually band together all the peasants, most of whom were residing in hilly areas. Chen Xuezhao observed in 1955 that it "was difficult [to organize mutual-aid teams] because the families were so spread out" in the hills surrounding West Lake.[80] The existing archival record shows that among fourteen production brigades under the West Lake District, thirteen were situated in the hills beside West Lake.[81] Because of its topographical condition, tea had historically been major money-making produce for most of those brigades: incomes generated from tea sales constituted over 60 percent of total revenues of the commune each year.[82]

Among the fourteen brigades, the Meijiawu Brigade (*Meijiawu dadui* 梅家坞大队) stood out for its worldwide reputation of producing *Longjin* tea. In 1954, the State Council designated Meijiawu as the exclusive tea producer and demanded it turn in the highest-quality tea every April as a gift in international exchange.[83] Moreover, it was nominated as a destination of political tourism to show foreign visitors the PRC's unique rural organization. Chen Xuezhao, for example, brought Jean-Paul Sartre (1905–1980) and Simone de Beauvoir (1908–1986) to pay a visit to Meijiawu in 1955.[84] Premier Zhou Enlai had been to Meijiawu five times since 1957.[85] Meijiawu's time-honored and world-renowned tea cultivation, according to the CCP propaganda apparatus, was reportedly given a new impetus—namely, pig manure—in the late 1950s and early 1960s. In a news story intended to publicize the brigade's record-breaking tea production in 1959, the author emphatically mentioned pig breeding's contribution to the remarkable growth of tea production: the number of pigs raised in the brigade reached two thousand in 1959, 50 percent more than in 1955. In consequence, four million kilograms of pig manure were generated. To ensure an adequate supply of manure, peasants moved pigpens to the hills close to tea plantations. As such, tea growers could apply fertilizer to tea fields three times, as opposed to just once a year, as previously. The writer thus summarized that the key to Meijiawu's success was "more pigs, more manure, and more tea" (*zhuduo, feiduo, chaduo* 猪多, 肥多, 茶多).[86] In another article, its writer provided a new rationality of breeding pigs in the hills: sows raised in hills near fields were free from threats of children's unpredictably mischievous actions and would not be prone to miscarriage. Therefore, the hilly areas of the People's Commune of West Lake were considered an apt location for pig rearing.[87]

The state propaganda machine illustrated not only Meijiawu but also the entire People's Commune of West Lake as the exemplar of the new countryside in socialist China. In an article published in 1959 that preached the notion, "West Lake is beautiful, but the People's Commune of West Lake is even more beautiful," the unchallenged supremacy of agricultural collectivization was said to manifest itself in not only the skyrocketing increase of the commune's tea and grain production but also the remarkable growth of the swine population. In the closing year of the 1950s, according to the authors, the People's Commune of West Lake reared over ten thousand pigs, half of which had been sold to the state. The swine population density was over one head per *mu* of arable land.[88] To set up the People's Commune of West Lake as the model pig-rearing unit across China, an article published in the *People's Daily* in the same year further bloated the number: 2.2 head per *mu* of land.[89] Although such data could hardly be accurate at the height of the Great Leap Forward campaign, at least we know that the Meijiawu Brigade, whose swine population density was reportedly 2.13 head per *mu*, was close to the entire commune's statistical average.[90]

The Nanshan Brigade

Despite Meijiawu's international reputation as the mecca of *longjin* tea, it was its neighbor, the Nanshan Brigade, that stole the show since the mid-1950s amid a countrywide pig-raising campaign. While Meijiawu's villagers raised slightly over two pigs per *mu* of field, the ratio in Nanshan amounted to 4.3 in the same period.[91] Located in the hills (mainly the Jade Emperor Mountain) south of West Lake and near the revered Jingci Temple (*Jingci si* 净慈寺), Nanshan was a tiny brigade with an insignificant amount of arable land under the People's Commune of West Lake's control. Its per capita cultivated land was merely 0.43 *mu* or 0.029 hectares in 1963,[92] as opposed to 0.049 hectares in the Hangzhou area in the same year.[93] Historically, it lacked natural resources, with the exception of some woods in the Jade Emperor Mountain. It also paled in comparison with Meijiawu and other lakeside villages with a tea-producing tradition. Hence, Nanshan had been in an economically disadvantaged position among all the villages surrounding West Lake. Shortly before 1949, over 100 out of its 130 households lived on tourism in the West Lake area: its dwellers eked out a living by carrying sedan chairs for affluent tourists.[94] Therefore, Nanshan fell into the category of an area without a history of raising pigs, where the central government had vowed to start a swine-breeding culture afresh.[95]

With the abolition of marketized tourism in Hangzhou after 1949, Nanshan's economic and social structure underwent dramatic changes. Without sizable rice fields and tea plantations, the local cadres began to focus on pig breeding as the backbone of the village's economy in the early 1950s. Very soon, Nanshan's accomplishments caught the provincial government's attention. Chen Bing 陈冰 (1920–2008), then director of the Propaganda Department of the Provincial Party Committee in Zhejiang, sought to establish Nanshan as a star cooperative that spoke the loudest in the propaganda-campaign project of swine breeding.[96] The first article that allowed Nanshan to grab the limelight before a national audience was published by the Xinhua News Agency in October 1956. This essay put emphasis on Nanshan's experimentation with breeding its own piglets:

> In the past, all piglets were purchased from [pig farms] in other places. The cost was high, and those piglets were not satisfactory. After the establishment of the cooperative, [its members] proceeded to breed and nurture [their own piglets]. In the past ten months, . . . members of the cooperative no longer needed to buy piglets from outside.
>
> [The cooperative] adopts a "collectively owned but privately raised" (*gongyou siyang* 公有私养) approach. . . . The cooperative implements a policy of "the more [pigs one] breeds, the more [one] earns" (*duoyang duode* 多养多有) and rewarding the villagers whose pigs' weights exceed the stipulated weight. . . . [The policy] immensely improves the members' motivation for breeding pigs. . . . The incomes from selling hogs and other revenues are distributed to the members on a regular basis. Ding Jinquan 丁金泉 was rearing four pigs before September and [thereby] received an advance of about six yuan [per pig]. After September, he claimed another sixteen to receive an advance of nine yuan [per pig].[97]

This news story was the earliest account that lent Nanshan national fame. Yet, it was also a highly informative document that explicated the predicaments of as well as the successes in pig rearing in rural China as a whole during the 1950s and 1960s. First, transactions of piglets had long been monopolized by private traders before the late 1950s. In a meeting held in Zhejiang in December 1955, Ma Yinchu

马寅初 (1882–1982), the preeminent economist, reported that piglets were overpriced in the market: their unit price was usually four times higher than that of the adult swine. The price was set artificially high because "private businessmen" took full control over the sales of piglets.[98] In this sense, Nanshan's breeding of its own piglets was hailed as the triumph of the socialist economy over the market economy. Second, epidemics remained a major concern. While Nanshan boasted of "not having a single pig die of diseases in five years" because of the hard work of homegrown veterinarians,[99] peasants across China had yet to foster an awareness of the necessity of vaccinating hogs, as I have shown in the previous section. In a report filed in 1959, on the one hand, Nanshan's members kept cleaning pigpens regularly. On the other hand, adult pigs were vaccinated twice or three times a year, and a piglet received the first vaccine shot twenty days after its birth. Additional vaccines would be available in case of emergency.[100] The contrast between Nanshan's capacity to regularly vaccinate its pigs and the universal shortage of vaccines across China revealed the workings of a propaganda-campaign project. Namely, the government's unlimited support warranted the sustainable success of a few model or star units—such as Nanshan—that had assumed the role of the face of the project.

Third and most significantly, the 1956 essay touched on a key issue of pig breeding, namely private versus public breeding of pigs. In the mid- and late 1950s, all articles or reports purporting to retell Nanshan's success story highlighted the indispensability of raising pigs by individual households rather than collectively or in state-owned pig farms. A *Hangzhou Daily* news report dated March 27, 1957, for example, gave full details about individual pig-breeding households' responsibilities and benefits:

> This cooperative (Nanshan) adopts the "publicly owned, but privately raised" approach to rear pigs. The cooperative focuses on breeding piglets, which are to be distributed to members [after small pigs grow up].... In this period, the cooperative provides each pig with 1,500 kg of green fodder.... Pigs tended by cooperative members are classified into three categories. In a nine-month-long rearing period, a grown-up category-one pig is expected to weigh one hundred kilograms, a category-two one 92.5, and a category-three one eighty-five. If a pig exceeds the limit, [the weight of meat equivalent to] sixty percent of the surplus is to be given out to reward the cooperative member. If [a pig's] weight is lower than the limit, the cooperative member is to pay the penalty... The remuneration the Cooperative gives its members who breed pigs is eight workpoints (*gongfen* 工分) per month (Previously, it was five workpoints).[101]

Therefore, Nanshan's policy was akin to, but not identical with, the "household contract system" that would prevail in China in the wake of the Cultural Revolution. Mark Selden summarizes that the household contract system was carried out in the following ways: First, "[l]and use rights are contracted to households by the village for specified periods." Second, the state "controls supply and price of critical inputs such as fertilizer, seeds, and oil." Third, villages under the household contract system "provide a range of services to farmers." Lastly, the state "creates and restricts markets."[102] In Nanshan's case, similarly, it was the rights over pigs that were contracted to households. The cooperative controlled the supply of one "critical input"—pig fodder—and provided services, such as disease control and epidemic prevention. Finally, salable adult hogs in Nanshan were subject to compulsory sale to the state. Ironically, therefore, all such propaganda works intended to boast of the advantage of the commune system unfailingly conveyed a message that the individualized way of pig rearing and tangible rewards both in cash and in kind proved crucial to Nanshan's success.

Lastly, Ding Jinquan's (b. 1926?) role as a model member of the cooperative was underscored in the Xinhua News Agency report in 1956. One year later, Ding would be promoted as the director of the cooperative.[103] Ding's reputation as an outstanding pig breeder finally obtained nationwide recognition in 1957, when he was elected as the "national model worker in agriculture" (*quanguo laodong mofan* 全国劳动模范). The application form showed that the Nanshan Cooperative had reared 115 sows and 715 piglets with a survival rate of 91 percent (650) under Ding's leadership. It is thus clear that Ding's candidacy principally resulted from Nanshan's standing as a model unit of pig farming in Zhejiang Province.[104] In 1959, Ding's name was mentioned in the national media outlets. A news story in the *People's Daily* highlighted his experimenting with feeding pigs with green fodder (*qing siliao* 青饲料). The report lauded Ding for playing an exemplary role in collecting green fodder in the mountains and waters. A blended swine feed with 70 percent of green fodder and 30 percent of small rice bran or soybean curb residue could provide adult pigs with sufficient nutrition. As a consequence, the members of Nanshan were reassured that pig breeding did not consume an excessive amount of grain. Moreover, Nanshan was also reclaiming a sixty-*mu* field to cultivate pumpkins, yams, and radish as fodder.[105]

By 1959, when Ding reached the apex of his fame as a star agricultural worker/pig breeder, the shortage of food began to beset the entire nation, giving rise to a burning sense of urgency to find alternative food for pigs in order to save grain. As a matter of fact, similar news stories filled the pages of the *People's Daily* in that period. In 1959, for example, a report in the *People's Daily* gave publicity to another model worker in Zhejiang who excelled at feeding pigs with weeds and vegetables.[106] Such news stories were, however, not based on conscientious studies but were generated as political expediency to reduce the pressure of inadequate supply of pig feed rather than to bring forward a viable proposal of supplying necessary nutrition to swine. The same newspaper, in actuality, had published an editorial earlier in 1956 opposing the exclusive use of coarse or green fodder because it would preclude pigs from gaining weight and prolong the breeding time, hence vastly wasting pig food.[107]

Despite its self-contradictory comments, the *People's Daily*, the CCP's mouthpiece, succeeded in establishing Ding Jinquan as a model worker known to the whole nation. Meanwhile, Ding also accumulated enormous political capital because of his achievement in pig breeding. By 1962, Ding was further elected as one of the thirty-seven standing members of the Political Consultative Conference in Hangzhou.[108] The making of Ding Jinquan as a role model or a Stakhanovite gave a new dimension to a propaganda-campaign project that previous chapters have not addressed. Lewis Siegelbaum notes that "the use of Stakhanovites as expediters and propagandists" both popularized the citizens' quality of diligence and self-sacrifice in a socialist society and allowed a socialist state to discipline managerial and engineering-technical personnel.[109] In the context of Mao-era China, Laikwan Pang notes, a model worker or *mofan* 模范 was a sublime figure who contributed to weaving "the ideological quilt together" by embodying "Maoist ideology and encourage[ing] the people to imitate them for the acquisition of the revolutionary spirit." While Pang focuses on the model that "the revolutionary masses could not become" and that "stood beyond the ordinary people,"[110] the model that Ding and his like incarnated was clearly an attainable goal for the "revolutionary masses" in an age when ordinary people were mobilized to remedy China's grievous deficiency in technology, means of production, and daily necessities.

Shortly after launching the media campaign of propagating Ding Jinquan as a competent leader, the local government in Hangzhou managed to find another model among the rank-and-file members of the People's Commune of West Lake. In a brochure published in Hangzhou in 1960, Sun Cui'e 孙翠娥, a twenty-year-old woman, was advertised as a veteran pig breeder. According to the pamphlet, Sun was designated to this position in 1957 and had been rearing pigs for three years. During this period, she succeeded in raising fifty-nine sows, which had produced 1,017 piglets. Since July 1959, the survival rate of piglets had reached 100 percent. Sun was portrayed as a committed new-generation woman who was ready to sacrifice her well-being for the public good of the commune. She spent the prime of her youth in the pigpen. She even internalized pig breeding as the ultimate significance of her life: her gender attributes were thereby neutralized. When asked whether her longtime labor in the pigpen would prevent her from pursuing female beauty, Sun firmly responded, "The most beautiful [people] are [those who] rear pigs for the masses."[111]

Swine and the Collectivization Movement

The year (1960) when the pamphlet was distributed saw the culmination of the agricultural collectivization movement during the Great Leap Forward. Sun Cui'e was portrayed in the media as a swine breeder working in the collectivized piggery affiliated with the People's Commune of West Lake. In this sense, Sun's image of self-sacrifice served a propagandistic purpose of preaching large-scale, centralized pig farming in particular and the campaign of collectivizing the countryside across the country in general. Between 1959 and 1961, communes and brigades in the Hangzhou area rallied to collectivize pig rearing by reversing the long-held policy of "publicly owned but privately raised." Consequently, pig farms with over one thousand hogs mushroomed.[112] Elsewhere in China, local governments went so far as to establish "ten-thousand-pig" farms at the height of this collectivization campaign. In Dongtai 东台 County of Jiangsu, for example, thousands of pigs of different breeds were driven to a newly built farm. However, measures of disinfection and epidemic prevention were not imposed accordingly. By 1960, this collectively owned pig farm ran out of business following the breakout of swine enzootic pneumonia.[113] Such a highly centralizing way of rearing pigs began to draw criticism in national media outlets as early as 1959.[114] More recently, researchers conclude that Chinese peasants and CCP cadres were "materially and technologically unprepared for" running highly centralized pig farms, and thereby the failure was inevitable.[115]

In Hangzhou, the government policy to collectivize swine breeding by establishing "one thousand-pig farms" sapped the peasants' morale and therefore dealt a stinging blow to pig breeding. The year-end pig inventories took a nosedive from 1957 (907,800) to 1961 (571,100).[116] Even Premier Zhou Enlai came to realize the collectivization movement's damage to pig breeding in the West Lake area. In his visit to Meijiawu in December 1960, Zhou was deeply concerned that the number of pig-rearing households fell from three to one in this brigade and thus reiterated the importance of raising pigs in individual households of the villagers.[117] Sha Wenhan, the disgraced ex-provincial governor of Zhejiang,[118] and his wife, Chen Xiuliang 陈修良 (1907–1998), happened to live in suburban Hangzhou in exile after 1957. Chen discovered that neither collectively owned pig farms nor poultry farms were sustainable. In chicken farms, the population of young chickens was decimated because of deficiency in food and water. Large pig farms were subject to the assault of deadly epidemic diseases. Chen was acutely aware that centralized pig or poultry farms entailed scientific management and up-to-date technologies, neither of which were available in China then. More importantly, the poorly motivated peasants had been reluctant to rear pigs together at the outset. Chen further discovered that one important factor behind their low morale was the abolition of the private plot.[119]

The possession of the private plot, as discussed earlier in this chapter, had long been a de facto reward to pig breeders. In theory, private plots were distributed to swine-breeding households for the sake of producing pig feed, such as melons and squashes. In reality, however, they functioned as private property in the age of collectivization and communization. In his study on the Chinese peasants' passive resistance to collectivization during the Great Leap Forward, Gao Wangling finds that holding and even expanding private plots was a manifestation of the peasants' "counteraction" vis-à-vis a highly interventionist state. Such "counteractions"—including possessing private plots, hiding crops, and secretly partitioning public properties—effectively neutralized the Party-state's established guidelines of mobilizing the peasants to give up on their private properties.[120]

The private plot had been a sticking point throughout the seventeen years prior to the Cultural Revolution. The CCP's policy makers dwelled on a dilemma between luring the reluctant peasants into the pig-breeding business by granting them private plots and maximally building up the momentum for collectivizing lands and private properties. Given swine's indispensable role in livestock husbandry, agriculture, and industry, the PRC state was usually willing to compromise and accommodate the pig-breeding peasants' needs. In June 1957, for example, the National People's Congress approved the State Council's amendment to the regulation in relation to the Advanced Agricultural Cooperative to meet pig breeders' demand for additional lands:

> Based upon the needs and local conditions, the Agricultural Cooperatives shall distribute more lands to cooperative members to grow pig feed. The amounts of such land assigned to cooperative members shall be determined by the heads of swine raised by individual households. Such lands [for pig feed] . . . and lands distributed to the cooperative members to grow vegetables shall not exceed ten percent of the acreage per person.[121]

It merits mentioning here that vegetables, according to Gao Wangling, were also in essence anticollectivistic because they, unlike grain, were not harvested once in a season. They required dispersion, rather than concentration, of labor as they could be reaped in multiple crops each year. Therefore, the peasants across Mao's China were unwilling to grow vegetables in publicly owned fields.[122]

Once the communes confiscated such private plots for vegetables and pig fodder in the late 1950s and early 1960s, the peasants were instantly demoralized. As shown above, the Hangzhou government's program of expanding publicly owned pig farms led to the abrupt reduction of the swine population in this area. Confronted with the setback of swine breeding, the *People's Daily* published an editorial on August 6, 1960, reminding the leadership of the communes of the advantages of private parties in raising pigs.[123] The Hangzhou government responded in 1962, mandating the closure of publicly owned, large-scale pig farms, and once again resorted to the rhetoric of "giving priority to private breeding" (*yi siyang weizhu* 以私养为主). Individual swine-breeding households were rewarded with grain and chemical fertilizer for their production of pigs and animal waste, a scheme similar to one that the Nanshan Cooperative had created back in the mid-1950s. In consequence, the annual growth of the swine population reached 18.3 percent between 1962 and 1965.[124]

Swine, the Cultural Heritage, and Tourism

The pig-rearing campaign sponsored by local political authorities exemplified the local governments' commitment to making West Lake a productive space. Nevertheless, productive activities, such as pig farming, cultivating cash crops, and enhancing industrial production, in the West Lake area were held accountable for deteriorating water quality in the lake. By the late 1970s and early 1980s, researchers concluded that West Lake's water had undergone longtime pollution and had become a eutrophic (*fu yingyang hua* 富营养化) body of water.[125] What I did not mention in Chapter 1 is the fact that a eutrophic waterbody actually provides an optimal condition for fish farming. An investigation in 1983 showed that the lake's water was filled with nutrients, some of which were partially caused by the waste of pigs and other animals, to such a degree that no additional fish food was needed.[126] The emphasis on the productiveness in the lakeside area, however, ran counter to the central government's plan to build up a scenic city in Hangzhou as a destination of political tourism. Here, the two propaganda projects inevitably clashed with each other. This rang particularly true in the early 1970s because of the PRC's eagerness to develop a rapport with the United States and other Western-bloc countries. Under those circumstances, local CCP cadres entered into a serious discussion of improving the lake's water quality to avoid grave "international repercussions" in 1973.[127]

While lake water's turbidity and unpleasant odor inflicted damage on the city's tourism, pig breeding in formerly tourist sites and historical relics similarly bemused and exasperated visitors and cultural preservationists alike. As the 1957 essay cited at the beginning of the chapter illustrated, the presence of pigs in Xu Xilin's graveyard was condemned as blasphemy against this 1911 Revolution martyr. Its author reported that other CCP cadres had attempted to dissuade the Zhejiang Department of Agriculture from requisitioning Xu Xilin's tomb but were squarely rejected. In order to refute those officials' theory that it was the pig, not Xu Xilin, that was indispensable to socialism, the writer emphatically remarked,

> Socialism needs them (the anti-Manchu revolutionaries) badly. There was only one Xu Xilin in China since the creation of the world. His revolutionary accomplishments and spirits are still of great significance to educate the next generation.... Xu Xilin and the historical relics are not like breeding ducks and pigs: they can't be reproduced. Therefore, it is absolutely [necessary] to protect the historical relics.[128]

Underlying the author's viewpoint was the inherent contradiction between the rhetoric of making productive cities in China and building up Hangzhou as a city of culture and tourism by virtue of preserving the city's cultural tradition. Given the vital importance of safeguarding Hangzhou's historical heritage, even the diehard apologists of the Zhejiang Department of Agriculture felt guilty for using an anti-Qing revolutionary martyr's burial site as an exhibition hall. Despite this, the department still decided to strike back by pointing out some errors and typos in the *Wenhui Daily* essay. In a letter dated May 4, 1957, in the *Wenhui Daily*, the writer from the Zhejiang Department of Agriculture clarified that because of the tight schedule in preparing the agricultural expo, the department could not possibly find an alternative location to Xu Xilin's tomb, which the Zhejiang Department of Industry had long occupied and used as the site of industrial expos. Meanwhile, when the agricultural expo was underway, not a single Hangzhou-based cadre filed a complaint. The writer then confirmed that the department was mulling over closing the expo ahead of time to allow for the restoration of Xu's grave.[129]

This letter thus disclosed an open secret that graveyards in the Solitary Hill area had been requisitioned as the sites of various expos ever since the opening years of the PRC. Between April and July 1951, the Zhejiang Provincial Display and Exchange Convention of Local and Special Products (*Zhengjiang sheng tutechan zhanlan jiaoliu dahui* 浙江省土特产展览交流大会) was held beside West Lake. In this three-month-long period, some time-honored tourist and cultural sites were chosen as exhibition halls, such as the Xiling Society for the Art of Seal Cutting (*Xiling yinshe* 西泠印社), General Yue Fei's 岳飞 (1103–1142) mausoleum, and the Temple of Phoenix and Grove (*Fenglin si* 凤林寺). Among them,

Xu Xilin's graveyard was converted into the showrooms of the "Engineering Gallery."[130] The 1951 expo's organizers built chambers in the graveyard, considerably altering its structure.[131] Between September and October 1952, when another expo opened, Xu's tomb and other sites of Solitary Hill continued to be appropriated as the locations for the galleries of industrial products.[132] After the expo, the Zhejiang Museum (*Zhejiang bowuguan* 浙江博物馆) refashioned it into a storeroom.[133] Thus, it was no surprise that the writer of the abovementioned letter felt it well-justified for the department to "temporarily" occupy Xu's tomb because it had been a long-established practice since 1951.

Figure 4.1. Xu Xilin's tomb. The tomb was moved away from Solitary Hill in late 1964 and was reconstructed in a distant suburban region (see Chapter 5). *Photo taken in August 2017.*

The Zhejiang Department of Agriculture soon drew fresh criticism. Song Yunbin 宋云彬 (1897–1979), chair of the Federation of Literary and Art Circles of Zhejiang (*Zhejiang wenxue yishu jie lianhehui* 浙江文学艺术界联合会), joined the chorus to protest the government's occupation of Xu Xilin's tomb. Song, first of all, blamed the Department of Agriculture's staff for blaspheming this 1911 Revolution martyr by displaying pigs in his graveyard. Then, Song rejected the excuse that local cadres in Hangzhou had never complained about setting up a showroom in Xu's graveyard. Song remembered that a vice director of the Zhejiang Department of Culture had tried to draft a letter urging the Department of Agriculture to change the location of the exhibition but was finally silenced. At the end of Song's essay, he condemned the leadership of the Department of Agriculture for being opinionated and ignorant of China's history.[134] Song had long been known as a staunch advocate of preserving the cultural heritage in Zhejiang. He had gained a reputation for battling local CCP cadres to protect a Buddhist pagoda in Longquan 龙泉 County and tombs in the Solitary Hill area beside West Lake in the mid-1950s, as I shall show in the following chapter. The rally for saving Xu Xilin's tomb turned out to be Song's last fight before being stigmatized as a "Rightist" later in 1957.[135]

The resounding cry for restoring Xu Xilin's grave soon captured the attention of the Hangzhou municipal government. In May 1957, the staff of the Hangzhou Bureau of Gardening Administration officially requested to reinstate Xu's tomb by driving away occupants and dismantling all temporary structures therein.[136] It took another four years before Xu Xilin's tomb was finally cleared for reopening to tourists and visitors. To commemorate the fiftieth anniversary of the 1911 Revolution, a report filed by the Zhejiang Department of Culture stated, pigpens in Xu Xilin's graveyard had been removed in the second half of 1961.[137] It is thus conceivable that pig breeding had lasted for at least a decade in the burial site of this 1911 Revolution hero. As a matter of fact, Xu Xilin's tomb was not the only graveyard where pigs were raised. The grave of Yu Qian 于谦 (1398–1457), a patriotic general who single-handedly saved the Ming dynasty from the Oirat Mongols' attack in 1449, and the shrine dedicated to him had for a decade been occupied by the villagers of the People's Commune of West Lake. An investigation carried out in late 1961 found that not only had new buildings been constructed in it, but the hall of Yu's memorial temple was converted to a pig-breeding stall.[138]

The fight for space between pigs and the deceased historical figures was testimony to the inherently contradictory city planning of Hangzhou during Mao's time. Before the 1980s, the Hangzhou government never ceased to pursue the agenda of making the city a productive space, despite the Soviet specialist's suggestion and the political necessity of building Hangzhou as a tourist city for visitors at home and abroad. Hence, the two propaganda projects—pig breeding and political tourism—proved mutually incompatible. The former posed a genuine threat to the preservation of Hangzhou's historical relics, such as ancient tombs, and contributed to damaging the environment, both of which tarnished the city's reputation as a must-go destination for tourists.

Meanwhile, pig breeding, known for its pivotal role in the PRC's effort to attain the goal of agricultural self-sufficiency, was in reality at odds with the CCP's most important agricultural policy, namely, the collectivization movement. This chapter has shown that unvaccinated pigs' vulnerability to epidemic diseases when raised in densely populated pig farms and farmers' preference of breeding pigs in individual households in order to acquire and retain private plots challenged the very cause of agricultural collectivization. In other words, pigs, domestic animals carrying strong economic and political ramifications in socialist China, turned out to be anti-socialist by nature. Dali Yang argues that decollectivization in post-Mao China could be traced back to the Great Leap Famine, during which "significant belief adjustment" was fostered in the population, leading to the "demands for rural institutional change (that is, decollectivization)."[139] The case study of pig breeding, however, demonstrates that ruptures of the commune system had already been visible at the height of the Great Leap Forward movement.

The policy pronouncement of the collectivizing campaign could not drown out peasants' voices that cried out for private ownership of pigs and retention of private plots. The agency peasants and pig breeders had was indeed nonpurposive: their motives were to maximize their economic gains as they negotiated with local authorities. Meanwhile, swines' agency to prosper in household pigpens and languish or even perish in collectivized pig farms legitimized and reinforced the villagers' preference of individuation of their work. While most existing scholarly works focus on the peasants' survival techniques or "wheeling and dealing" to "defraud the state" and thereby counter the collectivization movement,[140] this chapter highlights the collusion between humans and nonhuman creatures—swine—in obstructing and undermining the propaganda-campaign project of pig breeding, whose goal was set, ironically, to exhibit the advantage of the collectivization movement in the countryside in Mao's China.

CHAPTER FIVE

"Ghosts as Neighbors"
The Campaigns of Removing Tombs in the West Lake Region, 1956–1965

Pigs vying for space with tombs in the West Lake region during the 1950s and 1960s was a telltale sign of the CCP authorities' ambivalent attitudes toward myriads of graves that dotted the lakeshore. Sociologist Fei Xiaotong 费孝通 (1910–2005) complained in 1956 that West Lake had long been a "public cemetery" (*gongmu* 公墓).[1] Fei's observation found an echo in an article penned by writer and journalist Rong Dingchang 荣鼎昌 (pseudonym: Huang Shang 黄裳, 1919–2012), who recognized that the coexistence of the "living people" and "dead people" had been a defining character of West Lake for centuries.[2] The prevalence of burial sites in the lakeside area was a testimony to a process of reconfiguring the space of Hangzhou and West Lake since the 1911 Revolution, when the city wall was gradually dismantled, repositioning the lake from Hangzhou's remote outskirts to the heart of the city.[3] Accordingly, the lakeshore tombs, which had previously been erected outside the city wall of Hangzhou, were found to occupy the city's central place. Understandably, a sense of discomfort would creep in when city dwellers, as well as visitors, realized that they were staying side by side with dead souls. As early as the 1930s, for example, celebrated popular novelist Zhang Henshui 张恨水 (1895–1967) voiced his uneasiness with West Lake, a place replete with all kinds of tombs.[4]

The graves, according to Craig Clunas, had historically been considered "public sites" in imperial China.[5] This rings particularly true of the tombs on West Lake's shore as they had long been integrated into the lake's landscape, variously evoking heroic or sentimental emotions. A writer in 1961 concluded that the tombs leavened West Lake thanks to the circulation of patriotic epics, heartbreaking love stories, and well-received literary masterpieces associated with them.[6] Without a doubt, the sites where those heroic or romantic souls were laid to rest were the embodiments of such epics and tales. In dogmatic Maoists' opinion, meanwhile, sloughing off the "feudal tradition"—the burying and worshipping of ancient celebrities included—necessitated the materialization of China's modernization.[7] Therefore, the value of the tombs was consistently open to debate during the Mao years.

This chapter documents a tug-of-war between preservationists and iconoclastic Maoists in the two decades prior to the Cultural Revolution. As an unwavering opponent of the tombs, Mao gave an order in 1956 to remove the graves in the Solitary Hill area, but the decree was met with stiff opposition and ended up being nullified by Premier Zhou Enlai. It was not until 1964 and 1965 that practically all lakeside tombs were wiped out. Although radical Maoists could temporarily triumph over those taking a soft line in the mid-1960s, Mao's inability to eliminate all signs of the past—tomb, archway, monument, and temple—provided a stark contrast to his overwhelming power in refashioning Beijing. In the PRC's capital city, Mao was able to create "both the past and present" and "stood for both past and present, the people and history."[8] Hung Wu's observation shows, first of all, that the spatial and temporal reconfigurations were intertwined and mutually supportive in Mao's era. Second, such reconfigurations served ideological and, therefore, propaganda purposes by popularizing a peculiar conception of temporality, through which the past or its denial was utilized to legitimate both the present and the future of this young republic.

Mao and staunch Maoists, however, found themselves embroiled in a war of attrition in their attempt to spatially reconstruct the West Lake area by ridding the lake of the tombs, the very symbol of this lake's temporal dimension. The limitation of Mao's power to rebuild West Lake resulted, first and foremost, from the boisterous dissenting voices from both the central and local governments. Not only non-CCP intellectuals and social activists but also Party cadres on various levels ignored the outcry against the tombs. Premier Zhou, for example, contradicted Mao's edict to cleanse West Lake on various occasions, especially during the 1956 campaign. Zhou took up a rigid preservationist stance based upon two political considerations: the necessity of unifying and pacifying people of differing ideological orientations and preserving West Lake as a site for political tourism to advance the very cause of Mao's world revolution. Such a confrontation seemed to attest to an innate contradiction in the conception of historical time in communist regimes. While Denise Ho has emphasized only one temporal dimension—namely "historic continuity"—in creating a new socialist culture,[9] Evgeny Dobrenko offers a more complicated picture by portraying the duality of such temporality in a communist society: the "destruction and museumification" of the past lived side by side.[10] Here, it is vital to understand the different attitudes of preservationists and iconoclasts toward the tombs not as competing opinions but as two sides of the same coin of the CCP authorities' pursuit of contemporary political agendas through rereading and reinterpreting history.

Second, the Soviet experts' suggestions on building Hangzhou as a city of leisure and tourism and the policies of preserving traditional culture posed a grave problem to ambitious iconoclasts and effectively bulwarked assaults from radical Maoists on the tombs beside West Lake.[11] Third, even though Maoists scored a decisive victory to relocate or destroy all lakeside tombs in 1964 and 1965, political tourism, which importantly included displaying China's rich cultural tradition, would revive in less than a decade. The tombs, an indispensable component of West Lake and an embodiment of a perfect combination of "masculinity" (nationalistic heroism) and "feminine" beauty (sentimentalism in West Lake–related love stories) of the lake, would quickly undergo revivification. The iconoclastic campaign to annihilate those tombs proved unsuccessful, in no small part, because of the autonomy of the lake and the tombs: West Lake's lasting enchantment resides in a constant interplay between human and nonhuman elements, environmental and cultural factors, and the living and the dead in the past millennia.

Here, the tombs were not merely physical sites subject to protection or erasure. A tomb is, according to Eugene Wang, "topos," both "a locus" and "a topic." Given that a topos is "etched in collective memory by its capacity to inspire writings on it and the topical thinking it provoked," its physical feature is of tangential significance, as it was predestined to undergo construction and rebuilding in history.[12] For the tombs of Su Xiaoxiao 苏小小, a well-known courtesan during the Southern Qi dynasty (*Nanqi* 南齐, 479–502), and Lin Bu 林逋 (Lin Hejing 林和靖, 967 or 968–1028), a renowned hermit and poet during the Song dynasty, the absence of their bodies remains, and the authenticity of those historical figures do not matter. They have long been topoi in memories, writings, paintings, and performing arts that collectively define West Lake and augment its worldwide reputation. Namely, the lake has lent legitimacy to the dead, and conversely, the tombs have glorified and animated the lake. In other words, the lake and the tombs had coevolved, and their ties could not be easily severed.

Such a lake-tomb symbiosis leads to the argument I put forward throughout the book: the agency of nonhuman things. The tombs certainly differ from water, microbes, trees, pests, and pigs I have discussed thus far in that they are wholly artificial objects. However, the tombs on the lakeshore possessed agency in Mao's time and beyond, for their very existence and ability to spark controversies over how to remember China's past defined its capacity to govern humans' thoughts and activities and thereby (re)shaped the CCP's politico-cultural policies. In other words, they "acted back on" humans.[13] Simonetta Falasca-Zamponi notes that the historical narrative, as embodied in the tombs here, both tells about "actions" in history and "at the same time generate[s]" actions. It both represents and produces power.[14] In this sense, the lakeshore tombs did have agency beyond the control of their creators, maintainers, and destroyers. As Jane Bennett posits, "man-made items" have the ability "to exceed their status as objects and to manifest traces of

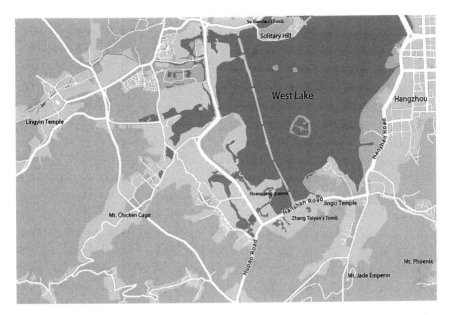

Figure 5.1. The map of the West Lake area with an emphasis on locations mentioned in this chapter.

independence or aliveness, constituting the outside of our own experience."[15] Therefore, it was the aggregation of both human and nonhuman agencies that contributed to diminishing, disempowering, and defying radical Maoists' efforts to impose their will and advance their agenda against the dead souls.

The Tombs after the Communist Takeover

Shortly after the CCP took over Hangzhou, the provincial and municipal governments were committed to physically transforming the city but failed to develop a long-term plan. Some of the policies devised and implemented contradicted one another. On the one hand, the government displayed a willingness to restore various scenic spots to build Hangzhou into a city for sightseeing. Lin Bu's grave was, for example, rebuilt in 1950. Plum trees were planted in line with Lin's widely known poems about plum blossoms.[16] Renamed "The Return of Cranes to the Plum Blossom Forest" (*Meilin guihe* 梅林归鹤), the grave became one of the earliest scenic sites reopened to the public by the government.[17] On the other hand, however, an urgent need for space to make Hangzhou a "productive city" inevitably prompted local officials to encroach upon former tourist sites. As shown in the preceding chapter, a 1951 agricultural expo was held in Hangzhou, for which purpose the government requisitioned various sites at Solitary Hill, General Yue Fei's Shrine, Bai's Causeway, the Temple of Phoenix and Grove, and Xu Xilin's graveyard.[18]

Xu's tomb would continue to be appropriated as the locus of different exhibitions as late as 1957. The writer who exposed the occupation of Xu's tomb presumed that most CCP cadres had equated destroying historical relics with doing away with superstition.[19] It thus came as no surprise that the government was pursuing an unequivocal agenda of cleansing religious or superstitious elements by cracking down on ancient buildings and institutions. During the early 1950s, when the land reform campaign was in full swing in Hangzhou, a great number of time-honored religious constructions were torn down, and many Buddha statues with artistic values were shattered to pieces.[20] Most of Hangzhou's Buddhist and Daoist monasteries were evacuated. James Gao notes that the number of monks plummeted in the opening years of the 1950s.[21] The Jingci Temple, a monastery with a millennium-long history, which had long evoked poetic sentiments, was entirely occupied by the army, and its priests were all forcibly relocated.[22] The graveyard of Wang Wenhua 王文华 (1887–1921), a Guizhou warlord best known for his anti-Yuan Shikai 袁世凯 (1859–1916) activism in the 1910s, was appropriated and reused as the location of a kindergarten.[23]

The fate of Wang Wenhua's and Xu Xilin's graveyards testify to the CCP's initial commitment to ridding the lake of graves. The very first mandate issued by the Hangzhou municipal government in the wake of the CCP's takeover ruled that burying the deceased in the "public land" (*gongdi* 公地) was unpermitted.[24] Just like many other policies and campaigns initiated by the communist regime immediately after the Civil War, the ban on burying the dead beside the lake was not the CCP's creation but merely a reiteration of the rulings of the previous government. In May 1948, for example, the Nationalist Party's municipal government of Hangzhou published a similar ruling.[25] By comparison, the CCP's injunction seemed more flexible. Peasants living in the surrounding groves were allowed to be buried in eight designated locations in the name of protecting the forests.[26] A report filed in 1951 suggested that interring body remains should be banned outright during seasons when hills were closed.[27] For the existing tombs, the Hangzhou Bureau of Urban Construction filed a proposal in 1952, promising to eradicate all the tombs at Solitary Hill except those with "historical and commemorative significance" (*lishi jinian yiyi* 历史纪念意义).[28] Removing tombs usually served an ideological purpose of banishing superstitious thoughts, but sometimes the decision was reached for practical reasons. The occupation of the graves of Wang Wenhua and Xu Xilin, as noted earlier, was intended to help the governments obtain ampler space. In another case, the local government mandated confiscating stones from the cemetery of a certain Jiang 蒋 family and, therefore, demanded all the tombs therein to be relocated from the lakeshore in 1959.[29]

The Burial of Zhang Taiyan

The ban on erecting new tombs in the West Lake area faced a stiff test when Zhang Taiyan's 章太炎 (1869–1936) family filed an application to bury Zhang in a formerly privately owned land south of West Lake shortly after the founding of the PRC. Zhang, one of the greatest philologists and philosophers in modern China and a staunch anti-Qing revolutionary, passed away in Suzhou on the eve of the Sino-Japanese War. The Nationalist Party government immediately allocated funds to perform a funeral for Zhang.[30] Although Tang Guoli 汤国黎 (1883–1980), Zhang's widow, had already purchased a piece of land on the southern shore of West Lake as the burial site, and the Republican government promised to arrange a state funeral there, Zhang's casket stayed in Suzhou until the early 1950s principally because of the prolonged Sino-Japanese War and the ensuing Civil War. Since 1949, as the situation in China stabilized, Tang entertained the idea of burying Zhang Taiyan's body remains by West Lake close to the mausoleum of Zhang Cangshui 张苍水 (1620–1664), a renowned anti-Manchu Ming loyalist and Zhang Taiyan's role model. At this point, however, Tang felt dismayed to find that, first of all, the municipal government had nationalized this piece of land, and local peasants had transformed it into a plant nursery with no prior notice. Second, the Hangzhou municipal government's injunctions against establishing tombs beside the lake had come into force.[31]

Tang Guoli's initial communication with political authorities in Zhejiang and Hangzhou proved futile. All CCP bureaucrats cited injunctions to squarely reject the Zhang family's application and suggested that Tang consider alternative sites. In response, the persevering Tang launched a massive lobbying campaign by rallying Zhang's friends and students across the country. In January 1950, Shen Junru 沈钧儒 (1875–1963), president of the Supreme People's Court of the PRC, and Ma Xulun 马叙伦 (1885–1970), minister of education, jointly wrote a letter to Tan Zhenlin, chair of Zhejiang, demanding special accommodations for the Zhang family. Although he hailed Zhang as an "anti-imperialist sage" (*fandi zheren* 反帝哲人), Tan refused to address the issue of building a grave for Zhang but only agreed to help Tang secure land tax exemption.[32]

Throughout 1951, Tang Guoli paid visits to the plot she had purchased in Hangzhou and kept consulting with numerous scholars and politicians. After many meetings and talks, those who supported the Zhang family finally generated a scheme that all parties could accept: after Zhang Taiyan's funeral, Tang would give up on the ownership of the mausoleum, and the government would step in to manage it as a historic relic. In the following two years, however, this proposal evoked no response from the Beijing government.[33] After three years, the wait was finally over when Premier Zhou responded to a letter from Tian Heng 田橫 (1893–1982), Zhang Taiyan's disciple. Tian had written Zhou on Tang Guoli's behalf shortly after the Liberation, but it took quite a long time before Zhou replied and eventually gave the long-overdue nod. Hence, the Zhang family and Zhang's friends and students were galvanized to make preparations for Zhang's funeral beside West Lake. In March 1954, Song Yunbin wrote to the State Council of the PRC urging a speedy resolution of the issue of Zhang's funeral.[34] In December of the same year, Song delivered Sha Wenhan, then governor of Zhejiang Province, a long letter reconfirming Zhang's status as a "cultural celebrity in history" (lishi wenhua mingren 历史文化名人) who deserved a spot on the lakeshore.[35] Sha responded by allocating a fund of fifty-nine million (equivalent to 5,900) yuan for the grave and the funeral.[36]

Song Yunbin served as one of the officiants at the funeral service on April 3, 1955, a sunny but chilly day in the wake of a storm. When the ceremony started at nine o'clock in the morning, Song delivered an address on behalf of the Chinese People's Political Consultative Conference of Zhejiang.[37] Members of other government institutions and Zhang Taiyan's funeral committee also spoke to commemorate Zhang. The number of attendees at the ritual amounted to over eighty, including Jiangsu- and Zhejiang-based officials and Zhang Taiyan's acquaintances.[38] After the funeral, the Hangzhou municipal government took over the grave as planned. A public funeral to commemorate this great scholar and anti-Manchu revolutionist was conducive to the CCP's propaganda campaign to win the support of social notables with a diverse array of backgrounds. Unsurprisingly, not only did the funeral receive full media coverage, but Zhang Taiyan's mausoleum would also gain publicity immediately after that.

The government-sponsored tourist guide, *Famous Historic Sites of West Lake* (*Xihu shengji* 西湖胜迹), for example, moved quickly to juxtapose Zhang's tomb with other time-honored scenic sites as early as mid-1955.[39] The Hangzhou municipal government also acted promptly. In June 1956, the grave gained official recognition as a "Class A Heritage Site under Hangzhou's Protection" (*Hangzhou shi yiji wenwu baohu danwei* 杭州市一级文物保护单位). The existing archive record shows that its category was "Revolutionary Commemoration" (*gemin jinian* 革命纪念), and the rationality of preserving and protecting the grave was Zhang's status as a "great scholar, thinker, and revolutionary in the late Qing." The Hangzhou Bureau of Gardening Administration was the designated institution to

Figure 5.2. Zhang Taiyan's tomb. *Photo taken in August 2017.*

maintain it.[40] By defining the grave as cultural heritage or *wenwu* 文物, as Denise Ho finds, the CCP drew on a long-standing tradition in the twentieth century of treating "cultural relics as national patrimony" that highlighted the PRC's continuity in Chinese history and thereby legitimated its very existence.[41]

Despite a high-profile effort to enshrine Zhang Taiyan as a revolutionist, the Hangzhou government failed to secure the necessary upkeep funds. Zhang's son publicly complained in 1957 that when he swept the tomb, he only saw the burial site overgrown with weeds and graffiti on the tombstone. He thus felt upset by the stark contrast between the lively atmosphere at the burial ceremony and the desolate scene after only two years.[42] What he failed to understand was the workings of a propaganda-campaign project: the authorities usually privileged the launching of such a program, which tended to garner greater attention from the media and the general population, over the long process of sustaining and maintaining. With such a complaint, however, the municipal government agreed to coordinate with different bureaus to discuss finding special funds for maintaining not only Zhang's grave but also other tombs with historical significance in the West Lake area.[43]

In spite of the municipal government's promise, a secret plan to destroy or relocate it was brewing. By 1960, the Zhang family withstood high pressure because of the "Project of Constructing [Mt.] Nanping" devised and carried out by the Zhejiang Provincial Public Security Department (Zhejiang sheng gong'an ting 浙江省公安厅). In response, Tang Guoli firmly opposed the elimination of Zhang's tomb.[44] The disputes between Tang and Zhejiang's public security officers lasted for four years. A letter from the Zhejiang Public Security Department to the Hangzhou municipal government stated the following:

> [As far as] the issue of moving tombs of Zhang Taiyan and Zhang Cangshui [is concerned], it has been repeatedly suggested by Wang Fang 王芳, Director-General [of the Department of Public Security]. [We] need to urgently dispose of the two tombs of Zhang and Zhang. . . . There are two plans: [first,] filling and leveling up the tombs and erecting monuments for commemoration; second, moving [the two tombs].
> Given the two tombs[' status as] historical relics under the protection, [we] can't dispose of them in a rush . . . Tang Guoli has rejected in writing [the proposal of moving the tombs].
> A letter jointly signed by twelve individuals from Hangzhou to the Bureau of Gardening Administration also says no [to the proposal].

Facing boisterous protests, the provincial and municipal governments finally decided to compromise. On February 4, 1964, a public announcement was made that no further plans were afoot to relocate the two tombs.[45]

The 1956 Incident of Removing Tombs in Solitary Hill

The incident of Zhang Taiyan's grave in the early 1960s bore testimony to CCP cadres' discrepant views on treating tombs in particular and historical relics in general throughout the Mao era. Among the Party's top leadership, the controversy was raging in a similar fashion. Mao Zedong, for example, had long been hostile to religious sites and superstitious practices. James Gao notes that Mao never mentioned the Lingyin Temple (*Lingyin si* 灵隐寺) when he composed poems about its nearby hills, "from where he could get a bird's-eye view of the temple." Gao thereby concludes, "the Party's policy on religion was very ambiguous."[46] Compared to his ambivalent attitude toward religious facilities, Mao loudly protested against the existence of numerous tombs in the West Lake area. During a conversation in 1956, Mao lamented that he was "living [in a place] with ghosts being [his] neighbors." Mao's complaint prompted some of Zhejiang's leaders to take action immediately to remove all tombs close to Mao's residence.[47]

This short-lived and ill-fated campaign of ridding West Lake of tombs started on February 21, 1956. Overnight, Hangzhou's citizens were dumbfounded to see the disappearance of the tombs of Qiu Jin 秋瑾 (1875–1907), Xu Xilin, and other historical figures without a trace.[48] Within a few days, most tombs were to be relocated to a cemetery in Mount Chicken Cage (Jilong shan 鸡笼山).[49] Such a surprise attack set off howls of protests. Song Yunbin, astonished and infuriated, instantly made a phone call to Premier Zhou Enlai, reporting the ongoing tomb removal campaign in Hangzhou. As an influential scholar in Zhejiang and a celebrity in the cultural circle, Song had been known as a stout defender of China's traditional culture vis-à-vis the CCP's antitraditional iconoclasm. On the eve of the Anti-Rightist Movement in 1957, he openly accused the CCP leadership in Zhejiang Province of being ignorant of and indifferent to China's classical literature and arts.[50] Such opinions would be cited as evidence of Song's ill-intentioned attacks on the Party and haughty disdain for CCP cadres at the height of the Anti-Rightist Movement.[51]

Song Yunbin's criticism of CCP cadres' mismanagement of China's historical heritage resulted from his personal experiences over the 1950s. Although he joined the choir of those singing high praise of a new West Lake belonging to the "laboring people" in the early 1950s,[52] Song soon found local cadres' heartless sabotage of cultural relics—exemplified by the incident of demolishing a pagoda in Longquan, as mentioned in the previous chapter—disgusting and intolerable. In 1957, for example, Song authored two articles centering on the issue of graves: one in defense of Xu Xilin's mausoleum in Solitary Hill, calling for dismantling temporary or permanent structures imposed upon it[53] and the other responding to sociologist Fei Xiaotong's resounding cry for a tomb-free West Lake.[54] It is thus understandable that Song reacted swiftly to contact the premier when witnessing the unfolding of the campaign of removing tombs beside West Lake in 1956.

Premier Zhou Enlai was initially left uninformed about the chaos in Hangzhou. Upon receiving requests from different sources, including Song Yunbin, he quickly pursued an investigation and asked Sha Wenhan to restore all the tombs.[55] Zhou promised not to castigate or punish anyone involved in the campaign but only hoped that all the tombs could be recovered on the grounds that those historical relics had constituted a part of West Lake's scenery, and some people still felt a strong attachment to them. Zhou further confirmed that the State Council would cover all the expenditures incurred by the restoration effort.[56]

Premier Zhou Enlai had consistently been an ardent defender of China's historical and cultural heritage in no small part because of his responsibility for handling foreign affairs. Given Hangzhou's significance in the PRC's political tourism, the tombs and temples beside West Lake were indispensable props. To this end, some Buddhist monasteries, particularly the Lingyin Temple Mao seemed to loathe, underwent repair and restoration during the 1950s following a brief period of confusion. The Lingyin Temple remained little affected at the height of iconoclasm during the Cultural Revolution, thanks to Zhou's mobilization of workers and militias to guard the temple against the rebellious Red Guards' vandalism.[57] Foreign visitors variously felt fascinated or grew upset by the CCP government's self-Orientalist effort to display China's "traditional culture." A tourist from England even questioned the necessity of devoting massive "manpower and equipment in that town to rebuilding that vast edifice of the Buddhist temple" when China was "in great need for housing and factories."[58] In a similar fashion, French writer Jules Roy (1907–2000) lamented in the 1960s that the lake was overcrowded with tombs. Or, in his own words, Hangzhou "was a mournful city, half dead."[59]

The tombs and historical accounts or fairy tales associated with them, nevertheless, helped to popularize an image of the Chinese nation with a long history and a peace-loving tradition. Simon Leys (the pseudonym for Belgian Sinologist Pierre Ryckmans [1935–2014]), who visited China numerous times between the 1950s and the 1970s, for example, noted that Su Xiaoxiao's tomb had historically been "the site of a poetic and sentimental pilgrimage, so famous that it had become a stop in visits to" West Lake.[60] Therefore, Premier Zhou Enlai expressly suggested that the Hangzhou municipal government not dismantle Su Xiaoxiao's tomb and the pavilion attached to it in 1957. For the tombs of the anti-Qing martyrs, Zhou reiterated their raison d'être by relating their revolutionary heroism to China's century-long anti-imperialist and antifeudal struggles. In a public meeting held in Hangzhou in 1957, Zhou hailed Hangzhou as one of the birthplaces of the Chinese revolution because of the anti-Qing activities undertaken by a galaxy of turn-of-the-century heroes or heroines, such as Qiu Jin, Xu Xilin, Zhang Taiyan, and Su Manshu 苏曼殊 (1884–1918), all of whom had been buried in the West Lake area. Zhou emphatically pointed out that their images had also been on display on the Monument to the People's Heroes at Tiananmen Square.[61]

Zhou Enlai's intervention entirely altered the plan of getting rid of the tombs on the lakeshore. Sha Wenhan, Zhejiang's provincial governor whom Zhou directly contacted, faced a terrible dilemma. On the one hand, it was Jiang Hua 江华 (1907–1999), secretary of the CCP Committee in Zhejiang, who faithfully followed Mao Zedong's instructions and proceeded to remove the tombs.[62] Hence, Sha would take the risk of not bending to Mao's will. On the other hand, Sha was a proven preservationist of cultural relics. Also, in 1955, for example, Sha disapproved of a proposition to demolish the statue of Chen Qimei 陈其美 (1878–1916), an anti-Qing and anti–Yuan Shikai revolutionary and Chiang Kai-shek's (1887–1975) mentor, in Huzhou, Zhejiang.[63] Torn between Mao and Zhou and unwilling to clash openly with Jiang Hua, Sha finally reached a decision, against his will, to scapegoat himself and issue an official apology for rashly launching the campaign of removing the graves at Solitary Hill.[64] This incident pitted not only Mao against Zhou but also Jiang Hua, Mao's most intimate subordinate in Zhejiang, against Sha on the provincial level. The Jiang-Sha antagonism finally exploded in 1957, leading to violent intraparty strife and Sha's eventual purge.[65] Anyhow, Sha temporarily resolved the 1956 crisis because of Premier Zhou's backing, and the campaign of removing tombs was brought to a screeching halt only a week after it began.

The "Great Cultural Cleanup" in 1964

The Antitomb Voices

The premature termination of the 1956 campaign signaled the temporary failure of Mao's stance of cleansing his beloved West Lake of burial sites. The 1956 incident pitted Mao and his followers against scholars and more pragmatic CCP officials. To say that all intellectuals and writers opposed Mao's call for ridding tombs would be an exaggeration. As noted earlier, Fei Xiaotong published an essay in the *People's Daily* several months after the incident, openly questioning the raison d'être of countless tombs on the lakeshore. In Fei's understanding, West Lake was supposed to be an "epic" (*shishi* 史诗), but unfortunately, it performed its function as a mammoth cemetery.[66] In October 1956, Fei published a six-thousand-character-long follow-up essay to clarify his viewpoint that West Lake was in need of improvement in this new historical age. Su Xiaoxiao's and General Yue Fei's tombs could stay, but it would be better if they gave way to works with high artistic value by present-day artists.[67]

Fei Xiaotong's opinions resonated well with Mao. During a conversation with Fei a few years later, Mao recalled that when he was reading Fei's essays, he could hardly resist the urge to fly to meet with Fei to discuss removing those lakeside tombs.[68] As early as 1951, Mao overtly criticized West Lake for being populated by "too many dead people" and made it clear that living next to ghosts deeply troubled him.[69] Mao opposed ground burial for both ideological and economic reasons. In 1956, Mao stated, "the dead are vying for land with the living; before long, the living would have no land to farm." Consequently, Mao was among the first high-ranking CCP officials to publicly advocate for cremation.[70] Mao's viewpoint found an echo among peasants in Hangzhou. In a 1964 essay, a CCP cadre from a Hangzhou village lashed out against pre-Liberation landlords who "had grabbed lands, peasants' means of subsistence, under the excuse of building ancestral graves [in the locations with] good fengshui."[71] At times, Mao resorted to socioeconomic semantics to elaborate on his tactic of disposing of the tombs. Upon hearing of the news that the graveyards were cleared for constructing a botanic garden in Hangzhou in the mid-1950s, the overjoyed Mao stated, "We're taking the road of collectivization; so [we] should let them (ghosts) take the road of collectivization, too."[72]

Mao's hardline stance against tombs, though having antagonized scholars and CCP cadres on varying levels, struck a chord among leftists nationwide, especially writers with intimate relationships with Mao. Hu Qiaomu 胡乔木 (1912–1992), Mao's secretary between 1941 and 1969, has long been held accountable for the massive 1964 campaign of destroying most of the tombs beside West Lake. As early as 1961, Hu had already voiced his frustration that West Lake was replete with graves and cried for reform.[73] In late 1964, Hu composed a *ci*-poem that provided the impetus for a concerted effort to purify the lakeshore. The poem ends with the following lines:

> Clay idols are oppressing the mountains; pernicious body remains are ruining the water.
> ...
> Who would join me to brandish the Sword of Leaning Against the Sky and clear away those preposterous [things]?

The 1964 *ci*-poem, arguably Hu's most valued work in his life, fulfilled dual purposes. On the one hand, when Hu, Mao's secretary, showed it to Zhejiang's CCP leaders, the poem was widely interpreted as an unofficial decree issued by Mao. On the other hand, when Hu presented Mao with the poem, it served as a reminder that Mao had tabled the proposal many years before. As most observers and historians would choose to believe, consequently, the publication of this poem directly led to the outbreak of the campaign of demolishing the lakeside tombs in December 1964. In hindsight, however, Hu believed that he had been misunderstood, and his role in this campaign was overstated.[74]

In all fairness, Hu Qiaomu could not have singlehandedly pushed for a campaign of this magnitude in the final month of 1964. Well before the campaign started, local officials had already waged a media war against the graves, temples, monuments, and archways—namely, the symbols of feudalism and imperialism. Hangzhou's two major newspapers, *Zhejiang Daily* (*Zhejiang ribao*) and *Hangzhou Daily,* devoted enormous space for ordinary citizens, PLA soldiers, CCP cadres, and tourists to publish essays rallying to annihilate all relics with feudalistic and counterrevolutionary implications. This propaganda campaign started with the publication of an essay on November 11, 1964, in *Zhejiang Daily* demanding all Hangzhou dwellers "nurture proletarian [ideology] and eliminate bourgeois [ideology]" (*xingwu miezi* 兴无灭资) and carry forward a new socialist lifestyle. The newspaper's editor added an editorial note to the essay to display a burning sense of urgency of "eradicating the old and fostering the new" (*pojiu lixin* 破旧立新) in scenic sites so that s/he solicited letters and articles from the readers.[75]

While *Zhejiang Daily* would publish numerous essays or letters regarding the necessity of getting rid of feudal and imperialist legacies on the lake, *Hangzhou Daily* established a special column, "Eradicating the Old and Fostering the New; Altering Old Customs and Habits" (*Pojiu lixin, yifeng yisu* 破旧立新, 移风易俗), on November 28, 1964, as the home of a vast mass of similar essays. One reader analyzed that given West Lake as the "humanized nature," it had to reflect the sentiments and proclivities of certain classes. Therefore, it was imperative to display cultural artifacts that would highlight the "revolutionary passion" and the "lofty spirit and soaring determination of socialist construction" beside the lake.[76] Given that the zeitgeist should be a lofty revolutionary spirit, readers were quick to point out, tombs, monuments, and archways were nothing but a manifestation of the continued dominance of feudal bureaucrats, landlords, warlords, prostitutes, and Nationalist Party officials.[77]

The movement against the lakeshore tombs in late 1964 was, therefore, a distinctive propaganda-campaign project because, first, it was a top-down program disguised as a populist movement. Despite a resounding call to eliminate those burial sites, as I shall show in the case of Su Xiaoxiao's tomb, many tombs continued to enjoy remarkable popularity among Hangzhou's citizens and tourists alike. Second, it predated and contributed to a more massive campaign of smashing the "Four Olds" (old customs, old culture, old habits, and old ideas) during the Cultural Revolution. Lastly, it intersected with and somehow conflicted with other propaganda-campaign projects, such as the program of making Hangzhou a city of cultural heritage and sightseeing that was a key component part of China's foreign policies, and therefore created confusion and contradictions. Surely at this moment, the necessity of propagating a redefined view of China's history by obliterating the tombs outweighed the long-held diplomatic scheme.

The Tombs at Solitary Hill

Among all the lakeside tombs, those jamming together at Solitary Hill bore the brunt of scathing criticism in this campaign. A PLA soldier made a rough estimation that over twenty graves of different styles were "besieging" Solitary Hill. In his words, epitaphs and inscriptions were "emitting the stench of the reactionary ruling class."[78] Back in 1956, it was the tombs of the 1911 Revolution martyrs in front of the Hangzhou Hotel, right outside Solitary Hill, that irritated Mao and prompted him to lodge a "living-next-to-ghosts" complaint. Although the Mao-inspired 1956 campaign had been stillborn, controversies surrounding the graves at Solitary Hill never subsided. In 1961, the Zhejiang Provincial Committee of Cultural Relics Administration (*Zhejiang sheng wenwu guanli ju* 浙江省文物管理局) filed a detailed report on various tombs at Solitary Hill at the Zhejiang provincial government's request. The authors of the report suggested that the tombs of 1911 Revolution heroes—including anonymous soldiers of the Zhejiang Army during the battle of conquering Nanjing, Qiu Jin and her friends, Xu Xilin, Tao Chengzhang 陶成章 (1878–1912), Zhu Shaokang 竺绍康 (1877–1910), Su Manshu—be preserved because the revolution "overthrew the millennia-long feudal monarchism and [therefore] constituted a vital part of China's bourgeois-democratic revolution."[79]

By comparison, the necessity of keeping the graves of individuals irrelevant to the revolutionary causes was open to debate. Lin Bu's tomb, for example, had been recognized as Lin's cenotaph since the Yuan dynasty.[80] Despite this, the writers of the report proposed to keep it on the grounds that Lin had "left a lot of

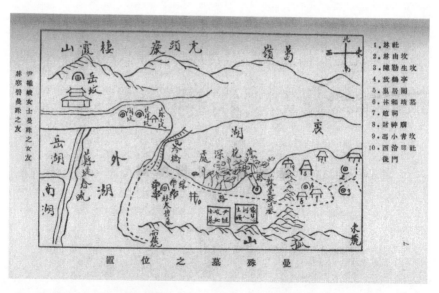

Figure 5.3. Tombs at Solitary Hill in the early twentieth century. *Reprinted from Liu Yazi* 柳亚子, *Su Manshu nianpu ji qita* 苏曼殊年谱及其他 (A chronicle of Su Manshu's life and other matters) (Shanghai: Beixin shuju, 1927), p. 7.

anecdotes, with which many people are familiar, making the tomb an integral part of Solitary Hill's landscape."[81] The tomb of Feng Xiaoqing 冯小青,[82] a legendary woman, known for her hapless marriage in the Ming, was even more controversial. The writers remarked that the accuracy of Feng's accounts had been a matter of debate, and the tomb was undoubtedly bogus. However, the report still found it worth preserving.[83] The value of tombs of ancient scholars and beauties, fictitious or not, was self-evident, for they had been long fused in West Lake's scenery. The looming importance of political tourism gave them a new lease of life, as they served as a showcase of China's enduring cultural legacy for an international audience. Among foreign visitors who cherished their memories of Solitary Hill, Michael Croft (1922–1986), an English actor and writer who visited China in the late 1950s, felt impressed by Lin Bu's tomb and "the spot where he planted his plum trees and kept his pet cranes,"[84] symbols of a carefree lifestyle.

The Issue of Su Xiaoxiao

Among scholars, heroes/heroines, and beauties lying at rest at Solitary Hill, Su Xiaoxiao sparked the most acrimonious dispute among CCP cadres, tourists, and the media. The legends about Su's love story had long lent inspiration to poets who mourned and commemorated this talented woman. For over a millennium, Su's tomb in Hangzhou was nothing but a small mound of earth. In 1784, a stone tomb was erected under the auspices of Emperor Qianlong.[85] In the 1840s, a Manchu general built a pavilion to protect the tomb and named it the "Pavilion of Admiring the Talent" (*Mucai ting* 慕才亭).[86] In the opening years of the PRC, Su's tomb not only survived but also figured prominently as a major tourist site. The tomb found emphatic mention in both editions (1954 and 1955) of the government-sponsored tourist guide, *Famous Historic Sites of West Lake*. Its author was unsure whether Su Xiaoxiao was an actual historical figure, nor did s/he believe that the tomb was her real burial place. Given her vigorous pursuit of the freedom of love, according to this tourist guide, Su gained recognition as a member of "the people" in ancient China worthy of commemoration because her story "reflected the people's strong desire for striving for freedom of love in a feudal society where women came under ruthless feudal oppression."[87]

In 1957, Su's tomb was officially classified as a Class B Heritage Site under Hangzhou's Protection. Its category was "Historical Commemoration" (*lishi jinian* 历史纪念).[88] Despite this, Su's grave sat uneasily with diehard left-wingers, including Chairman Mao. The tomb briefly fell victim to the 1956 campaign but underwent complete restoration because of Premier Zhou's intervention.[89] The political authorities' heavy hand aroused Simon Leys's displeasure. He resentfully stated, "Perhaps the ghost of that witty and beautiful woman troubled the sleep of some 'revolutionaries.'"[90] Mao and uncompromising Maoists certainly felt that this woman's ghost was still wandering around and haunting the city. The debate on the necessity of keeping the grave broke out intermittently throughout the 1950s and 1960s. In the abovementioned 1961 report, the tomb once again came under critical scrutiny. Luckily, the writers of the report viewed the tomb as a keeper because Su's story had reportedly penetrated deep into the people's hearts.[91]

In November 1964, when the whole society swiftly turned radical, and pressure on relocating the lakeside tombs was piling up, the Hangzhou municipal government pondered moving the graves of the 1911 Revolution heroes and heroines to a remote mountainous area.[92] Under this circumstance, Su Xiaoxiao's tomb failed to escape the fate of total destruction. However, local CCP cadres in Hangzhou made a last-ditch effort to keep some trace of the tomb by proposing removing the tomb but keeping the pavilion during a meeting on November 11, 1964.[93] The effort proved futile. In the following month, the public clamor for wiping off Su's tomb raged in the press. Some workers asserted that tombs of reactionary bureaucrats, landlords, and prostitutes were doing incredible harm to the younger generation.[94] *Hangzhou Daily*'s editorial note on December 4, 1964, refuted the theory that the tombs of Su and Lin Bu were an essential part of West Lake's landscape by comparing them to abscesses on human bodies.[95] Four days later, the editorialist pointed his/her finger squarely at Su, describing her as a fictitious figure concocted by some perverted feudal men of letters. Therefore, her tomb had become the lake's "malignant tumor."[96]

It is thus clear that Su Xiaoxiao would no longer be viewed as a member of "the people," and her story would not be interpreted as Chinese people's brave struggle for the freedom of love, as shown in the 1955 tourist guide. At this point, she gained a novel interpretation as the plaything of the feudal landlord or gentry class. The reclassification of Su's class was a testament to the ambiguity of class labels throughout Mao's time. Yiching Wu finds that individuals were entitled to select segments of their lives and choose from one of their multiple identities to determine their class classification in Mao's time.[97] Similarly, Jeremy Brown reminds us of the "dynamism, instability, extreme variation, and sheer confusion" of individuals' class status in the early PRC era.[98] In Su Xiaoxiao's case, such an utterly unstable and chaotic system could be applied to people both at present and in ancient times. The reassigning of Su's class identity dictated the status and the fate of her "tomb." Joseph Levenson contends that the CCP cherished the traditional culture of "nongentry" or those "loosely designated as 'the people.'"[99] The call for stripping Su Xiaoxiao of her membership of "the people" was reinforced by the confirmation that her tomb was associated with superstitious activities. Two local traffic policemen reported that older women were convinced that lying on the top of the tomb could relieve their backache, while young men and women scrambled to rub the tomb's exterior, praying for their happy marriages. Thus, the policemen concluded that the grave was tarnishing West Lake's reputation.[100]

The perceived revival of superstitious activities testifies to both the general population's favorable attitude toward the tomb and a relatively tolerant religious atmosphere beginning in the early 1960s. Holmes Welch finds that Buddhist temples attracted more devotees in the first half of this decade than the period before 1949.[101] Such a trend undoubtedly upset radical leftists. Hence, the clampdown on Su Xiaoxiao's burial site was itself a propaganda campaign to inform the locals of the government's commitment to battling religious beliefs and superstitious activities. On December 2, 1964, when *Zhejiang Daily* assembled a special column entitled "The Dirt Left by the Old Society—Su Xiaoxiao's Tomb" (*Jiushehui yiliu xialai de wuhou—Su Xiaoxiao mu* 旧社会遗留下来的污垢— 苏小小墓), readers and writers took issue with both the tomb and the couplets hung on the pavilion. An employee of a local museum accused the couplets of disseminating debauched feelings of "downfallen classes" (*moluo jieji* 没落阶级).[102] A Hangzhou urbanite outright denied the status of Su's tomb as "a place of historical interest and scenic beauty" (*mingsheng guji* 名胜古迹).[103] The discussion resumed the next day. One worker from Hangzhou presumed that Su's stories and couplets commemorating her would certainly preclude tourists from nurturing "revolutionary sentiments" (*geming de ganqing* 革命的感情).[104] The significance of dead souls in exerting impact on the living found an echo in an essay published in *Hangzhou Daily* on the same day. The writers of the essay—some workers from a local silk printing and dyeing firm—reminded their readers of the critical role of monument revolutionary martyrs in shaping the masses' revolutionary spirit as portrayed in a popular film of the day.[105] Evidently, virtually all contributors recognized that tombs—namely the nonhuman things and the human-made artifacts—had the capacity to affect humans.

The Great Cultural Cleanup

Su Xiaoxiao's tomb was among over thirty graves at Solitary Hill that suffered the fate of annihilation on December 2, 1964.[106] In hindsight, neither Hu Qiaomu's *ci*-poem nor public ire as expressed in the press played a decisive role in propelling the Hangzhou municipal government to take concerted action against the tombs. Removing the lakeside graves was, according to extant archival documents, a premeditated politico-cultural movement. As early as November 3, 1964, the Hangzhou Bureau of Gardening Administration filed a report in response to a request to relocate tombs of the 1911 Revolution martyrs and proposed four possible locations: Mount Phoenix (*Fenghuang shan* 凤凰山), Mount Jade Emperor,

Figure 5.4. The rebuilt tomb of Su Xiaoxiao with a pavilion. *Photo taken in August 2017.*

Mount Chicken Cage, and Solitary Hill. Mount Phoenix in the southeastern region of West Lake was geographically close to downtown Hangzhou. In this area, an old mausoleum had already been built in the first half of the twentieth century. Therefore, it would be easier and less expensive to construct a cemetery as the home of the tombs moved from Solitary Hill. Mount Jade Emperor, also located in the southeast of the lake, had easy access to transportation lines, but the cost of building a cemetery from scratch would be high. Mount Chicken Cage was situated in a distant region southwest of the lake and near a tea farm. It had been picked as the site to which tombs at Solitary Hill were relocated in 1956. Given its distance from the city and the shortage of necessary infrastructure, however, the estimated investment would be enormous. An isolated location in the eastern part of Solitary Hill would be another option. Evidently, the reporter(s) preferred Mount Phoenix.[107]

The Hangzhou Bureau of Gardening Administration submitted another report on December 19, 1964, drawing up a more detailed plan of relocating or demolishing those tombs. The officials reached a decision that the tombs of those related to the 1911 Revolution would be relocated to Mount Phoenix. The only exception was Su Manshu, whose tomb would be wiped off. The tombs of historical figures of imperial times, including Lin Bu and two generals subordinated to Yue Fei, would be kept intact. All other tombs at Solitary Hill, including that of Su Xiaoxiao, would be dismantled.[108] Obviously, the report writers continued to have Mount Phoenix in their minds as the most desired location for a new cemetery. In reply, the Zhejiang provincial government offered less radical plans a week later that would have minimized the impact of the campaign of removing tombs on West Lake's landscape.[109]

This report, dated November 26, 1964, featured two plans. Plan A would have allowed most tombs of 1911 Revolution heroes/heroines to stay beside West Lake. Qiu Jin's grave would be refashioned to make its design consistent with the overall architectural style in the adjacent area. The tombs of Tao Chengzhang and his colleague would be relocated to another site within the confines of the West Lake Scenic District. Plan B bore a resemblance to what the Hangzhou Bureau of Gardening Administration had proposed: moving all those tombs to Mount Phoenix. Su Xiaoxiao's tomb remained a perplexing puzzle. The writers, on the one hand, leaned toward removing the tomb. On the other hand, however, the report proposed to keep the pavilion intact because the pavilion was located right beside the Xiling Bridge (*Xiling qiao* 西泠桥), and "the combination of a pavilion and a bridge is a rare architectural style, matchless across the country." The writers brought forth an alternative plan—keeping both the tomb and the pavilion intact and only erasing couplets attached to them.[110]

The relatively moderate solution proposed by the provincial government provided a stark contrast to clarion calls for vigorous action against the tombs in the press throughout November 1964. To rally the hard-liners, Hu Qiaomu showed his *ci*-poem to the vice secretary and the director of propaganda of the CCP Committee in Zhejiang, reiterating Mao's decision to eradicate all lakeside tombs.[111] Hu's stance effectively silenced the moderates in the government. On December 2, 1964, a concerted effort was made to wipe off about thirty tombs and thirteen steles, pavilions, stone statues, and archways in the Solitary Hill region. The graves of 1911 Revolution martyrs, except that of Qiu Jin, were all moved to Mount Chicken Cage. Evidently, the authorities purposely selected the most distant and isolated location short-listed in the November 3 report, as noted earlier. Other tombs were smashed into pieces. Those graves containing body remains, such as that of Wang Wenhua, were moved to designated burial sites. The tombs of Lin Bu, Su Xiaoxiao, and Feng Xiaoqing were filled entirely and leveled up.[112] The cherished tomb of Su Xiaoxiao, according to Simon Leys, "disappeared completely, and no trace of it [was] left."[113]

Hu Qiaomu, a longtime advocate of the campaign, triumphantly wrote a letter to Mao Zedong and showed the latter his *ci*-poem, boasting of the success of the movement of tomb removal. In response, Mao expressed his dissatisfaction over the limited scope of the action:

> In the suburbs of Hangzhou and elsewhere, [people] are living next to ghosts. [West Lake] could not be cleaned up for several centuries. Nowadays, [the Hangzhou government] has only dug out a few piles of rotten bones and presumes that the problem has been resolved. [You're] underestimating the enemy.[114]

Without a doubt, Mao had viewed all the dead souls and their modern-day apologists as "the enemy" in urgent need of total destruction. In consequence, a more radical campaign across the West Lake area with greater momentum—known as the Great Cultural Cleanup—ensued in the next two months. By March 1965, 654 tombs were obliterated, only twenty-eight of which were moved to somewhere else.[115]

Despite the unfolding of the Great Cultural Cleanup, Premier Zhou remained unconvinced. Later in 1965, he continued to remark on the necessity of protecting the "cultural landscape with historical values" (*you lishi jiazhi de renwen jingguan* 有历史价值的人文景观) beside West Lake and giving the 1911 Revolution its due.[116] As the intellectuals' dissenting voices began to rise, the provincial government held a meeting on December 9, trying to appease or silence dissenters. Zhang Taiyan's son lamented that since Tao Chengzhang's tomb had been demolished, the same fate would soon befall his late father's recently constructed grave. A former air force officer under the Nationalist Party government poignantly pointed out that Lin Bu was nobody but a hermit. "If living in recluse was a sin, it means that one committed a crime as soon as s/he was born in the [old] society." A high school teacher called for making a full analysis of the historical heritage from the standpoint of both "the class viewpoint" (*jieji guandian* 阶级观点) and "the historical perspective" (*lishi guandian* 历史观念). He feared that considering practically all historical relics countrywide carried feudal implications, they could all be subject to total annihilation.[117]

The CCP's Historiography

The critics' opinions testify to changing interpretations of China's past and revolutions and the shifting historiography on the eve of the Cultural Revolution. As Huaiyin Li notes, "The recurrent ideological and political antagonism within the Chinese Communist Party and tensions between historians of different generations and social backgrounds" led to a transition from "disciplinization"—"the efforts to turn the revolutionary narrative developed by CCP historians into a standard representation of China's past"—to "radicalization"—an approach to push the revolutionary narrative to "its extreme form." Consequently, "historicism" (*lishi zhuyi* 历史主义), or "objectivity in historical research" in academia, gave way to more "radical historiography"—namely, "a simplistic dichotomy between good and evil, or the revolutionary and the counterrevolutionary."[118]

This revolutionary/counterrevolutionary binary provided the theoretical basis for a new historical interpretation, in which figures like the hermit Lin Bu could not stay neutral. A reader, for example, dismissed Lin as a parasitic man who "sat idle and raked in a profit" (*bulao erhuo* 不劳而获).[119] In other words, if he could not join in the revolutionary cause, he must have been a counterrevolutionary, and his tomb deserved to be torn down. As one abovementioned critic lamented, "[O]ne committed a crime as soon as s/he was born in the [old] society." Hence, Su Xiaoxiao's tales and the literary works dedicated to her were even more intolerable. Not only was she considered irrelevant to the laboring class, but poets and writers who had produced a myriad of literary and artistic works to commemorate her all hailed from questionable class backgrounds: they were landlords or their mouthpieces who promoted a "decadent and obscene" (*tuifei yinmi* 颓废淫靡) literary taste.[120] It was thus no surprise that Hu Qiaomu singled out Su in his effort to crack down on the lakeside tombs in late 1964.[121]

Such an assessment of Su Xiaoxiao offered a marked contrast to that in the mid-1950s. As noted earlier, *Famous Historic Sites of West Lake* portrayed Su Xiaoxiao's pursuit of free-choice love as a manifestation of the oppressed people's aspiration for freedom in feudal society.[122] As late as November 1961, the report filed by the Zhejiang Provincial Committee of Cultural Relics Administration continued to sing high praise of Su Xiaoxiao because she embodied a woman who fell victim to Confucian ethics but strove for her freedom in marriage. Therefore, Su's stories had enjoyed immense popularity among the people.[123] Hence the dramatic change in the CCP's assessment of Su Xiaoxiao's tomb within a decade was due to the changing definition of "the people." As Joseph Levenson indicates, the CCP deployed a class-based analysis approach by defining China's cultural tradition as that of "the nongentry" or "the people."[124] In this sense, the vicissitudes of the tombs of Su Xiaoxiao and Lin Bu resulted from political authorities' (re)interpretations of the category of "the people" and (re)defining of the boundary between the gentry and the nongentry.

By comparison, defining the nature of the 1911 Revolution that consistently pitted Mao and Maoist doctrinaires against those carrying out conciliatory cultural policies, such as Zhou Enlai, turned out to be a thornier problem. While the latter triumphed during the short-lived 1956 campaign, the former scored certain victory in 1964 and 1965, when the tombs of all 1911 Revolution martyrs but Qiu Jin were forced out of the West Lake region. The unabated controversy regarding the worthiness of those tombs throughout the pre–Cultural Revolution attests to the CCP's predicament of generating "modern history" in China. As Huaiyin Li has cogently argued, "China's 'modern history' itself has been an ongoing process full of uncertainties and yet to be finished." Because of such confusion and uncertainties,

> the historians in the twentieth century were burdened with rivaling ideologies, nationalist, liberalist, Marxist, Maoist, New left, or neoliberal. Their interpretations of history thus yielded a myriad of varying (and often contradictory) narratives and competing grand narratives, which frequently functioned to distort and obscure rather than illuminate the realities in the past.[125]

The constant tug-of-war between moderates and Maoist hard-liners surrounding the treatment of the tombs of heroes and heroines in relation to the 1911 Revolution was thus a testimony to two mutually contradictory historical narratives produced and adopted by CCP historians and leaders. This said, however, such a quarrel among the CCP's upper-echelon leaders did not necessarily stem from their diametrically different ideological orientations. Premier Zhou Enlai's "concessions to the Chinese past," for example, were tantamount to his theory of treating "tradition in its own right, not as a sop to the feelings of the backward."[126] Zhou and his colleagues restored China's past in a nearly self-Orientalist way for tactical reasons: he was more concerned about Hangzhou's status as a city of political tourism where China's rich historical heritage was on display. For the tombs related to the 1911 Revolution, Zhou was willing to incorporate the perceived "bourgeois revolution" into the broadest scope of the Chinese revolution in the past century in an attempt to win the hearts of all walks of society. In this sense,

Zhou's advocacy of preserving the tombs beside West Lake was merely a matter of expediency. Or, as I have posited, the two approaches were nothing but the two sides of the same coin: both resorted to the interpretations of China's past to legitimate the PRC regime.

Beginning in the mid-1960s, it was evident that Zhou Enlai's flexibility and tolerance gave way to uncompromising, dogmatic Maoism. Zhang Taiyan's tomb, kept intact during the 1964–1965 campaign, would be completely destroyed in the summer of 1966, as Zhang's son had pessimistically foreseen. Zhang's body remains were initially discarded in the wild but were later hastily buried. The expensive coffin also disappeared. The local peasants eventually turned the graveyard into a vegetable garden.[127] The same fate befell many other tombs under the CCP's protection in 1964 and 1965. The tomb of Yu Qian, minister of defense during the Ming dynasty, was removed because Yu's title had been interpreted as "minister of national defense" (*Guofang buzhang* 国防部长), a position assumed by Peng Dehuai 彭德怀 (1898–1974), the chief target of radical Maoists during the Cultural Revolution.[128] Even the grave and shrine of General Yue Fei, a national hero during the Song dynasty, underwent the fate of being demolished and "entirely ransacked."[129] It was not a coincidence that when Hangzhou's historical relics were undergoing massive destruction at the height of the Cultural Revolution, China's diplomatic relations with foreign countries quickly soured. Political tourism came to a halt and remained suspended until 1971.[130]

The competing discourses on China's past and revolutions manifested themselves in the culture wars surrounding the tombs in the West Lake area throughout Mao's time. Under the rubric of "using the past to serve the present" (*guwei jinyong* 古为今用), professional historians, CCP officers, and laypersons not only attempted to understand and redefine the past but also had to respond to and act upon China's imperial and modern histories as political justifications.[131] As Vera Schwarcz's study on a Chinese garden shows, "Voices from a distant past continue to speak about our predicament today."[132] For Mao Zedong and Maoist doctrinaires, the tombs were making so much noise that the specters disrupted their sleep.[133] But for Zhou Enlai and his like, the same tombs, the symbol of the nation's glorious cultural heritage and the memorial to revolutions in twentieth-century China, functioned as a way of unifying people of differing ideological persuasions and as a locus of performing diplomatic tourism. As I have stated, the two contradictory senses of temporality—Mao's doctrine to use the present to deny the past and Zhou's recourse to history to justify the present—both served the purpose of propaganda and political legitimation. Their uneasy coexistence, however, precluded the CCP from devising and implementing a consistent policy, and the pendulum constantly swung back and forth between the two extremes of preserving or demolishing those graves.

The radical program that obliterated all lakeside tombs popularized a Faustian mode of development, namely, burning all bridges to make a new society "so there can be no turning back."[134] Ironically, the very act of burning bridges or destroying the past resurrected the dead souls by lending the tombs "a living significance."[135] More importantly, it could well ruin Mao's revolutionary cause. The cleanup of West Lake seriously jeopardized political tourism, which was purported to promote Mao's rhetoric of the world revolution. After three tumultuous years, the PRC was inching closer toward rapprochement with the United States. Under these circumstances, CCP authorities were compelled to restore some relics and gardens beside West Lake for foreign tourists in the early 1970s, signifying the total failure of radical Maoists' attempt to banish all "old" elements from the lake. In reality, the suggestions of substituting the "new" elements—such as Mao's poems and exhibitions of oil paintings about the CCP's revolutionary history—for the "old" during the 1964 campaign hardly came to fruition.[136]

The tombs, archways, monuments, and temples—namely, the "old" and the dead—seemed irreplaceable because they gained recognition as a defining feature of the lake, essentially a humanized nature. Rong Dingchang noted that West Lake had historically been a locus for the living and the dead to coexist. Without the tombs, the scenery of West Lake would not have been complete. Newly constructed sites, such as the well-acclaimed *Huagang guanyu* park, proved no match for scenic spots with a longer history.[137] Song Yunbin contended in 1961 that West Lake appealed to tourists because the tombs of Yue Fei, Yu Qian, and Zhang Cangshui ennobled the lake with their heroics and great devotion to the country.[138] In the same year, a contributor to the *People's Daily* added that it was a potent combination of the abovementioned patriotic heroes, prolific poets and writers with their unforgettable literary works, and sentimental female protagonists in fairy tales, such as Su Xiaoxiao, that provoked tourists' intense interest in the lake.[139]

The specters of revolutionaries, writers, and beautiful and talented women still loomed on the horizon in spite of the massive 1964–1965 campaign to remove their tombs. The dead continued to shape historiography and sociocultural policies in post-Mao times. Gradually, the dead souls staged a comeback to West Lake. Zhang Taiyan's grave, for example, was moved back to its original site in 1983. A report submitted by the Hangzhou municipal government cited Zhang's status as a veteran of the 1911 Revolution and a maestro of sinology as evidence of the tomb's worthiness.[140] Qiu Jin's tomb, which failed to survive the Cultural Revolution, would also be moved from its site in Mount Chicken Cage back to Solitary Hill in the early 1980s.[141]

If there were few obstacles to restoring the graves of Qiu Jin, Zhang Taiyan, and Zhang Cangshui, a more bitter controversy was provoked over rebuilding the tomb and pavilion of Su Xiaoxiao, who could neither be related to nationalism nor conform to historiography based on the theory of class struggle. In 2004, four decades after its demolition, the Hangzhou government finally decided to reconstruct the same tomb and pavilion decorated with couplets, all of which had been denounced as the embodiment of the landlord class's perverted and decadent sentiments in 1964.[142] Instantly, Su's tomb featured as one of tourists' most favorite scenic spots. The old practice of rubbing the tomb came back, and a new practice of tossing coins toward the tomb was invented, inviting a writer's criticism of such vulgar and superstitious behavior. The same writer also felt regretful that the tombs related to historical figures during the 1911 Revolution, such as Su Manshu, did not gain the government's approval for rebuilding.[143]

The priority of Su Xiaoxiao's grave over those of 1911 Revolution heroes/heroines signified the final triumph of commercial tourism in China. The late 1970s saw the transformation from politicized tourism to a market-oriented one, and Hangzhou figured prominently as the harbinger of such a sweeping change.[144] In this sociocultural atmosphere, the peaceful coexistence of the dead and the living was undoubtedly the most lucrative way of managing West Lake. In other words, the ghosts did not easily go away despite radical Maoists' tireless rally against the tombs: they no longer trouble the living but sweeten the lake-related businesses and continue to provide an unambiguous definition of how West Lake should be and what it stands for. To be more precise, it is the constant interplay between the living and the dead that contributes to the making and development of West Lake. In a sense, the highly radical 1964 movement of removing all tombs was also an episode of such interplay, if in a more dramatic way, that shaped both the scene of the lake and human beings' relations with it. As Rong Dingchang commented, some tombs would disappear, and others would be preserved in a more "natural" way without much human intervention. The rise and fall of the tombs thus followed the law in their own rights.[145] Namely, human efforts might be able to alter such a law, but only temporarily.

Given the tombs' status as topoi or the interface between human imagination and their physicality, to completely eliminate them is to obliterate them on two levels, the physical and the discursive or imaginary. The campaigns of removing those tombs during Mao's time succeeded in destroying their physical features but fell short of erasing the memories of them. Or, to borrow Maurice Halbwachs's words, radical Maoists could remove "physical objects" but failed to eradicate "something of spiritual significance" in the collective memory.[146] If we view those tombs as "symbols" in Henri Lefebvre's sense, they are able to "introduce a depth to everyday life: presence of the past, individual or collective acts and dramas, poorly specified possibilities, and the more striking, beauty and grandeur."[147] In other words, they have succeeded in transforming or "appropriating" West Lake's space to evoke a collective sensibility. Hence, the building and rebuilding of them further boosted a collective memory, and this memory was decidedly associated with the specific localities. Thus, it was what Peter Carroll calls "sited memory."[148] Su Xiaoxiao's tomb and pavilion, for example, became a site of pilgrimage for both men of letters and ordinary people in search of romantic love after it was reconstructed in the Qing. It is, therefore, the unity of their physical features and the discourses that lends the masses a sense of authenticity. The comeback of numerous tombs to the West Lake area after 1980 thus throws light on the futility of human will to unilaterally shape the external world and the tombs' capacity to remold or even dictate the perspective of tourists, CCP cadres, and intellectuals alike.

Conclusion

Throughout this book, I have documented the CCP authorities' strenuous efforts to transform West Lake physically, culturally, and ecologically. All the programs discussed in the present book could fall into the category of the propaganda-campaign project. They generated concrete results—a deep body of water, a scenic public park, greener lakeside hills, a new economy of pig farming, and the temporal removal of the lakeshore tombs—and thereby helped the CCP attain some of its preset sociopolitical goals. Their success was visible—given the governments' enormous financial investment and labor input—though limited. Meanwhile, they constituted a vital part of state propaganda as they provided the general population with guidebooks to conceptualize what socialism was and understand how to participate in it in the PRC. They familiarized the PRC's citizens with the notions of mass mobilization of labor, voluntarism, economic self-sufficiency, agricultural collectivization, Stakhanovism, class-based views of history and realities, and world revolution in the Cold War age. Collectively, they helped the CCP to legitimize the new socialist regime domestically and internationally and rationalize all its efforts to fundamentally alter society, culture, nature, and historical memories in China.

The Party's self-proclaimed triumph over nature, history, and culture was an embodiment of "will," an essential component of Mao Zedong's philosophical thoughts. In his analysis of voluntarism or *zhuguan nengdong xing* in transforming or subjugating society and inanimate things in the world,[1] Mao juxtaposed the "conquest of nature" with humankind's "liberation from superstition."[2] The case studies provided in this book, nevertheless, present counterexamples of the CCP's imposition of its will on West Lake and its adjacent area. Throughout the book, I argue that "counteractions"—as opposed to conscious and purposive "resistance"—defined the "expressive" or "nonpurposive" agency that both human and nonhuman actors possessed and exercised. Here, this expressive and nonpurposive agency is understood in three ways. First, while Micah Muscolino highlights "a distinctive agency" of nonhuman entities (the Yellow River in his research) that refuses to bend to humans' will,[3] this book underscores the capacity of humans' and nonhumans' unconscious and unintentional actions or inactions to not only defy but also reshape and rework the Party's sociopolitical agendas. The dredging project came to an end a few years earlier than what planner Yu Senwen was lobbying for; the demand of visitors to *Huagang guanyu* for more sheltered areas for rest and tea consumption conflicted with the designer's intention to carve out more open spaces; the villagers in the afforestation movements were mobilized to catch pests but focused only on exchanging bugs for cash without putting in the maximal effort, further exacerbating pest infestation; unvaccinated pigs' massive deaths in collectivized pig farms dealt a blow to the Party's rural collectivization policy, partly contributing to decollectivization in the early 1960s; the campaign of removing lakeside tombs failed to blot out memories of heroes and heroines in the West Lake area, leading to the restoration of the destructed burial sites later. All those instances exemplify the nonpurposive agency capable of steering Party policies in different directions.

Second, the discussion of the expressive or nonpurposive agency in this book problematizes an artificial human/nonhuman divide and is thereby intended to unify human and nonhuman actors. Poachers of aquatic creatures in the *Huagang guanyu* park, tea growers who stole lands from mountain forests, pig breeders who attempted to retain or even expand their private plots in the name of feeding pigs, and Hangzhou urbanites who rubbed Su Xiaoxiao's tombs ran parallel with algae that proliferated in and reddened the lake in the mid-1950s, pine bugs that devastated trees, and viruses that killed pigs in collectively run swine farms. They were not self-conscious resisters to the CCP's sociopolitical agendas, but their actions or the lack thereof somehow undercut the authorities' endeavors to transform the West Lake area. More importantly, the emergence of the uncooperative or recalcitrant human and nonhuman actors was an outgrowth of the unfolding of those propaganda-campaign projects. The unity between human and nonhuman actors was thus akin to what Ling Zhang calls the "entanglements" of all "geological, physical, chemical, social, political, [and] cultural" entities. Just like Zhang, who rejects "the nature-culture binarism" by casting doubt on the possibility of differentiating "something natural" from "something cultural,"[4] I explore the human/nonhuman unity with an emphasis on those actors' nonpurposive agency.

Third, underscoring "a greater sense of interconnectedness between humanity and nonhumanity," as Jane Bennett posits, allows for a further investigation of those actors' enhanced "political potential."[5] It is tempting to argue that the political potential to defy the political authorities' agenda referred to the undesired or even dire consequences those human and nonhuman actors created: a polluted lake, a park of diverse uses, the expansion of tea plantations at the expense of forested lands, pest infestation of pine trees, or the marked loss of swine population because of either villagers' unwillingness to collectivize or the outbreak of epidemic diseases. However, to call those incidents and events failures or even disasters runs the risk of being anthropocentric.[6] From the angle of nonhuman things—namely, microbes lurking in the lake, bugs that devoured the trees, viruses that knocked down pigs, and unerasable memories of heroes and heroines in imperial Chinese—they benefited variously from the fiascoes of sociocultural projects launched by humans. Similarly, young men and women who made their trysts in the park or brought back goldfish or plankton; tea peasants who obtained, legally or not, pieces of land from forests; poachers who cut down trees to sell timber or firewood; villagers who caught easy bugs from the trees in exchange for cash; and peasants who were entitled to receive pork, private plots, and workpoints as rewards of their pig-breeding activities also reaped benefits from those programs. Their actions or inactions driven by self-interest, to a varying degree, jeopardized the propaganda-campaign projects discussed in this book.

It is thus fair to argue that the political potential of the agency at issue of both human and nonhuman actors resided in its capacity to affect, delegitimate, and alter Party policies, even if not in a purposeful and intentional way. I have repeatedly highlighted the nonpurposive nature of such agency because it provides a new perspective on power relations in Mao-era China, namely the futility of the resistance-accommodation paradigm. In a socialist regime, as Alexei Yurchak notes, such binaries as "oppression and resistance," "repression and freedom," "the state and the people," and "official culture and counterculture," had all been artificial and ex post constructions, and therefore, failed to shed light on individuals' lived experiences.[7] Following this line of thought, the entire book does not interpret the (in)actions of both humans and nonhumans as a manifestation of their resistance driven by political motives but more as their moves in response to the Party's agenda. Their agency was not "voluntaristic" but "expressive" in essence because it was the actions—or the lack thereof—that defined their intentions but not the other way round.

The agency exercised by both humans and nonhuman entities inflicted harm upon various propaganda-campaign projects designed to bring about spatial, cultural, and ecological changes to Hangzhou. Thus, the story about the CCP's less-than-successful effort to transform Hangzhou was in stark contrast to the Party's success in rebuilding Beijing, the PRC's capital. During his historic visit to China in 1972, President Richard Nixon made an apt comparison between the two cities:

"Peking [Beijing] is the head of China, but Hangchow [Hangzhou] is the heart of China."[8] What makes this comment intriguing was not Nixon's acute awareness of the comparable political significance of the two cities but the metaphorization of the two aspects of the propaganda-campaign project of city rebuilding in the PRC's early years. As the "head" or the face of the new republic, Beijing was necessarily refashioned into a predominantly political space, which "emphasized revolution, [but] not preservation."[9] In other words, its function as propaganda had to outweigh others. In contrast, Hangzhou, the beating "heart," symbolized the vitality of Mao's China and must perforce perform multiple, albeit mutually contradictory, functions. Hence, it became at once political, productive, cultural, discursive, and leisure space. The coexistence and interactions among a diverse array of spaces and competing agendas left much room for both local cadres' manipulation or negotiation and enabled other humans and nonhuman entities to variously undermine Party policies and/or obtain their benefits. In consequence, although Hangzhou was the capital of a "red province" in Zhejiang with "high party membership density" and therefore consistently came under the CCP's tight control,[10] the projects of transforming West Lake and the city could hardly reach all their goals.

Soon after China reopened its doors during the post-Mao era, Hangzhou has quickly evolved into a city of tourism, culture, and the fast-growing Internet economy, corresponding to a general trend of urban development in the world that recalibrates the functions of the city. As David Harvey observes, the "managerial" approach in urban administration prevalent across the globe in the 1960s gradually gave way to "entrepreneurial" forms in the closing years of the twentieth century and beyond. The city governments' newly acquired role as the coordinator, rather than the leader, centered on "investment and economic development with the speculative construction of place."[11] Accordingly, the projects launched in turn-of-the-century Hangzhou, such as the dredging of West Lake between 1999 and 2003, carried new socioeconomic ramifications: they were designed to build a scenic and pollution-free city to appeal to not only tourists but also investors and settlers.

The 1999–2003 project of dredging the lake, for which the PRC government invested 235 million yuan in order to dig a 2.35-meter-deep body of water, constituted a part of the ongoing ambitious campaign of pollution treatment and prevention in Hangzhou. Its target was at once to purify lake water and to reduce citywide smog and noise.[12] In 2003, the dredging project was completed, and the lakeshore region was remodeled. The revitalization of the West Lake region featured a wide range of subprojects, including the return of Su Xiaoxiao's tomb, as discussed in the preceding chapter. To further appeal to tourists and visitors, the

Figure 6.1. West Lake "gentrified." *Courtesy of Mr. Zhu Jiang* 朱绛.

Hangzhou municipal government made a bold decision to exempt them from admission fees in practically all lakeside scenic spots.

To rationalize the decision, a local official stated that the government's short-term goal was to attract tourists both at home and abroad, but the long-term target was to maximally "absorb investments and entrepreneurial talents" and lay the groundwork for the intake of multinational capital, the recruitment of leading experts, and the development of industry and commerce.[13] Hence, the turn-of-the-century program of remolding the lake played a central role in the gentrification of Hangzhou, a city committed to being a leading competitor in a globalized world. The Hangzhou government managed to fulfill its dual goals in the 2010s. In the space of a decade between 2002 and 2013, the tourism-related revenue in Hangzhou rose by 483.6 percent.[14] Meanwhile, Hangzhou has also been known as the home of a number of blockbuster high-tech enterprises, such as Alibaba.

It is thus fair to argue that the program of dredging West Lake between 1999 and 2003 was a new type of propaganda-campaign project not just to legitimate the PRC but to establish Hangzhou's identity as a heavyweight player in the global, interurban contest for capital investment and talent. The gentrification of Hangzhou and the city's enduring reputation as a destination for tourism, nevertheless, created a new ecological dilemma: the soaring land and real estate prices disallowed West Lake's dredgers from finding a low-cost location to store the excavated earth, while the lake's water was poised to be repolluted shortly after the dredging project ended due to the high population density of tourists in the lakeside area and the capacity of the cutting-edge dredging technologies to swiftly and irretrievably remove microbes—including water-purifying ones.[15] Once again, as David Harvey posits, every society is plagued by its "share of ecologically based difficulties."[16]

ABBREVIATIONS

HMA	Hangzhou shi dang'an guan 杭州市档案馆 [Hangzhou Municipal Archives].
SMA	Shanghai shi dang'an guan 上海市档案馆 [Shanghai Municipal Archives].
XHFJYL	Hangzhou shi yuanlin wenwu guanliju 杭州市园林文物管理局, ed. *Xihu fengjing yuanlin (1949-1989)* 西湖风景园林（1949-1989）[Landscape and gardening in West Lake, 1949-1989]. Shanghai kexue jishu chubanshe, 1990.
XHWXJC3	Wang Guoping 王国平, ed. *Xihu wenxian jicheng di 3 ce, Mingdai shizhi Xihu wenxian zhuanji* 西湖文献集成第3册 明代史志西湖文献专辑 [Collection of literatures about West Lake, book 3, special issue of literatures about West Lake in histories and gazetteers in the Ming]. Hangzhou: Hangzhou chubanshe, 2004.
XHWXJC8	Wang Guoping 王国平, ed. *Xihu wenxian jicheng di 8 ce, Qingdai shizhi Xihu wenxian zhuanji* 西湖文献集成第8册 清代史志西湖文献专辑 [Collection of literatures about West Lake, book 8, special issue of literatures about West Lake in histories and gazetteers in the Qing]. Hangzhou: Hangzhou chubanshe, 2004.
XHWXJC12	Wang Guoping 王国平, ed. *Xihu wenxian jicheng di 12 ce, Zhonghua renmin gongheguo chengli 50 nian Xihu wenxian zhuanji* 西湖文献集成第12册 中华人民共和国成立50年西湖文献专辑 [Collection of literatures about West Lake, book 12, special issue of literatures about West Lake in 50 years since the founding of the PRC]. Hangzhou: Hangzhou chubanshe, 2004.
XHWXJC13	Wang Guoping 王国平, ed. *Xihu wenxian jicheng, di 13 ce, Lidai Xihu wenxuan zhuanji* 西湖文献集成第13册 历代西湖文选专辑 [Collection of literatures about West Lake, book 13, special volume of essays on West Lake in all ages]. Hangzhou: Hangzhou chubanshe, 2004.

XHWXJC14 Wang Guoping 王国平, ed. *Xihu wenxian jicheng, di 14 ce, Lidai xihu wenxuan zhuanji* 西湖文献集成第14册 历代文选专辑 [Collection of literatures about West Lake, book 14, special volume of essays on West Lake in all ages]. Hangzhou: Hangzhou chubanshe, 2004.

ZPA Zhejiang sheng dang'an ju 浙江省档案局 [Zhejiang Provincial Archives].

Notes

Introduction

1. Hong, *Guangrong shuyu nimen*, pp. 113–115.
2. Huang, *Huang Yanpei shiji*, p. 339.
3. Van Fleit Hang, *Literature the People Love*, p. 7.
4. Wu, *Remaking Beijing*, p. 85.
5. Smith, *Thought Reform and China's Dangerous Classes*, p. 28.
6. Ibid., p. 222.
7. Le Bon, *The Psychology of Revolution*, p. 69.
8. Hong, *Guangrong shuyu nimen*, p. 128.
9. Volland, "Clandestine Cosmopolitanism," p. 186.
10. Kunakhovich, "Ties That Bind, Ties That Divide," p. 136.
11. Johnson, *China's New Creative Age*, p. 44.
12. Agamben, *Homo Sacer*, p. 176.
13. Gao, *The Communist Takeover of Hangzhou*, p. 216.
14. Ibid., pp. 155–156.
15. Dove, Sajise, and Doolittle, "Introduction," p. 21.
16. For example, Smil, *The Bad Earth*; Smil, *China's Environment Crisis*; and Shapiro, *Mao's War against Nature*, to name but a few.
17. Harvey, *Justice, Nature and the Geography of Difference*, p. 189.
18. de Pee and Lam, "Introduction," p. xiv.
19. Duan, *The Rise of West Lake*, p. 3.
20. *Zhejiang sheng Shuiwen zhi* bianzuan weiyuanhui, *Zhejiang sheng shuiwen zhi*, p. 137.
21. Wang, "Paradise for Sale," p. 8.
22. Ibid., p. 343.
23. "Ba xiaofei chengshi biancheng shengchan chengshi."
24. Rugg, *Spatial Foundations of Urbanism*, p. 314.
25. Gao, *The Communist Takeover of Hangzhou*, pp. 217–218.
26. Ibid., pp. 221–222.
27. Ye, *Mao Zedong yu Xihu*, p. 133.
28. Yu, "Hangzhou jiefang hou 17 nianjian de yuanlin jianshe," p. 153.
29. Zhao, "Wang Pingyi tongzhi zai Hangzhou," p. 4.
30. Nixon, *RN*, p. 573.
31. Hung, *Mao's New World*, p. 8. Such studies also include Wu, *Remaking Beijing*; Yu, *Chang'an Avenue and the Modernization of Chinese Architecture*; and Li, *China's Soviet Dream*.

32. For more information about the CCP's effort to make Beijing a political space, please also see Hung, *Politics of Control*, pp. 131–150.
33. Hung, *Mao's New World*, 18.
34. Kenez, *The Birth of the Propaganda State*, p. 8.
35. Brandenberger, *Propaganda State in Crisis*, p. 2.
36. Cheek, *Propaganda and Culture in Mao's China*, p. 14.
37. Denton, "What Do You Do with Cultural 'Propaganda' of the Mao Era?" p. 1.
38. Ibid.
39. Johnson, "Beneath the Propaganda State," p. 199.
40. Mittler, *A Continuous Revolution*, p. 12.
41. Kenez, *Cinema and Soviet Society from the Revolution to the Death of Stalin*, p. 224.
42. Kenez, *The Birth of the Propaganda State*, 253.
43. Kotkin, *Magnetic Mountain*, p. 236.
44. Kiaer and Naiman, "Introduction," p. 6.
45. Hung, *Mao's New World*, p. 2.
46. Petrone, *Life Has Become More Joyous, Comrades*, p. 1.
47. Kassymbekova, *Despite Cultures*, pp. 3–9.
48. Quoted in Chi, "The Red Detachment of Women," p. 153.
49. Hellbeck, "Working, Struggling, Becoming," p. 185.
50. Tang, *Chinese Modern*, pp. 165–195.
51. Vogel, *Canton under Communism*, p. 351.
52. Lieberthal, *Revolution and Tradition in Tientsin, 1949–1952*, p. 8. Ezra Vogel also finds that what the CCP did in the early 1950s "follow[ed] logically from pre-Liberation trends." See Vogel, *Canton under Communism*, p. 350.
53. Murphey, "Man and Nature in China," p. 330.
54. Scott, *Seeing Like a State*, p. 4.
55. Pietz, *The Yellow River*, p. 3; Gross, *Farewell to the God of Plague*, p. 240; Liu, *Gongdi shehui*, p. 9.
56. Smith, *Thought Reform and China's Dangerous Classes*, pp. 4–5.
57. Scott, *Seeing Like a State*, p. 2.
58. Brock and Wei, "Introduction," p. 29.
59. Koss, *Where the Party Rules*, pp. 3–6.
60. For example, Esherick, "Deconstructing the Construction of the Party-State," p. 1078; Lu, "Introduction," p. 3; Hershatter, *The Gender of Memory*, p. 14; He, *Gilded Voices*; Brown and Johnson, "Introduction," p. 3; Sun, "War against the Earth," pp. 252–253.
61. Westboy, "'Making Green the Motherland,'" p. 231.
62. Smil, *The Bad Earth*, p. 7; Shapiro, *Mao's War against Nature*, p. 1; Murray and Cook, *Green China*, p. 38; Marks, *China*, p. 276.
63. Hung, *Mao's New World*, p. 19.
64. Johnson, "Beneath the Propaganda State," p. 228.
65. He, *Gilded Voices*.
66. Tuan, "Thought and Landscape," p. 90.
67. Hershatter, *The Gender of Memory*, p. 4.
68. Ibid., pp. 287–288.
69. Anand, *Hydraulic City*, p. 12.
70. Yurchak, *Everything Was Forever, Until It Was No More*, p. 8.

71. Schmalzer, "On the Appropriate Use of Rose-Colored Glasses," p. 358.
72. Durdin, Reston, and Topping, *The New York Times Report from Red China*, p. 198.
73. "Guanyu Xihu fengjing qu de diaocha baogao," p. 287.
74. Murphey, "Man and Nature in China," p. 319.
75. Shapiro, *Mao's War against Nature*, p. 3.
76. For example, Wakeman, *History and Will*, p. 236; Rogaski, "Nature, Annihilation, and Modernity," p. 383; Smil, *The Bad Earth*, p. 7; Pietz, *The Yellow River*, p. 139; Sun, "War against the Earth," pp. 252–266.
77. Lynteris, *The Spirit of Selflessness in Maoist China*, p. 22.
78. Castree, "Socializing Nature," p. 4. Also see Evernden, *The Social Creation of Nature*, p. 59.
79. Bewell, *Natures in Translation*, p. 3.
80. Blackbourn, *The Conquest of Nature*, pp. 5–7.
81. Evernden, *The Social Creation of Nature*, p. 59.
82. Cronon, "Introduction," p. 34.
83. Lehtinen, "Modernization and the Concept of Nature," pp. 26–34.
84. Saito, *Karl Marx's Ecosocialism*, pp. 14–15.
85. Castree, "Marxism and the Production of Nature," pp. 26–28. Author's italics.
86. Williams, *Culture and Materialism*, pp. 109–110.
87. Smith, *Uneven Development*, p. 17.
88. Löwy, "What Is Ecosocialism?" p. 16.
89. Yurchak, *Everything Was Forever, Until It Was No More*, p. 10.
90. Bauman, *Modernity and Ambivalence*, pp. 263–264.
91. Pietz, *The Yellow River*, p. 15.
92. Shapiro, *Mao's War against Nature*, p. 8.
93. For example, Esherick, "Deconstructing the Construction of the Party-State," pp. 1078–1079; Shue, *The Reach of the State*, p. 70; Johnson, "Beneath the Propaganda State," p. 199; Shi, *Political Participation in Beijing*, p. 12; Zheng, *The Chinese Communist Party as Organizational Emperor*, p. 176.
94. For example, Perkins, *Market Control and Planning in Communist China*, p. 3; Harding, *Organizing China*, p. 31.
95. Bruno, *The Nature of Soviet Power*, p. 7.
96. Mitchell, *Rule of Experts*, p. 10.
97. Latour, *Politics of Nature*, p. 81.
98. Bennett, *Vibrant Matter*, p. 6. Author's italics.
99. Grusin, "Introduction," p. xi.
100. Chen, "The Human–Machine Continuum in Maoism," p. 161.
101. Latour, *The Pasteurization of France*, p. 35.
102. Mosse, "Introduction," p. 5.
103. Muscolino, *The Ecology of War in China*, p. 141.
104. Braden, "Review of *The Ecology of War in China: Henan Province, the Yellow River, and Beyond*," p. 785.
105. Anand, *Hydraulic City*, p. 230.
106. Knappett and Malafouris, "Material and Nonhuman Agency," p. xii.
107. Bowden, "Human and Nonhuman Agency in Deleuze," p. 60.
108. Jones and Cloke, "Non-Human Agencies," p. 80.

109. For example, recent scholarship on peasants' resistance to the agricultural collectivization movement has cited examples of not attending meetings and refusing to work (Friedman, Pickowicz, and Selden, *Revolution, Resistance, and Reform in Village China*, pp. 11–12), opposing the state-initiated disease-prevention programs (Gross, *Farewell to the God of Plague*, p. 12), altering the Party policies in the Great Leap Forward (Yang, *Calamity and Reform in China*, p. 14; Thaxton, *Catastrophe and Contention in Rural China*, p. 6), and killing livestock on the eve of the collectivization of peasants' personal belongings (Walker, *Planning in Chinese Agriculture*, pp. 61–62), to name but a few. In the urban areas, scholars have focused on massive protests launched by workers and students (Perry, "Shanghai's Strike Wave of 1957," pp. 1–27; Chen, "Against the State," p. 490); artists' appropriation of the Party's policies of cultural reform to reap personal benefits (He, "Between Accommodation and Resistance," pp. 524–549); and ordinary citizens' violation of dress code in their everyday life (Sun, "The Collar Revolution," pp. 773–795).

110. Castree and MacMillan, "Dissolving Dualisms," p. 213.
111. Gao, *Renmin gongshe shiqi zhong Zhongguo nongmin "fan xingwei" diaocha*, p. 3.
112. Ibid., pp. 170–172.
113. Latour, *Politics of Nature*, p. 81.
114. Mitchell, "Everyday Metaphors of Power," p. 562; Chatterjee et al., "Introduction," p. 3.
115. Kassymbekova, *Despite Cultures*, pp. 3–9.
116. Yurchak, *Everything Was Forever, Until It Was No More*, p. 24.
117. Johnston, *Being Soviet*, p. xxxiii.
118. Merchant, *Autonomous Nature*, p. 1.
119. Mosse, "Introduction," p. 7.
120. Lu, "Introduction," 3.
121. Wakeman, *History and Will*, p. 202.

Chapter 1. Water, Labor, and Microbes

1. Wu, "Jianguo chuqi Xihu shujun gongcheng jishi," pp. 78–79.
2. Yu, "Yu Senwen huiyi lu," p. 122.
3. Akutagawa, *Zhongguo youji*, p. 68.
4. Gao, *The Communist Takeover of Hangzhou*, p. 219.
5. Pietz, *The Yellow River*, p. 4.
6. Liu, *Gongdi shehui*, p. 12.
7. Courtney, "At War with Water," p. 1810.
8. Ibid., p. 1824.
9. Pietz, *The Yellow River*, pp. 3–4.
10. Shi, *Xihu zhi*, p. 49.
11. Yu, "Yu Senwen huiyi lu," p. 122.
12. Ibid.
13. For example, *Hangzhou Daily* (*Hangzhou ribao* 杭州日报) published two reports in five days between November 3 and 8, 1955, to rally a voluntary labor campaign on November 5 in which over 1,000 students, workers, government staff members, and soldiers participated. See "Benshi qingnian jiang canjia shujun Xihu de yiwu laodong"; "Benshi qingnian shujun Xihu yiwu laodong kaigong."
14. Gross, *Farewell to the God of Plague*, p. 240.

15. Jones and Cloke, "Non-Human Agencies," p. 3; Bowden, "Human and Nonhuman Agency in Deleuze," p. 75.
16. Latour, *Politics of Nature*, p. 81.
17. Gross, *Farewell to the God of Plague*, p. 11.
18. Pietz, *The Yellow River*, p. 6.
19. Zheng, *Hangzhou Xihu zhili shi yanjiu*, p. 146.
20. Shi, *Xihu zhi*, p. 67.
21. Wu et al., "Quanmian zhengxiu Xihu hu'an," p. 37.
22. Lin, "Meishu de Hangzhou," p. 497.
23. Zhang, *Bibo yingying*, pp. 53–54.
24. Yu, "Hangzhou jiefang hou 17 nianjian de yuanlin jianshe," p. 150.
25. Wu, "Jianguo chuqi Xihu shujun gongcheng jishi," p. 78.
26. "Hangzhou shi yuanlin jianshe shinian lai de zhuyao chengjiu (chugao)," p. 179.
27. Between 1953 and 1957, the overall investment in infrastructure in the entire province of Zhejiang amounted only to 190.51 million yuan. See *Zhejiang sheng zhengfu zhi xia*, p. 551.
28. ZPA, J163-002-305, p. 56.
29. Wu, "Jianguo chuqi Xihu shujun gongcheng jishi," p. 79.
30. "Shujun Xihu sheji renwushu," p. 569.
31. "Shujun Xihu gongcheng jihua," pp. 565–566.
32. Yu, "Yu Senwen huiyi lu," p. 72.
33. "Shujun Xihu gongcheng jihua," p. 565.
34. Ibid., pp. 565–566.
35. Ibid., pp. 566–568.
36. Ibid., p. 567.
37. Wu, "Jianguo chuqi Xihu shujun gongcheng jishi," p. 80.
38. Shi, *Xihu zhi*, p. 49.
39. Hangzhou shi difangzhi bianzhuan weiyuanhui, *Hangzhou shi zhi (dijiu juan)*, p. 212.
40. Gao, *The Communist Takeover of Hangzhou*, p. 34.
41. The rice quota listed in *Gazetteer of Hangzhou* [*Hangzhou shi zhi* 杭州市志] was inconsistent with the existing archival records. A survey in June 1950 showed that a worker participating in "work in exchange for relief" earned at least six to eight kilograms of rice per day. (See ZPA, J103-002-098-020, p. 20).
42. Hangzhou shi difangzhi bianzhuan weiyuanhui, *Hangzhou shi zhi (dijiu juan)*, p. 212.
43. Ibid.
44. ZPA, J103-002-098-020, p. 20.
45. Hangzhou shi difangzhi bianzhuan weiyuanhui, *Hangzhou shi zhi (dijiu juan)*, p. 212.
46. ZPA, J103-002-098-020, p. 20.
47. HMA, 071-001-0009, p. 16.
48. Ibid., pp. 16–22.
49. "Jiasu shujun Xihu gongcheng zuori kaishi jinxing."
50. Zhou Haiyan 周海燕 argues that such a correlation was initially established in the early 1940s when the CCP regime in Northern Shaanxi called for the massive organization of labor and preached self-sufficiency amid an unprecedented economic crisis. See Zhou, *Jiyi yu zhengzhi*, pp. 136–137.
51. HMA, 071-001-0009, p. 16.

52. As a matter of fact, reports abounded on prisoners' participation in Hangzhou's public projects in the early 1950s. For example, jailed monks from a Hangzhou Buddhist monastery were said to "go out to work on a road gang" each day. See Welch, *Buddhism under Mao*, p. 70.
53. HMA, 071-001-0009, pp. 9-11.
54. Ibid., p. 19.
55. Ibid., pp. 9-11.
56. Ibid., p. 15.
57. Ibid., p. 9.
58. Ibid., pp. 10-13.
59. "Benshi qingnian jiang canjia shujun Xihu de yiwu laodong."
60. "Benshi qingnian shujun Xihu yiwu laodong kaigong."
61. Ibid.
62. "Qingnian men wei meihua Xihu de yiwu laodong ri."
63. "Liheng he Tiyuchang he jiangke tiqian tianping."
64. Wu, "Jianguo chuqi Xihu shujun gongcheng jishi," p. 80.
65. Ibid.
66. "Hangzhou shi yuanlin guanli ju wei jiansong 'Shujun Xihu de liangnian guihua' de baogao," pp. 577-579.
67. ZPA, J163-002-430, pp. 50-56.
68. Wu, "Jianguo chuqi Xihu shujun gongcheng jishi," p. 81.
69. "Shujun Xihu gongcheng jihua," p. 567.
70. "Shujun Xihu sheji renwushu," p. 570.
71. Chen, *Nanwang de nianyue*, p. 8.
72. "Hangzhou shi banyun Xihu ni gongzuo zongjie," p. 571.
73. Ibid., p. 572.
74. HMA, 071-001-0009, p. 3.
75. Ibid., pp. 3-5.
76. Bennett, *Vibrant Matter*, p. viii.
77. Wu, "Jianguo chuqi Xihu shujun gongcheng jishi," p. 80.
78. Hangzhou shi difangzhi bianzhuan weiyuanhui, *Hangzhou shi zhi (disan juan)*, p. 609.
79. *Hangzhou shi shuili zhi* bianzuan weiyuanhui, *Hangzhou shuili zhi*, p. 185.
80. HMA, 071-002-0003, p. 18.
81. Shi, *Xihu zhi*, pp. 74-78.
82. *Hangzhou shi shuili zhi* bianzuan weiyuanhui, *Hangzhou shuili zhi*, p. 185.
83. HMA, 071-002-0028, p. 2.
84. Tang et al., "Gaishan Xihu shuiti wenti de shijian yu tantao," p. 434.
85. Shi, *Xihu zhi*, p. 117.
86. Ibid., p. 69.
87. Mao, "Hangzhou Xihu de huanjing shuiwen tiaojian yu shuiti fuyingyanghua wenti," p. 162.
88. Liu, Mao, and He, "Hangzhou Xihu shuizhi tezheng jiqi zonghe pingjia," pp. 310-315.
89. Shi, *Xihu zhi*, p. 49.
90. Mao, "Hangzhou Xihu de huanjing shuiwen tiaojian yu shuiti fuyingyanghua wenti," p. 1.
91. Liu, Mao, and He, "Hangzhou Xihu shuizhi tezheng jiqi zonghe pingjia," p. 309.

92. HMA, 071-002-0028, pp. 2–3.
93. Ibid., pp. 3–5.
94. Zheng, *Hangzhou Xihu zhili shi yanjiu*, p. 145.
95. Tang et al., "Gaishan Xihu shuiti wenti de shijian yu tantao," p. 434.
96. Gao, *The Communist Takeover of Hangzhou*, p. 220.
97. Tang et al., "Gaishan Xihu shuiti wenti de shijian yu tantao," p. 439.
98. "Shi Xihu hushui bianqing de shiyan baogao," pp. 542–544.
99. Ibid., pp. 543–544.
100. Ibid., p. 544.
101. Ibid., pp. 544–545.
102. Gross, *Farewell to the God of Plague*, p. 11.
103. Schmalzer, *The People's Peking Man*, p. 9.
104. "Dangqian Xihu shuizhi ehua de qingkuang fanying," p. 546.
105. "Shi Xihu hushui bianqing de shiyan baogao," p. 544.
106. Tang et al., "Gaishan Xihu shuiti wenti de shijian yu tantao," p. 434.
107. Ibid.
108. Yu, "Yu Senwen huiyi lu," p. 566.
109. ZPA, J163-002-430, pp. 25–27.
110. Ibid., pp. 28–33.
111. Ibid., pp. 33–34.
112. Ibid., pp. 50–58.
113. Ibid., p. 77.
114. Gray, "Mao in Perspective," p. 664.
115. Murphey, "Man and Nature in China," p. 330.
116. Smil, *The Bad Earth*, p. 97.
117. Kenez, *Cinema and Soviet Society from the Revolution to the Death of Stalin*, p. 224.
118. In the 2000s, West Lake's water quality has been consistently rated to "exceed V class" or severe pollution in numerous tests. See Zheng, *Hangzhou Xihu zhili shi yanjiu*, p. 40.
119. Zheng, *Hangzhou Xihu zhili shi yanjiu*, pp. 143–147.
120. Merchant, *Autonomous Nature*, pp. 1–4.
121. Mosse, "Introduction," p. 7.

Chapter 2. "Watching Fish at the Flower Harbor"

1. "Huanggang guanyu."
2. "Hangzhou shi yuanlin jianshe shinian lai de zhuyao chengjiu (chugao)," p. 183.
3. Zhao, *Zhongguo xiandai yuanlin*, p. 50.
4. Hunt, *Greater Perfections*, p. 113.
5. David Blackbourn argues, "What we call landscape are neither natural nor innocent; they are human constructs." See Blackbourn, *The Conquest of Nature*, p. 16.
6. Malpas, "Place and the Problem of Landscape," p. 17.
7. Hayden, *Russian Parks and Gardens*, p. 231.
8. Ivanova, *Parks of Culture and Rest in the Soviet Union*, p. 9.
9. Ho, *Curating Revolution*, p. 13.
10. Pack, *Tourism and Dictatorship*, p. 5.
11. Hollander, *Political Pilgrims*, p. 17.

12. Hung, *Mao's New World*, pp. 8–19.
13. For example, Shuishan Yu showed how architects used architectural space to preach socialist nationalism. See Yu, *Chang'an Avenue and the Modernization of Chinese Architecture*, p. 57. Tsung-yi Pan argued that the PRC state-sponsored commemorative architecture and practices at Tiananmen Square materialized the CCP's memory of national salvation and revolutionary tradition. See Pan, "Constructing Tiananmen Square as a Realm of Memory." Also see Li, *China's Soviet Dream*, pp. 91–108.
14. Gao, *The Communist Takeover of Hangzhou*, p. 218.
15. de Certeau, *The Practice of Everyday Life*, p. 117.
16. Brown, "Moving Targets," p. 381, n4.
17. Gao, *The Communist Takeover of Hangzhou*, p. 5.
18. Wu, *Remaking Beijing*, p. 9.
19. Clunas, *Fruitful Sites*, p. 102.
20. Scholars have long found that the CCP had to negotiate and compromise with specialists of various fields to advance its social and economic agendas in Mao's China. For example, Perkins, *Market Control and Planning in Communist China*, p. 3; U, *Disorganizing China*, p. 59.
21. Ho, *Curating Revolution*, p. 214.
22. Zhongguo jianzhu wenhua zhongxin, *Zhongwai jingguan*, p. 35.
23. Nora, *Realms of Memory*, p. 1. Lee Hui-shu argued that West Lake had become a "site of memory" immediately after the Song dynasty collapsed. Lee, "*Xihu qingqu tu* yu Lin'an shengjing tuxiang de zaixian," p. 184.
24. Carroll, *Between Heaven and Modernity*, p. 15.
25. Link, *The Use of Literature*, p. 285.
26. Rotenberg, *Landscape and Power in Vienna*, p. 4.
27. de Certeau, *The Practice of Everyday Life*, p. 117.
28. Mitchell, "Introduction," pp. 1–4.
29. Olwig, *Landscape, Nature, and the Body Politic*, p. 216.
30. de Certeau, *The Practice of Everyday Life*, p. 115.
31. Yang and Shinji, "Chūgoku Kōshū 'Seiko jikkei' no hensen kara mita fūkeichi no seiritsu katei," p. 465.
32. Tian, "Xihu youlan zhi," p. 47. Also, Li et al., *Xihu zhi*, p. 234.
33. Chen, "Xihu shijing de youlai he xianzhuang," p. 116.
34. Wang and Wu, "Cong wenxue dao huihua," p. 70.
35. Duan, "The Ten Views of West Lake," p. 172.
36. Lee, "*Xihu qingqu tu* yu Lin'an shengjing tuxiang de zaixian," p. 184.
37. Zhai and Zhai, "Hushan bianlan," pp. 630–631.
38. Song, "Huagang guanyu zongheng tan," p. 28.
39. Li et al., *Xihu zhi*, pp. 42–43.
40. Ibid., p. 234.
41. Wang, *Yuan Ming Qing sanwen xuan*, p. 436.
42. Shen, *Xihu zhizuan*, p. 150.
43. Hu, "Huagang guanyu gongyuan," p. 77.
44. Li, *Hangzhou tonglan*, p. 27.
45. Gao, *The Communist Takeover of Hangzhou*, p. 218.
46. Sun and Hu, "Hangzhou Huagang guanyu gongyuan guihua sheji," p. 19.
47. Hung, *Mao's New World*, p. 263.

48. Hu, "Huagang guanyu gongyuan," p. 78.
49. "Hangzhou shi yuanlin jianshe gongzuo baogao (1949–1955) (jielu)," pp. 172–173.
50. "Xihu fengjing jianshe wunian jihua," pp. 84–91.
51. "Guanyu Xihu fengjing zhengjian gongzuo jihua de baogao," p. 262.
52. Fu, *Hangzhou fengjing chengshi de xingcheng shi*, pp. 105–124.
53. Shi, *Xihu zhi*, pp. 160–161.
54. Wu et al., "Xihu ji huanhu diqu de bianqian he gongyuan lüdi de kaituo," p. 77.
55. Huang, *Shanchuan, lishi, renwu*, p. 42.
56. Wu et al., "Xihu ji huanhu diqu de bianqian he gongyuan lüdi de kaituo," p. 77.
57. Ibid.
58. Shi, *Shijie mingyuan shengjing 1 Yingguo, Aierlan*, p. 5.
59. Meng and Chen, *Zhongguo fengjing yuanlin mingjia*, p. 191.
60. Ibid., p. 196.
61. Huang, *Shanchuan, lishi, renwu*, p. 42.
62. For example, Sun, *Yuanlin yishu yu yuanlin sheji*, p. 3.
63. Kenez, *The Birth of the Propaganda State*, p. 255. See also Naiman, "Introduction," p. xii.
64. Here, I gain insight from the Nazi experience. Frank Uekoetter argues that conservationists in Nazi Germany were surprisingly free in expressing their opinions on conservation because "it was difficult, if not impossible, to deduce an authoritative conservation ethic from the key pillars of Nazi ideology." See Uekoetter, *The Green and the Brown*, p. 10.
65. Sun and Hu, "Hangzhou Huagang guanyu gongyuan guihua sheji," p. 19.
66. Zhao, *Zhongguo xiandai yuanlin*, p. 49.
67. Ci, *Dialectic of the Chinese Revolution*, p. 41.
68. Here, I follow Stanislaus Fung and Mark Jackson to translate *jie* as "borrowing." See Fung and Jackson, "Four Key Terms in the History of Chinese Gardens," p. 24.
69. Sun and Hu, "Hangzhou Huagang guanyu gongyuan guihua sheji," pp. 20–22.
70. Yu, "Yu Senwen huiyi lu," pp. 73–88.
71. Zhou and Chen, *Shanghai gongyuan sheji shilue*, p. 38.
72. Sun, *Yuanlin yishu yu yuanlin sheji*, p. 3.
73. Wang, "The Politics of Private Time," p. 156.
74. Ren, *Meili de Xihu*, pp. 24–25.
75. SMA, B119-2-629, p. 41.
76. *Xihu shengji*, p. 63.
77. Shi, *Xihu zhi*, p. 125.
78. Hollander, *Political Pilgrims*, p. 287.
79. Parish, *Village and Family in Contemporary China*, p. 1.
80. Huadong shifan daxue Zhongguo dangdaishi yanjiu zhongxin, *Zhongguo dangdai minjian shiliao jikan 11 Sha Wenhan gongzuo biji 1949–1954 nian*, p. 440.
81. "Hadini Sujianuo furen daoda Hangzhou, Zhejiang sheng shengzhang Zhou Jianren he furen huanyan Yindunixiya guibin."
82. "Fulao maoyu manyou Xihu mingsheng, wanjian guankan Gai Jiaotian mingju 'Ehu cun.'"
83. "Mao Zedong he zhongyang shouzhang tan yuanlin lühua wenti," p. 1.
84. Gao, *The Communist Takeover of Hangzhou*, p. 107.
85. Wu et al., "Xihu ji huanhu diqu de bianqian he gongyuan lüdi de kaituo," p. 70.
86. Ma, *Waijiaobu wenge jishi*, p. 278.

87. HMA, 71-004-0059, pp. 7-31.
88. Shi, *Xihu zhi*, p. 115.
89. Volland, "Clandestine Cosmopolitanism," p. 186.
90. Kahn and Feuerwerker, "The Ideology of Scholarship," p. 2.
91. Liu, *Jiecanglou shichao*, p. 155.
92. Wang, *Wang Tuizhai shixuan*, p. 59.
93. Fan, *Zhou Shoujuan wenji zhencang ban shang*, p. 633.
94. Wu, *Xihu fengjingqu mingsheng bolan*, p. 110.
95. Liu, *Jiecanglou shichao*, p. 155.
96. Gu, *Wentan zayi quanbian san*, p. 355.
97. Shen, *Shen Congwen quanji 24 shuxin xiudingben*, p. 330.
98. "Hangzhou shi yuanlin jianshe gongzuo baogao (1949–1955) (jielu)," p. 175.
99. Sun and Hu, "Hangzhou Huagang guanyu gongyuan guihua sheji," p. 24.
100. "Zhanduan Tao Zhu shenjin zhiwuyuan de heishou," p. 9.
101. Carroll, *Between Heaven and Modernity*, p. 15.
102. Yu, *Caozhou mudan*, p. 72.
103. Yu, "Xihu jijing."
104. "Hangzhou shi yuanlin jianshe gongzuo baogao (1949–1955) (jielu)," p. 175.
105. Wu et al., "Xihu ji huanhu diqu de bianqian he gongyuan lüdi de kaituo," pp. 70–71.
106. Yequ, "Yeyou yougan, xiangcun zaji."
107. Wang, "Huagang guanyu," pp. 168–169.
108. Hung, *Politics of Control*, p. 148.
109. Lu, "Xihu he haizi men."
110. Zhou, "Hangzhou fengwu."
111. Difeng, "Huagang guanyu xinjing."
112. "Zhejiang sheng shengzhang Zhou Jianren juxing yanhui, huanying Xihanuke qinwang deng guibingbin."
113. Zhou and Chen, *Shanghai gongyuan sheji shilue*, p. 38.
114. Sun and Hu, "Hangzhou Huagang guanyu gongyuan guihua sheji," p. 24.
115. Wang, Lin, and Liu, "Guji gengyun, momo fengxian," p. 28.
116. HMA, 71-002-0058, p. 59.
117. Enyedi, "Urbanization under Socialism," pp. 102–104.
118. "Nixon and Chou Stroll and Go Boating in Hangchow."
119. Kiaer and Naiman, "Introduction," pp. 2–6.
120. Brown and Johnson, "Introduction," p. 2; Brown, "Moving Targets," p. 381, n4.

Chapter 3. Forests, Propaganda, and Agency

1. Guowuyuan fazhi bangongshi, *Zhonghua renmin gongheguo fagui huibian 1958–1959 di 4 juan*, p. 226.
2. Zhao, *Zhongguo xiandai yuanlin*, pp. 107–108.
3. "Xiang dadi yuanlin hua qianjin."
4. Zhao, *Zhongguo xiandai yuanlin*, p. 20.
5. Scott, *Seeing Like a State*, p. 14; Lee, "Postwar Pines," p. 321.
6. Shi, *Xihu zhi*, p. 114.
7. In the words of the *People's Daily*'s editorial dated February 17, 1956, the rural cooperatives should play a leading role in this movement. Hence, this editorial established a firm

connection between the "making green the motherland" and the ongoing collectivizing movement across the country. See "Lühua zuguo."
   8. Scott, *Seeing Like a State*, pp. 11–12.
   9. Rajan, *Modernizing Nature*, pp. 51–53.
   10. Skaria, "Timber Conservancy, Desiccationism and Scientific Forestry," pp. 596–597.
   11. Westboy, "'Making Green the Motherland,'" p. 236.
   12. Menzies, *Forest and Land Management in Imperial China*, p. 52.
   13. Westboy, "'Making Green the Motherland,'" p. 231.
   14. For example, Shapiro, *Mao's War against Nature*, p. 1; Smil, *The Bad Earth*, p. 7; Marks, *China*, p. 270; Murray and Cook, *Green China*, p. 38; Gardner, *Environmental Pollution in China*, p. 25.
   15. Murray and Cook, *Green China*, p. 38.
   16. Schmalzer, "On the Appropriate Use of Rose-Colored Glasses," p. 358.
   17. Ho, *Curating Revolution*, p. 13.
   18. Spirn, *The Language of Landscape*, pp. 17–20.
   19. HMA, 071-004-0038, pp. 13–18.
   20. "Hangzhou shi jianshe ju yuanlin guanli chu 1950 nian linye gongzuo zongjie baogao (jielu)," p. 406.
   21. Volland, *Socialist Cosmopolitanism*, p. 9.
   22. For example, an article published in *Zhejiang Daily* on June 19, 1955, informed its readers that half of Taiwan's woodlands had been deserted, while timber reserves plummeted by 40 percent between 1945 and 1955. See "Zai Jiang Jieshi maiguo jituan tongzhi xia de Taiwan."
   23. Hangzhou shi dang'an guan, *Minguo shiqi Hangzhou shi zhengfu dang'an shiliao huibian (yijiu erqi nian—yijiu sijiu nian)*, pp. 525–527.
   24. Zhongguo linye bianji weiyuanhui, *Xin Zhongguo de linye jianshe*, p. 31.
   25. Nanqu, Xiqu guanlichu, "Xihu shanqu hulin he fengshan yulin de chubu baogao," p. 71.
   26. "Hangzhou shi jianshe ju yuanlin guanli chu 1950 nian linye gongzuo zongjie baogao (jielu)," pp. 407–409.
   27. "Zhejiang sheng renmin zhengfu wei zhishi baohu Xihu fengjingqu banfa wuxiang you," p. 5.
   28. Nanqu, Xiqu guanlichu, "Xihu shanqu hulin he fengshan yulin de chubu baogao," p. 72.
   29. The very first regulation promulgated by the Hangzhou municipal government specified that no tombs could be built in either public or private lands in the West Lake scenic zone without special authorization. See "Hangzhou shi renmin zhengfu guanyu gongbu *Xihu fengjingqu guanli tiaoli* de tonggao," p. 4.
   30. Nanqu, Xiqu guanlichu, "Xihu shanqu hulin he fengshan yulin de chubu baogao," p. 72.
   31. Ibid., p. 75.
   32. "Gaizao zhong de Xihu."
   33. Lu, "Xihu he haizi men."
   34. Huadong shifan daxue Zhongguo dangdaishi yanjiu zhongxin, *Zhongguo dangdai minjian shiliao jikan 12 Sha Wenhan gongzuo biji 1955 nian*, p. 452.
   35. Hangzhou shi linye zhi bianzuan weiyuanhui, *Hangzhou shi linye zhi*, p. 251.
   36. Gross, *Farewell to the God of Plague*, p. 240.
   37. Westboy, "'Making Green the Motherland,'" p. 239.
   38. Thomas and Packham, *Ecology of Woodlands and Forests*, pp. 131–133.
   39. Wang, *Zhongguo shumu wenhua yuanliu*, p. 1.

40. Hangzhou shi dang'an guan, *Minguo shiqi Hangzhou shi zhengfu dang'an shiliao huibian (yijiu erqi nian—yijiu sijiu nian)*, p. 525.
41. Zhongguo linye bianji weiyuanhui, *Xin Zhongguo de linye jianshe*, p. 32.
42. Huang, "Shuitu baochi shuzhong jieshao zhiqi maweisong," p.10.
43. Hou, *1930 niandai guomin zhengfu de zaolin shiye*, p. 82.
44. Hangzhou shi yuanlin guanli ju, "Yuanlin jiehe shengchan hao, Xihu fengjing mianmao xin," p. 4.
45. ZPA, J115-003-010, p. 56.
46. Powers, "When Is a Landscape Like a Body?" pp. 17-20.
47. Lee, "Postwar Pines," p. 321.
48. "Hangzhou shi yuanlin jianshe shinian lai de zhuyao chengjiu (chugao)," p. 183.
49. Clark, *Moscow, the Fourth Rome*, p. 4.
50. ZPA, J115-003-010, p. 56.
51. *Hangzhou nongye zhi*, p. 676.
52. "Hangzhou shi jianshe ju yuanlin guanli chu 1950 nian linye gongzuo zongjie baogao (jielu)," p. 80.
53. Smil, *China's Environment Crisis*, p. 59.
54. HMA, 071-002-0003, p. 19.
55. ZPA, 002-998-196523, p. 4.
56. ZPA, 115-003-010, pp. 68-69.
57. Kathirithamby-Wells, "The Implications of Plantation Agriculture for Biodiversity in Peninsular Malaysia," p. 63.
58. ZPA, J115-003-010, pp. 8; 59.
59. Cheng, *Zenyang zhongzhi maweisong*, pp. 5-15.
60. Gao, *Senlin ziyuan jingying guanli yanjiu*, p. 231.
61. ZPA, J115-003-010, p. 59.
62. Jack Westboy's relatively conservative estimation shows that the percentage was 5, while Robert Marks posits that between 5 and 9 percent of lands across the country were covered by forests. See Westboy, "'Making Green the Motherland,'" pp. 231-232; Marks, *China*, p. 276.
63. Zhonggong zhongyang wenxian yanjiushi, Guojia linye ju, *Mao Zedong lun linye*, p. 78.
64. "Lühua zuguo."
65. *Jianguo yilai zhongyao wenxian xuanbian (di 10 ce) (1957 nian)*, pp. 646-647.
66. Guowuyuan fazhi bangongshi, *Zhonghua renmin gongheguo fagui huibian 1958-1959 di 4 juan*, p. 226.
67. "Hangzhou shi yuanlin jianshe qingkuang he yuanlin hua guihua de chubu yijian," pp. 101-103.
68. "Xihu shanqu zaolin lühua de qingkuang," p. 440.
69. Hangzhou shi yuanlin guanli ju, "Yuanlin jiehe shengchan hao, Xihu fengjing mianmao xin," pp. 6-9.
70. "Hangzhou shi yuanlin jianshe qingkuang he yuanlin hua guihua de chubu yijian," p. 100.
71. "Guanyu Xihu fengjing qu de diaocha baogao," p. 286.
72. "Guanyu Xihu fengjing qu nei gongchang, danwei banqian qingkuang ji jinhou gongzuo de yijian," p. 821.
73. Welch, *Buddhism under Mao*, p. 43.
74. "Hangzhou shi renmin zhengfu jianshe ju dui Xihu fengjingqu guanli de yijian," pp. 6-7.

75. Shi, *Xihu zhi*, p. 815.
76. Dai and Luo, "Hangzhou yuanlin fagui yilanbiao," p. 494.
77. ZPA, J117-005-067, p. 33.
78. "Tuoshan chuli linmu rushe wenti shi dangqian fangzhi luankan lanfa de guanjian," pp. 1-2.
79. Wang, "Weishenme lingxing shumu buyao rushe?" p. 1.
80. Huadong shifan daxue Zhongguo dangdaishi yanjiu zhongxin, *Zhongguo dangdai minjian shiliao jikan 14 Sha Wenhan gongzuo biji 1957-1958 nian*, p. 272.
81. "Hangzhou shi renmin zhengfu jianshe ju dui Xihu fengjingqu guanli de yijian," p. 442; HMA, J115-003-010-055, p. 4.
82. ZPA, J116-006-033, p. 33.
83. HMA, 071-006-011, p. 8.
84. Yu, "Hangzhou jiefang hou 17 nianjian de yuanlin jianshe," pp. 154-156.
85. HMA, 071-004-0038, pp. 13-15.
86. *Hangzhou nongye zhi*, p. 666.
87. Murray and Cook, *Green China*, p. 49.
88. Marks, *China*, p. 270.
89. Shi, *Xihu zhi*, pp. 115-117.
90. Xin, *Dianran jiyi*, p. 51.
91. HMA, 071-005-0012, pp. 2-3.
92. "Xihu fengjingqu jianshe jihua dagang (chugao)," p. 78.
93. Huadong shifan daxue Zhongguo dangdaishi yanjiu zhongxin, *Zhongguo dangdai minjian shiliao jikan 14 Sha Wenhan gongzuo biji 1957-1958 nian*, p. 92.
94. "Jiejue Xihu jianshe yu kuozhan chadi de maodun."
95. Zhang, "Yuanlin jianshe de qige maodun."
96. "Jiejue Xihu jianshe yu kuozhan chadi de maodun."
97. *Hangzhou nongye zhi*, p. 639.
98. "Hangzhou shi yuanlin jianshe shinian lai de zhuyao chengjiu (chugao)," p. 180.
99. ZPA, J116-020-064, p. 46; J116-018-345, p. 108.
100. ZPA, J116-016-066, p. 415.
101. ZPA, J116-008-007, p. 7.
102. "Xihu shanqu zaolin lühua de qingkuang," p. 441.
103. ZPA, J115-003-010, pp. 55-56.
104. "Guanyu Xihu fengjing qu de diaocha baogao—sheng, shi jingji diaocha zu diaocha cailiao zhi'er," p. 287.
105. Watkins, *Trees, Woods and Forests*, p. 205.
106. Scott, *Seeing Like a State*, p. 20.
107. Nanjing linye daxue linye yichan yanjiushi, *Zhongguo jindai linye shi*, pp. 266-267.
108. Zhejiang sheng linye zhi bianzuan weiyuanhui, *Zhejiang sheng linye zhi*, p. 468.
109. Ye, "Buyao ba songmaochong chiguo de songshu dou kanle."
110. Que, "Fangzhi songmaochong," p. 415.
111. HMA, 071-004-0038, pp. 19-22.
112. Ibid., p. 23.
113. "Jiangshan xian Miaolizhen xiang Geshan she kaizhan zhi songmaochong de qingkuang jieshao," p. 39.
114. Johnston, *Being Soviet*, p. xxiv.

115. Ye, "Buyao ba songmaochong chiguo de songshu dou kanle."
116. Jiang, "Ganxie Sulian zhuanjia dui Zhejiang linye gongzuo de bangzhu," p. 2.
117. Shanghai kunchong yanjiusuo, "Zhongguo de songganjie," p. 14; "Riben songganjie de xin tiandi—yinban piaochong de chubu yanjiu," p. 1.
118. Zhejiang sheng songganjie yanjiu xiezuo zu, "Songganjie de yanjiu," p. 18.
119. ZPA, J117-019-133, p. 1; J117-019-370, p. 57.
120. ZPA, J117-019-133, pp. 1–2. Another source indicates that *Matsucoccus matsumurae* actually damaged 667 hectares of pine forests in the West Lake mountainous area. See "Maweisong de xin haichong—songganjie," p. 32.
121. Shi, *Xihu zhi*, p. 815.
122. "Maweisong de xin haichong—songganjie," p. 32.
123. "Yijiuqisan nian songganjie fangzhi yanjiu xiezuo huiyi jiyao," p. 13.
124. "Riben songganjie de xin tiandi," p. 1; Shanghai kunchong yanjiusuo, "Zhongguo de songganjie," p. 14.
125. ZPA, J117-019-133, p. 2.
126. HMA, 071-004-0038, pp. 13–18.
127. Rajan, *Modernizing Nature*, pp. 50–51.
128. Shlapentokh, *Public and Private Life of the Soviet People*, p. 154.
129. Wright, *Passport to Peking*, p. 380.
130. Schmalzer, "On the Appropriate Use of Rose-Colored Glasses," p. 358.

Chapter 4. Socialist Pigs

1. Anderson, *Capitalist Pigs*, p. 5.
2. Saraiva, *Fascist Pigs*, pp. 3–11.
3. *Mao Zedong sixiang wansui (1958–1960)*, pp. 261–262.
4. E. C. Ellis and S. M. Wang find that Chinese farmers began to use manure as fertilizer in approximately 500 CE. See Ellis and Wang, "Sustainable Traditional Agriculture in the Tai Lake Region of China," p. 181.
5. Schmalzer, *Red Revolution, Green Revolution*, pp. 115–116.
6. Christopher Isett finds that farmers in Jiangnan in the Qing preferred to apply beancake fertilizers over manure and canal sludge because of the intensive labor input. See Isett, *State, Peasant, and Merchant in Qing Manchuria, 1644–1862*, p. 236.
7. Gross, *Farewell to the God of Plague*, p. 240.
8. Zhonghua renmin gongheguo di'er shangyebu shipin shangyeju, *Woguo fazhan yangzhu shengchan de cankao ziliao*, p. 5.
9. Hu, "Yazi he shehui zhuyi, lishi wenwu he mixin, zhu he Xu Xilin."
10. Ibid.
11. Walder, *China under Mao*, p. 85.
12. Shue, *The Reach of the State*, p. 70; Kelliher, *Peasant Power in China*, pp. 239–243; Manning and Wemheuer, "Introduction," p. 19.
13. Friedman, Pickowicz, and Selden, *Revolution, Resistance, and Reform in Village China*, pp. 11–12.
14. Gao, *Renmin gongshe shiqi zhong Zhongguo nongmin "fan xingwei" diaocha*, p. 3.
15. Ibid.
16. Chan, "Women's Work and Women's Food in Lineage Land," p. 86.

17. Ellis and Wang, "Sustainable Traditional Agriculture in the Tai Lake Region of China," p. 185.
18. Skinner, "Vegetable Supply and Marketing in Chinese Cities," pp. 737–754.
19. Walker, *Planning in Chinese Agriculture*, pp. 43–55.
20. Platte, "The Private Sector in China's Agriculture," p. 82.
21. Du, *Jinzhi*, pp. 3–5.
22. Schmalzer, "Breeding a Better China," p. 19.
23. Chan and Unger, "Grey and Black," p. 456.
24. Zhonghua renmin gongheguo di'er shangyebu shipin shangyeju, *Woguo fazhan yangzhu shengchan de cankao ziliao*, pp. 1–3.
25. Nongyebu xumu shouyi si, *Zhongguo dongwu yibing zhi*, p. 186.
26. Zhonghua renmin gongheguo di'er shangyebu shipin shangyeju, *Woguo fazhan yangzhu shengchan de cankao ziliao*, p. 4.
27. Nongyebu xumu shouyi si, *Zhongguo dongwu yibing zhi*, p. 186.
28. Huadong shifan daxue Zhongguo dangdaishi yanjiu zhongxin, *Zhongguo dangdai minjian shiliao jikan 12 Sha Wenhan gongzuo biji 1955 nian*, p. 457.
29. Zhonghua renmin gongheguo di'er shangyebu shipin shangyeju, *Woguo fazhan yangzhu shengchan de cankao ziliao*, pp. 3–7.
30. Walker, *Planning in Chinese Agriculture*, pp. 61–62.
31. Huadong shifan daxue Zhongguo dangdaishi yanjiu zhongxin, *Zhongguo dangdai minjian shiliao jikan 12 Sha Wenhan gongzuo biji 1955 nian*, p. 456.
32. "Daliang yangzhu."
33. Zhonghua renmin gongheguo di'er shangyebu shipin shangyeju, *Woguo fazhan yangzhu shengchan de cankao ziliao*, p. 9.
34. Walker, *Planning in Chinese Agriculture*, pp. 66–67.
35. Zhonghua renmin gongheguo di'er shangyebu shipin shangyeju, *Woguo fazhan yangzhu shengchan de cankao ziliao*, p. 8.
36. Gao, *Nongye hezuohua yundong shimo*, p. 193.
37. Deng, "Guanyu guoying nongchang wenti he fazhan yangzhu wenti," p. 3.
38. "Duo yangzhu, yang haozhu."
39. Xiao-Planes, "A Dissenting Voice against Mao Zedong's Agricultural Policy," pp. 1–9.
40. Deng, "Guanyu guoying nongchang wenti he fazhan yangzhu wenti," p. 2.
41. "Duo yangzhu, yang haozhu."
42. Zhonghua renmin gongheguo di'er shangyebu shipin shangyeju, *Woguo fazhan yangzhu shengchan de cankao ziliao*, p. 11.
43. "Duo yangzhu, yang haozhu."
44. *Hangzhou nongye zhi*, pp. 198–199.
45. Ibid., p. 761.
46. Nongyebu xumu shouyi si, *Zhongguo dongwu yibing zhi*, p. 186.
47. Ibid.
48. *Hangzhou nongye zhi*, p. 57.
49. Ibid., pp. 758–761.
50. Nongyebu xumu shouyi si, *Zhongguo dongwu yibing zhi*, p. 186.
51. Zhao, *Zhongguo yangzhu dacheng*, p. 11.
52. Schmalzer, *Red Revolution, Green Revolution*, p. 103.
53. Ibid., p. 116.

54. Marks, *China*, pp. 267-269.
55. Zhonghua renmin gongheguo di'er shangyebu shipin shangyeju, *Woguo fazhan yangzhu shengchan de cankao ziliao*, p. 7.
56. Schell, *In the People's Republic*, p. 206.
57. *Hangzhou nongye zhi*, pp. 61-65.
58. Marks, *China*, p. 269.
59. Xi, "Zhufen shi hao feiliao."
60. Guan and Holley, *Hog Manure Management, the Environment and Human Health*, pp. 1-2.
61. Ibid., p. 125.
62. Key, McBride, and Ribaudo, *Changes in Manure Management in the Hog Sector: 1998-2004*, p. 7.
63. Li and Wu, *Shengwu fuzhisuan feiliao shengchan yu yingyong*, p. 92.
64. *Hangzhou nongye zhi*, pp. 96-97.
65. Ibid., p. 758.
66. Hu, "Zhufei de jiazhi," p. 19.
67. *Hangzhou nongye zhi*, p. 261.
68. Thomas Lyons noted in the 1970s that only 7.5 percent of the total output of pork entered the interprovincial market. (See Lyons, "Interprovincial Trade and Development in China, 1957-1979," p. 232.) His observation hinted at the fact that most provinces, if not all, in Mao's China had the capacity to raise enough pigs to feed the local population.
69. Zhongguo xumu shouyi xuehui, *Zhongguo xumu shouyi xuehui cankao ziliao xuanji zhu chuanranbing fangzhi wenti*.
70. Chen, "Shanghai nongcun de yimu di yitou zhu yundong," p. 14.
71. Nongyebu xumu shouyi si, *Zhongguo dongwu yibing zhi*, p. 186.
72. Zhongguo xumu shouyi xuehui, *Zhongguo xumu shouyi xuehui cankao ziliao xuanji zhu chuanranbing fangzhi wenti*, p. 71.
73. "Xihu gongshe meimu youzhu yituo duo."
74. Skinner, "Vegetable Supply and Marketing in Chinese Cities," p. 747.
75. Chen, *Cangsang jubian de quyu jishi*, p. 55.
76. Yi and Gong, "Gonshe xianhua yan Xihu—Zhejiang Hangzhou Xihu renmin gongshe xianjing," p. 729.
77. Hangzhou shi difangzhi bianzhuan weiyuanhui, *Hangzhou shi zhi (dishi juan)*, p. 97.
78. Chen, *Cangsang jubian de quyu jishi*, p. 55.
79. Ibid., pp. 56-57.
80. Chen, *Surviving the Storm*, p. 31.
81. "Hangzhou shi yuanlin jianshe shinian guihua buchong yijian (jielu)," p. 154.
82. Yi and Gong, "Gonshe xianhua yan xihu," p. 730.
83. Chen, *Cangsang jubian de quyu jishi*, p. 56.
84. Chen, *Surviving the Storm*, p. 43.
85. Shi, *Xihu zhi*, p. 115.
86. Hangzhou shi techanju, "Xihu gongshe shiyue dui muchan 320 jin longjing cha," p. 13.
87. Shang, "Ditou yangzhu haochu duo," p. 32.
88. Yi and Gong, "Gonshe xianhua yan xihu," pp. 730-731.
89. "Zhejiang daliang zengyang jiaqin jiachu."
90. Hangzhou shi techanju, "Xihu gongshe shiyue dui muchan 320 jin longjin cha," p. 13.

91. ZPA, J116-017-140-122, p. 122.
92. ZPA, J116-017-331, p. 164.
93. *Hangzhou nongye zhi,* p. 97.
94. ZPA, J116-017-140, p. 122.
95. Zhonghua renmin gongheguo di'er shangyebu shipin shangyeju, *Woguo fazhan yangzhu shengchan de cankao ziliao,* p. 3.
96. Hu, "Dao shenghuo zhong qu," p. 91.
97. *Xinhua she xinwen gao,* p. 26.
98. Huadong shifan daxue Zhongguo dangdaishi yanjiu zhongxin, *Zhongguo dangdai minjian shiliao jikan 12 Sha Wenhan gongzuo biji 1955 nian,* p. 419.
99. ZPA, J116-001-114, p. 40.
100. Ibid., pp. 43-44.
101. Zhang, "Nanshan she yangde zhu youda youfei." Workpoint or *gongfen* was an egalitarian remuneration system widely adopted in collectives in Mao's China. Originally set up based on villagers' "overall attitude towards laboring well, whatever the nature and quantity of their labor," the system led to confusion, controversies, and favoritism, demoralizing the members of collectives. See Li, "Everyday Strategies for Team Farming in Collective-Era China," p. 92.
102. Selden, "Household, Cooperative, and State in the Remaking of China's Countryside," p. 18.
103. Quanguo nongye zhanlan hui, *1957 nian quanguo nongye zhanlan hui ziliao huibian xia,* p. 718.
104. ZPA, J116-001-082, p. 26.
105. "Duowei qingcu siliao zhufei zhuzhuang, Zhejiang tuiguang Nanshan shengchan dui yong qing siliao yanghzu jingyan."
106. "Zhu Ruixiang shizhan yangzhu benling."
107. "Daliang yangzhu."
108. Hangzhou shi zhengxie zhi bianzuan weiyuanhui, *Hangzhou shi zhengxie zhi 1950-2002,* p. 23.
109. Siegelbaum, *Stakhanovism and the Politics of Productivity in the USSR, 1935-1941,* p. 297.
110. Pang, *The Art of Cloning,* p. 194.
111. Zhonggong Zhejiang shengwei xumu shengchan weiyuanhui, *Hongse siyang yuan,* pp. 88-89.
112. *Hangzhou nongye zhi,* p. 761.
113. Wang, "'Yangzhu xiaoqu' bushi 'daban jiti zhuchang,'" p. 23.
114. Song, "Dui renmin gongshe jiti yangzhu ruogan wenti de yijian," p. 121.
115. Zhang and Zhang, "Dui 'zhu wei liuchu zhishou' ji 'siyang weizhu' de zai renshi," p. 18.
116. *Hangzhou nongye zhi,* p. 261.
117. Ye, *Zhou Enlai yu Xihu,* p. 45.
118. Sha Wenhan was purged after he lost an intraparty struggle with Jiang Hua, the CCP leader in Zhejiang, in the 1957 Anti-Rightist Movement. See Forster, "Localism, Central Policy, and the Provincial Purges of 1957-1958," pp. 193-196.
119. Qin and Ya, *Sha Wenhan yu Chen Xiuliang,* p. 42.
120. Gao, *Renmin gongshe shiqi zhong Zhongguo nongmin "fan xingwei" diaocha,* pp. 2, 135.

121. Zhonghua renmin gongheguo di'er shangyebu shipin shangyeju, *Woguo fazhan yangzhu shengchan de cankao ziliao*, p. 17.
122. Gao, *Renmin gongshe shiqi zhong Zhongguo nongmin "fan xingwei" diaocha*, p. 129.
123. "Fazhan yangzhu ye bixu gongyang weizhu gongsi bingju."
124. Hangzhou shi difangzhi bianzhuan weiyuanhui, *Hangzhou shi zhi (dishi juan)*, p. 503.
125. Mao, "Hangzhou Xihu de huanjing shuiwen tiaojian yu shuiti fuyingyanghua wenti," p. 162.
126. Shi, *Xihu zhi*, p. 76.
127. "Huiyi jiyao," p. 280.
128. Hu, "Yazi he shehui zhuyi, lishi wenwu he mixin, zhu he Xu Xilin."
129. "Laixin zhaodeng."
130. Shi, *Xihu zhi*, p. 96.
131. HMA, 071-001-0024, p. 145.
132. Shi, *Xihu zhi*, p. 97.
133. HMA, 071-001-0024, p. 145.
134. Haining shi dang'an ju (guan), *Song Yunbin wenji (di'er juan)*, p. 311.
135. Chen, *Chen Xiuliang wenji*, pp. 552-553.
136. HMA, 071-001-0024, pp. 145-149.
137. ZPA, J101-013-207, p. 8.
138. Ibid., p. 10.
139. Yang, *Calamity and Reform in China*, p. 14.
140. Dikötter, *Mao's Great Famine*, p. 198.

Chapter 5. "Ghosts as Neighbors"

1. Fei, "Wei Xihu buping."
2. Huang, *Shanchuan, lishi, renwu*, p. 61.
3. Fu, *Hangzhou fengjing chengshi de xingcheng shi*, pp. 63-64.
4. Zhang, "Xihu shi keyan," p. 472.
5. Clunas, *Fruitful Sites*, 131.
6. Yu, "Xihu jijing."
7. Rofel, *Other Modernities*, 25.
8. Wu, *Remaking Beijing*, p. 34.
9. Ho, *Curating Revolution*, p. 246.
10. Dobrenko, *Stalinist Cinema and the Production of History*, p. 9.
11. Gao, *The Communist Takeover of Hangzhou*, p. 220.
12. Wang, "Tope and Topos," pp. 488-489.
13. Laurier and Philo, "X-Morphising," p. 1061.
14. Falasca-Zamponi, *Fascist Spectacle*, p. 2.
15. Bennett, *Vibrant Matter*, p. xvi.
16. Shi, *Xihu zhi*, p. 681.
17. Wu et al., "Xihu ji huanhu diqu de bianqian he gongyuan lüdi de kaituo," p. 73.
18. Shi, *Xihu zhi*, p. 96.
19. Hu, "Yazi he shehui zhuyi, lishi wenwu he mixin, zhu he Xu Xilin."
20. Leng and Zhu, "Xihu sishi nian de bianqian yu fansi," p. 420.
21. Gao, *The Communist Takeover of Hangzhou*, p. 227.

22. "Hangzhou shi renmin zhengfu jianshe ju dui Xihu fengjingqu guanli de yijian," p. 7.
23. Wu et al., "Xihu ji huanhu diqu de bianqian he gongyuan lüdi de kaituo," p. 73.
24. "Hangzhou shi renmin zhengfu guanyu gongbu *Xihu fengjingqu guanli tiaoli* de tonggao," p. 4.
25. Hangzhou shi dang'an guan, *Minguo shiqi Hangzhou shi zhengfu dang'an shiliao huibian (yijiu erqi nian—yijiu sijiu nian)*, p. 525.
26. "Hangzhou shi zhengxie chengjian weiyuanhui guanyu jianjue shazhu Xihu fengjingqu muzang manyanfeng de jianyi baogao," p. 757.
27. "Hangzhou shi jianshe ju yuanlin guanli chu 1950 nian linye gongzuo zongjie baogao (jielu)," p. 418.
28. "Xihu fengjing jianshe wunian jihua," p. 83.
29. HMA, 071-001-0024, p. 28.
30. Tang, *Zhang Taiyan nianpu changbian (yijiu yijiu nian—yijiu sanliu nian)*, pp. 975-976.
31. Shen, *Zhang Taiyan yu Tang Guoli*, pp. 66-68.
32. Ibid., p. 67.
33. Ibid., pp. 66-68.
34. Haining shi dang'an ju (guan), *Song Yunbin riji (zhongce)*, p. 491.
35. Shen, *Zhang Taiyan yu Tang Guoli*, pp. 68-70.
36. Huadong shifan daxue Zhongguo dangdaishi yanjiu zhongxin, *Zhongguo dangdai minjian shiliao jikan 12 Sha Wenhan gongzuo biji 1955 nian*, p. 246.
37. Haining shi dang'an ju (guan), *Song Yunbin riji (zhongce)*, p. 506.
38. Shen, *Zhang Taiyan yu Tang Guoli*, p. 66.
39. *Xihu shengji*, pp. 56-57.
40. "Zhejiang sheng Hangzhou shi renmin weiyuanhui guanyu gongbu benshi wenwu baohu danwei ji youguan wenwu baohu gongzuo de tongzhi," p. 670.
41. Ho, *Curating Revolution*, p. 214.
42. HMA, 071-001-0024, p. 176.
43. Ibid., pp. 172-177.
44. Shen, *Zhang Taiyan yu Tang Guoli*, p. 72.
45. HMA, 071-001-0058, pp. 1-4.
46. Gao, *The Communist Takeover of Hangzhou*, p. 230.
47. Huang, *Huang Yuan huiyi lu*, p. 271.
48. Chen, *Chen Xiuliang wenji*, p. 553.
49. Shi, *Xihu zhi*, p. 115. However, this chronicle mistakes the year of the campaign as 1955.
50. Chen, *Chen Xiuliang wenji*, p. 552-553.
51. Yu et al., "Cong 'kuanggu weiyou' tanqi," p. 13.
52. Haining shi dang'an ju (guan), *Song Yunbin wenji (di'er juan)*, pp. 258-259.
53. Chen, *Chen Xiuliang wenji*, p. 553.
54. Song Yunbin, "Xihu shangde san'ge fen."
55. Huang, *Huang Yuan huiyi lu*, p. 271.
56. Chen, "Gemin lingxiu zai Xihu de huodong jishi," 369.
57. Leys, *Chinese Shadows*, p. 101; Shi, *Xihu zhi*, p. 116.
58. Wright, *Passport to Peking*, p. 291.
59. Roy, *Journey through China*, p. 192.

60. Leys, *Chinese Shadows*, pp. 99-100.
61. Chen, "Gemin lingxiu zai Xihu de huodong jishi," p. 369.
62. Huang, *Huang Yuan huiyi lu*, p. 271.
63. Haining shi dang'an ju (guan), *Song Yunbin riji (zhongce)*, p. 505.
64. Huang, *Huang Yuan huiyi lu*, p. 271.
65. Forster, "Localism, Central Policy, and the Provincial Purges of 1957-1958," pp. 193-196.
66. Fei, "Wei Xihu buping."
67. Li, "*Hangzhou ribao* chuangkan de qianqian houhou," p. 218.
68. He, "Xihu huimu fengbo yu Hu Qiaomu de yishou ci," p. 47.
69. "Mao zhuxi guanhuai yuanlin lühua gongzuo (xu)," p. 1.
70. Liu, *Zhonggong dangshi shangde naxie ren yu shi*, p. 215.
71. Lu, "Jue buneng yu 'gui' weilinglin."
72. Chen, "Gemin lingxiu zai Xihu de huodong jishi," p. 368.
73. "Dasi fanmai fengzixiu heihuo, wei ziben zhuyi fubi mingluo kaidao," p. 22.
74. He, "Xihu huimu fengbo yu Hu Qiaomu de yishou ci," pp. 266-269.
75. Liu, "Fengjing qu yeyao pojiu lixin."
76. Sima, "Fengjing, shihua he shidai jingshen."
77. For example, Fan, "Buneng rongxu zhexie fenmu jixu dianwu dahao hushan"; Cao, Yu, and Zhang, "Jiefangjun zhanshi shuo: zhexie chenshi fugu ying rengdao lajixiang li qu"; and Xu, Ruan, and Chen, "Lao gongren shuo: women yaowei xiayidai xiangxiang."
78. Chen, "Yingdang laige dasaochu."
79. ZPA, J101-013-207, pp. 12-19.
80. Zhang, *Tao'an mengyi, Xihu xunmeng*, p. 166.
81. ZPA, J101-013-207, p. 20.
82. Feng Xiaoqing was said to be a native of Yangzhou and a concubine of a rich businessman in Hangzhou. As the businessman's principal wife grew jealous of her, Xiaoqing was forced to live as a recluse in Solitary Hill and eventually died of grief at the age of eighteen. See Zhang, *Tao'an mengyi, Xihu xunmeng*, p.183.
83. ZPA, J101-013-207, pp. 20-22.
84. Croft, *Red Carpet to China*, p. 206.
85. Shen, *Fusheng liuji*, p. 70.
86. Liang, "Langji congtan; xutan; santan," p. 433.
87. *Xihu shengji*, p. 32.
88. "Zhejiang sheng Hangzhou shi renmin weiyuanhui guanyu gongbu benshi wenwu baohu danwei ji youguan wenwu baohu gongzuo de tongzhi," p. 672.
89. Chen, "Gemin lingxiu zai Xihu de huodong jishi," p. 369.
90. Leys, *Chinese Shadows*, p. 99.
91. ZPA, J101-013-207, p. 20.
92. HMA, 71-003-0019, pp. 19-27.
93. Ibid., p. 88.
94. Xu, Ruan, and Chen, "Lao gongren shuo."
95. "Chedi saochu wugou, suqing fandong jieji sixiang yingxiang."
96. "Xihu fengjingqu dali pojiu lixin."
97. Wu, *The Cultural Revolution at the Margins*, p. 46.
98. Brown, "Moving Targets," p. 53.
99. Levenson, *Confucian China and Its Modern Fate, A Trilogy*, p. 139.

100. Wu and Chen, "Xilingqiao pan mianmu yixin."
101. Welch, *Buddhism under Mao*, p. 307.
102. Zhou, "Bu yingdang rang ta jixu sanbu dusu."
103. Mao Cai, "Zhe bushi shenme mingsheng guji."
104. Zhang, "Relie yonghu da saochu."
105. Xu, Ruan, and Chen, "Lao gongren shuo."
106. HMA, 71-002-0058, p. 99.
107. ZPA, J101-015-265, p. 9.
108. HMA, 071-003-0019, p. 19.
109. ZPA, J101-015-265, p. 1.
110. Ibid., pp. 1-2.
111. He, "Xihu huimu fengbo yu Hu Qiaomu de yishou ci," p. 266.
112. HMA, 071-003-0019, p. 99.
113. Leys, *Chinese Shadows*, p. 100.
114. Zhongyang wenxian yanjiushi, *Jianguo yilai Mao Zedong wengao*, p. 81.
115. He, "Xihu huimu fengbo yu Hu Qiaomu de yishou ci," p. 272.
116. Ye, *Zhou Enlai yu Xihu*, p. 52.
117. HMA, 071-003-0019, pp. 101-102.
118. Li, *Reinventing Modern China*, pp. 19-22.
119. Lu, "Shi nongchuang, bushi 'xuerou.'"
120. "Chedi saochu wugou, suqing fandong jieji sixiang yingxiang."
121. He, "Xihu huimu fengbo yu Hu Qiaomu de yishou ci," p. 266.
122. *Xihu shengji*, p. 32.
123. ZPA, J101-013-207, p. 19.
124. Levenson, *Confucian China and Its Modern Fate, A Trilogy*, p. 139.
125. Li, *Reinventing Modern China*, pp. 2-9.
126. Levenson, *Confucian China and Its Modern Fate, A Trilogy*, p. 137.
127. Shen, *Zhang Taiyan yu Tang Guoli*, pp. 73-74.
128. Huang, *Shanchuan, lishi, renwu*, p. 61.
129. Qu, "Xihu yuanlin jianshe sishinian," p. 6. Also, Leys, *Chinese Shadows*, p. 99.
130. Keith Forster argues that some of Zhou's pre-Cultural Revolution policies made a comeback in the early 1970s. (See Forster, *Rebellion and Factionalism in a Chinese Province*, p. 114). Also, Ma, *Waijiaobu wenge jishi*, p. 278.
131. Chen, "Use the Past to Serve the Present; the Foreign to serve China," p. 225.
132. Schwarcz, *Place and Memory in the Singing Crane Garden*, p. 1.
133. Leys, *Chinese Shadows*, p. 99.
134. Berman, *All That Is Solid Melts into Air*, p. 76.
135. Ho, "To Protect and Preserve," p. 94.
136. HMA, 71-003-0019, pp. 71-72.
137. Huang, *Shanchuan, lishi, renwu*, pp. 37-42.
138. Haining shi dang'an ju (guan), *Song Yunbin wenji (di'er juan)*, p. 304-305.
139. Yu, "Xihu jijing."
140. "Hangzhou shi guihua ju, Hangzhou shi wenguan hui guanyu Zhang Taiyan, Zhang Cangshui mu baohu fang'an de han," p. 725.
141. Han, "Fang Qiu Jin mu."
142. "Hangzhou shi fujian 'Su Xiaoxiao mu' he 'Wu Song mu.'"

143. Wu, "Hu Qiaomu he Xihu," p. 157.
144. Ma, *Waijiaobu wenge jishi*, p. 309.
145. Huang, *Shanchuan, lishi, renwu*, p. 41.
146. Halbwachs, "The Legendary Topography of the Gospels in the Holy Land," p. 204.
147. Stanek, *Henri Lefebvre on Space*, p. 118.
148. Carroll, *Between Heaven and Modernity*, p. 15.

Conclusion

1. Lu, "Introduction," p. 3.
2. Wakeman, *History and Will*, p. 236.
3. Muscolino, *The Ecology of War in China*, p. 141.
4. Zhang, *The River, the Plain, and the State*, p. 15, n24.
5. Bennett, "The Force of Things," p. 367.
6. Chris Courtney cautions against the anthropocentric tendency in scholarly discussion of natural disasters, such as floods. See Courtney, *The Nature of Disaster in China*, p. 9.
7. Yurchak, *Everything Was Forever, Until It Was No More*, pp. 5–6.
8. Wilson, *The President's Trip to China*, p. 129.
9. Wu, *Remaking Beijing*, p. 8.
10. Koss, *Where the Party Rules*, p. 6.
11. Harvey, "From Managerialism to Entrepreneurialism," pp. 4–8.
12. Yuan, "Bishui qingliu geng yiren."
13. Fang, "Mianfei yige hu, jihuo yige cheng."
14. Ibid.
15. Zheng, *Hangzhou Xihu zhili shi yanjiu*, pp. 141–147. Zheng Jin 郑瑾 finds that the contents of nitrogen and phosphorus have steadily risen in the 2000s.
16. Harvey, *Justice, Nature and the Geography of Difference*, p. 189.

Bibliography

Agamben, Giorgio. *Homo Sacer: Sovereign Power and Bare Life.* Translated by Daniel Heller-Roazen. Stanford, CA: Stanford University Press, 1998.
Akutagawa Ryūnosuke 芥川龍之介 (Jiechuan longzhijie). *Zhongguo youji* 中国游记 [A report on the journey of Shanghai]. Translated by Qin Gang 秦刚. Beijing: Zhonghua shuju, 2007.
Anand, Nikhil. *Hydraulic City: Water and the Infrastructures of Citizenship in Mumbai.* Durham, NC: Duke University Press, 2017.
Anderson, J. L. *Capitalist Pigs: Pigs, Pork, and Power in America.* Morgantown, WV: West Virginia University Press, 2019.
Bauman, Zygmunt. *Modernity and Ambivalence.* Cambridge, UK: Polity Press, 1991.
"Ba xiaofei chengshi biancheng shengchan chengshi" 把消费城市变成生产城市 [Transforming consumerist cities into productive cities]. *Renmin ribao* 人民日报, March 17, 1949.
Bennett, Jane. "The Force of Things: Steps toward an Ecology of Matter." *Political Theory* 32, 3 (June 2004): 347–372.
———. *Vibrant Matter: A Political Ecology of Things.* Durham and London: Duke University Press, 2010.
"Benshi qingnian jiang canjia shujun Xihu de yiwu laodong" 本市青年将参加疏浚西湖劳动 [The youth in town will perform voluntary labor to dredge West Lake]. *Hangzhou ribao* 杭州日报, November 3, 1955.
"Benshi qingnian shujun Xihu yiwu laodong kaigong" 本市青年疏浚西湖义务劳动开工 [The youth in town began to perform voluntary labor to dredge West Lake]. *Hangzhou ribao* 杭州日报, November 8, 1955.
Berman, Marshall. *All That Is Solid Melts into Air: The Experience of Modernity.* New York: Penguin Books, 1988.
Bewell, Alan. *Natures in Translation: Romanticism and Colonial Natural History.* Baltimore: Johns Hopkins University Press, 2017.
Blackbourn, David. *The Conquest of Nature: Water, Landscape, and the Making of Modern Germany.* New York: W. W. Norton, 2006.
Bowden, Sean. "Human and Nonhuman Agency in Deleuze." In *Deleuze and the Non/Human,* edited by Jon Roffe and Hannah Stark, 60–80. London: Palgrave MacMillan, 2015.
Braden, Peter. "Review of *The Ecology of War in China: Henan Province, the Yellow River, and Beyond.*" *The Journal of Asian Studies* 77, 3 (August 2018): 785–786.

Brandenberger, David. *Propaganda State in Crisis: Soviet Ideology, Indoctrination, and Terror under Stalin, 1927–1941*. New Haven, CT: Yale University Press, 2011.

Brock, Darryl E., and Chunjuan Nancy Wei. "Introduction: Reassessing the Great Proletarian Cultural Revolution." In *Mr. Science and Chairman Mao's Cultural Revolution*, edited by Chunjuan Nancy Wei and Darryl E. Brock, 1–39. Lanham, MD: Lexington Books, 2014.

Brown, Jeremy. "Moving Targets: Changing Class Labels in Rural Hebei and Henan, 1960–1979." In *Maoism at the Grassroots: Everyday Life in China's Era of High Socialism*, edited by Jeremy Brown and Matthew D. Johnson, 51–76. Cambridge, MA: Harvard University Press, 2015.

Brown, Jeremy, and Matthew D. Johnson. "Introduction." In *Maoism at the Grassroots: Everyday Life in China's Era of High Socialism*, edited by Jeremy Brown and Matthew D. Johnson, 1–15. Cambridge, MA: Harvard University Press, 2015.

Bruno, Andy. *The Nature of Soviet Power: An Arctic Environmental History*. Cambridge, UK: Cambridge University Press, 2016.

Carroll, Peter J. *Between Heaven and Modernity: Reconstructing Suzhou, 1895–1937*. Stanford, CA: Stanford University Press, 2006.

Cao Peiwei 曹佩伟, Yu Gaokun 俞高坤, and Zhang Jixian 张继贤. "Jiefangjun zhanshi shuo: zhexie chenshi fugu ying rengdao lajixiang li qu" 解放军战士说: 这些陈尸腐骨应扔到垃圾箱里去 [PLA soldiers say: Those decayed bodies and rotten bones should be thrown into trash cans]. *Hangzhou ribao* 杭州日报, December 3, 1964.

Castree, Noel. "Marxism and the Production of Nature." *Capital and Class* 24, 3 (2000): 5–36.

———. "Socializing Nature: Theory, Practice, and Politics." In *Social Nature: Theory, Practice, and Politics*, edited by Noel Castree and Bruce Braun, 1–21. Malden, MA: Blackwell, 2001.

Castree, Noel, and Tom MacMillan. "Dissolving Dualisms: Actor-Networks and the Reimagination of Nature." In *Social Nature: Theory, Practice, and Politics*, edited by Noel Castree and Bruce Braun, 208–224. Malden, MA: Blackwell, 2001.

Chan, Anita, and Jonathan Unger. "Grey and Black: The Hidden Economy of Rural China." *Pacific Affairs* 55, 3 (Autumn, 1982): 452–471.

Chan, Wing-hoi. "Women's Work and Women's Food in Lineage Land." In *Merchants' Daughters: Women, Commerce, and Regional Culture in South China*, edited by Helen E. Siu, 77–100. Hong Kong: Hong Kong University Press, 2010.

Chatterjee, Choi, David Ransel, Mary Canender, and Karen Petrone. "Introduction: The Genesis and Themes of Everyday Life in Russia Past and Present." In *Everyday Life in Russia Past and Present*, edited by Choi Chatterjee, David Ransel, Mary Canender, and Karen Petrone, 1–13. Bloomington: Indiana University Press.

"Chedi saochu wugou, suqing fandong jieji sixiang yingxiang" 彻底扫除污垢 肃清反动阶级思想影响 [Thoroughly cleaning up the dirt; eliminating influences of reactionary class thoughts]. *Hangzhou ribao* 杭州日报, December 4, 1964.

Cheek, Timothy. *Propaganda and Culture in Mao's China: Deng Tuo and the Intelligentsia*. Oxford, UK: Clarendon Press, 1997.

Chen, Feng. "Against the State: Labor Protests in China in the 1950s." *Modern China* 40, 5 (2014): 488–518.

Chen Hanmin 陈汉民. "Gemin lingxiu zai Xihu de huodong jishi" 革命领袖在西湖的活动纪实 [A true record revolutionary leaders' activities in West Lake]. XHFJYL, 365–370.

———. "Xihu shijing de youlai he xianzhuang" 西湖十景的由来和现状 [The origins of the ten vistas of West Lake and their current status]. XHFJYL, 116–118.

Chen Pixian 陈丕显. "Shanghai nongcun de yimu di yitou zhu yundong" 上海农村的一亩地一头猪运动 [A movement of one pig per *mu* of land in the countryside in Shanghai]. *Hongqi* 红旗 4 (February 1960): 11–16.

Chen, Tina Mai. "The Human–Machine Continuum in Maoism: The Intersection of Soviet Socialist Realism, Japanese Theoretical Physics, and Chinese Revolutionary Theory." *Cultural Critique* 80 (Winter 2012): 151–182.

———. "Use the Past to Serve the Present; the Foreign to Serve China." In *Words and Their Stories: Essays on the Language of the Chinese Revolution*, edited by Ban Wang, 205–225. Leiden, the Netherlands: Brill, 2011.

Chen Xiuliang 陈修良. *Chen Xiuliang wenji* 陈修良文集 [Chen Xiuliang's anthology]. Shanghai: Shanghai shehui kexue chubanshe, 1999.

Chen Xuezhao 陈学昭. *Nanwang de nianyue* 难忘的年月 [The unforgettable years]. Guangzhou: Huacheng chubanshe, 1983.

———. *Surviving the Storm: A Memoire*. Translated by Ti Hua and Caroline Greene. Armonk, NY: M. E. Sharpe, 1990.

Chen Ye 陈野. *Cangsang jubian de quyu jishi* 沧桑巨变的区域纪实 [A veritable record of a world of changes in a region]. Hangzhou: Zhejiang renmin chubanshe, 2009.

Chen Yuxian 陈玉先. "Yingdang laige dasaochu—guanyu Xihu fengjingqu de fen, bei, ji'nianta dengdeng" 应当来个大扫除— 关于西湖风景区的坟、碑、纪念塔等等 [In need of a great cleaning—on tombs, steles, memorial towers, and so on in the West Lake scenic district]. *Zhejiang ribao* 浙江日报, December 2, 1964.

Cheng Chongde 程崇德. *Zenyang zhongzhi maweisong* 怎样种植马尾松 [How to plant the horsetail pine]. Beijing: Zhongguo linye chubanshe, 1956.

Chi, Robert. "The Red Detachment of Women: Resenting, Regendering, Remembering." In *Socialist Imaginations: Utopias, Myths, and the Masses*, edited by Stefan Arvidsson, Jakub Beneš, and Anja Kirsch, 152–159. London: Routledge, 2019.

Ci, Jiwei. *Dialectic of the Chinese Revolution: From Utopianism to Hedonism*. Stanford, CA: Stanford University Press, 1994.

Clark, Katerina. *Moscow, the Fourth Rome: Stalinism, Cosmopolitanism, and the Evolution of Soviet Culture, 1931–1941*. Cambridge, MA: Harvard University Press, 2011.

Clunas, Craig. *Fruitful Sites: Garden Culture in Ming Dynasty China*. London: Reaktion Books, 1996.

Courtney, Chris. "At War with Water: The Maoist State and the 1954 Yangzi Floods." *Modern Asian Studies* 52, 6 (2018): 1807–1836.

———. *The Nature of Disaster in China: The 1931 Yangzi River Flood*. Cambridge, UK: Cambridge University Press, 2018.

Croft, Michael. *Red Carpet to China*. London: Longmans, Green and Co., 1958.

Cronon, William. "Introduction: In Search of Nature." In *Uncommon Ground: Rethinking the Human Place in Nature,* edited by William Cronon, 23–56. New York: W. W. Norton, 1996.

Dai Shanzhong 戴善忠 and Luo Ping 络平. "Hangzhou yuanlin fagui yilanbiao" 杭州园林法规一览表 [A general table of regulations on gardening in Hangzhou]. XHFJYL, 493–501.

"Daliang yangzhu" 大量养猪 [Put in greatest effort to raise pigs]. *Renmin ribao* 人民日报, February 25, 1956.

"Dangqian Xihu shuizhi ehua de qingkuang fanying" 当前西湖水质恶化的情况反映 [Feedback on the worsened water quality in West Lake]. XHWXJC12, 546–548.

"Dasi fanmai fengzixiu heihuo, wei ziben zhuyi fubi mingluo kaidao" 大肆贩卖封资修黑货, 为资本主义复辟鸣锣开道 [Recklessly selling contraband goods of feudalism, capitalism, and revisionism to beat gongs and clear the way for the restoration of capitalism]. *Yuanlin gemin* 园林革命 6 (1968): 18–22.

de Certeau, Michel. *The Practice of Everyday Life.* Translated by Steven Rendall. Berkeley: University of California Press, 2011.

Deng Zihui 邓子恢. "Guanyu guoying nongchang wenti he fazhan yangzhu wenti" 关于国营农场问题和发展养猪问题 [On the issues of state-owned farms and developing pig rearing]. *Zhongguo nongken* 中国农垦 6 (February 24, 1957): 1–3.

Denton, Kirk A. "What Do You Do with Cultural 'Propaganda' of the Mao Era?" *The PRC History Review* 4, 2 (August 2019): 1–45.

de Pee, Christian, and Joseph Lam. "Introduction." In *Senses of the City: Perceptions of Hangzhou and Southern Song China, 1127–1279,* edited by Joseph S. C. Lam, Shuen-fu Lin, Christian de Pee, and Martin Powers, xiii–xxv. Hong Kong: Chinese University of Hong Kong Press, 2017.

Dikötter, Frank. *Mao's Great Famine: The History of China's Most Devastating Catastrophe, 1958–1962.* New York: Walker, 2010.

Difeng 荻风. "Huagang guanyu xinjing" 花港观鱼新景. *Hangzhou ribao* 杭州日报, December 4, 1964

Dobrenko, Evgeny. *Stalinist Cinema and the Production of History: Museum of the Revolution.* Translated by Sarah Young. Edinburgh: Edinburgh University Press, 2008.

Dove, Michael R., Percy E. Sajise, and Amity A. Doolittle. "Introduction: Changing Ways of Thinking about the Relations between Society and Environment." In *Beyond the Sacred Forest: Complicating Conservation in Southeast Asia,* edited by Michael R. Dove, Percy E. Sajise, and Amity A. Doolittle, 1–34. Durham, NC: Duke University Press, 2011.

Du Xinhao 杜新豪. *Jinzhi: Zhongguo chuantong feiliao zhishi yu jishu shijian yanjiu (10–19 shiji)* 金汁：中国传统肥料知识与技术实践研究 (10–19世纪) [Compost gold: A study on the traditional knowledge of fertilizers and the technological practices (10th–19th centuries)]. Beijing: Zhongguo nongye kexue jishu chubanshe, 2017.

Duan, Xiaolin. *The Rise of West Lake: A Cultural Landmark in the Song Dynasty.* Seattle: Washington University Press, 2020.

———. "The Ten Views of West Lake." In *Visual and Material Cultures in Middle Period China*, edited by Patricia Buckley Ebrey and Shih-shan Susan Huang, 151–189. Leiden, the Netherlands: Brill, 2017.

"Duo yangzhu, yang haozhu" 多养猪, 养好猪 [Rearing more pigs and rearing pigs well]. *Hangzhou ribao* 杭州日报, March 29, 1957.

"Duowei qingcu siliao zhufei zhuzhuang, Zhejiang tuiguang Nanshan shengchan dui yong qing siliao yangzhu jingyan" 多喂青粗饲料猪肥猪壮, 浙江推广南山生产队用青饲料养猪经验 [Feeding more green and crude fodder to [make] pigs bigger and stronger; Zhejiang is popularizing the experience of the Nanshan Production Brigade to raise pigs with the green fodder; in Xiapu County, each commune and brigade has established a base area for the fodder to rear pigs massively]. *Renmin ribao* 人民日报, November 24, 1959.

Durdin, Tillman, James Reston, and Seymour Topping. *The New York Times Report from Red China*. New York: Quadrangle Books, 1971.

Ellis, E. C., and S. M. Wang. "Sustainable Traditional Agriculture in the Tai Lake Region of China." *Agriculture, Ecosystems and Environment* 61 (1997): 177–193.

Enyedi, György. "Urbanization under Socialism." In *Cities after Socialism: Urban and Regional Change and Conflict in Post-Socialist Societies*, edited by Gregory Andrusz, Michael Harloe, and Ivan Szelenyi, 100–118. Oxford, UK: Blackwell, 1996.

Esherick, Joseph W. "Deconstructing the Construction of the Party-State: Gulin County in the Shaan-Gan-Ning Border Region." *China Quarterly* 140 (December 1994): 1052–1079.

Evernden, Neil. *The Social Creation of Nature*. Baltimore and London: Johns Hopkins University Press, 1992.

Falasca-Zamponi, Simonetta. *Fascist Spectacle: The Aesthetics of Power in Mussolini's Italy*. Berkeley: University of California Press, 1997.

Fan Boqun 范伯群. *Zhou Shoujuan wenji zhencang ban shang* 周瘦鹃文集珍藏版上 [Zhou Shoujuan's anthropology, collector's edition, no. 1]. Shanghai: Wenhui chubanshe, 2015.

Fan Wensheng 范文生. "Buneng rongxu zhexie fenmu jixu dianwu dahao hushan" 不能容许这些坟墓继续玷污大好湖山 [(We shall) not allow those tombs to smear the beautiful lake and mountains]. *Hangzhou ribao* 杭州日报, December 2, 1964.

Fang Min 方敏. "Mianfei yige hu, jihuo yige cheng" 免费一个湖 激活一座城 [(With) a lake free of admission fees, a city is revitalized], *Renmin ribao* 人民日报, November 9, 2015.

"Fazhan yangzhu ye bixu gongyang weizhu gongsi bingju" 发展养猪业必须公养为主公私并举 [To develop swine breeding, it is necessary to give priority to public raising, but to focus simultaneously on public and private (breeding)]. *Renmin ribao* 人民日报, August 6, 1960.

Fei Xiaotong 费孝通. "Wei Xihu buping" 为西湖不平 [Speaking out against injustice on behalf of West Lake]. *Renmin ribao* 人民日报, July 26, 1956.

Forster, Keith. "Localism, Central Policy, and the Provincial Purges of 1957–1958: The Case of Zhejiang." In *New Perspectives on State Socialism in China*, edited by Timothy Cheek and Tony Saich, 191–233. Armonk, NY: M. E. Sharpe, 1997.

———. *Rebellion and Factionalism in a Chinese Province: Zhejiang, 1966–1976*. Armonk, NY: M. E. Sharpe, 1990.

Friedman, Edward, Paul G. Pickowicz, and Mark Selden. *Revolution, Resistance, and Reform in Village China*. New Haven, CT: Yale University Press, 2005.

Fu Shulan 傅舒兰. *Hangzhou fengjing chengshi de xingcheng shi: Xihu yu chengshi xingtai guanxi yanjin guocheng yanjiu* 杭州风景城市的形成史：西湖与城市形态关系演进过程研究 [History of the making of Hangzhou as a landscape city: A study of the developmental process of the morphological relation between West Lake and the city]. Nanjing: Dongnan daxue chubanshe, 2015.

"Fulao maoyu manyou Xihu mingsheng, wanjian guankan Gai Jiaotian mingju 'Ehu cun'" 伏老冒雨漫游西湖名胜，晚间观看盖叫天名剧"恶虎村" [Voroshilov tours scenic spots at West Lake in the rain, and watches Gai Jiaotian's famous operatic play, *Village of Evil Tiger*, at night]. *Renmin ribao* 人民日报, April 28, 1957.

Fung, Stanislaus, and Mark Jackson. "Four Key Terms in the History of Chinese Gardens." *International Conference on Chinese Architectural History* (August 7–10, 1995): 21–33.

"Gaizao zhong de Xihu" 改造中的西湖 [West Lake in transformation]. *Zhejiang ribao* 浙江日报, May 17, 1950.

Gao Huamin 高化民. *Nongye hezuohua yundong shimo* 农业合作化运动始末 [The whole story of the collectivization movement in the countryside]. Beijing: Zhongguo qingnian chubanshe, 1999.

Gao, James Z. *The Communist Takeover of Hangzhou: The Transformation of City and Cadre, 1949–1954*. Honolulu: University of Hawai'i Press, 2004.

Gao Wangling 高王凌. *Renmin gongshe shiqi zhong Zhongguo nongmin "fan xingwei" diaocha* 人民公社时期中国农民"反行为"调查 [An investigation into the Chinese peasants' "counteraction" during the times of the people's commune]. Beijing: Zhonggong dangshi chubanshe, 2006.

Gao Zhaowei 高兆蔚. *Senlin ziyuan jingying guanli yanjiu* 森林资源经营管理研究 [Studies on the administration and management of forestry resources]. Fuzhou, Fujian sheng ditu chubanshe, 2004.

Gardner, Daniel K. *Environmental Pollution in China: What Everyone Needs to Know*. Oxford, UK: Oxford University Press, 2018.

Gray, Jack. "Mao in Perspective." *China Quarterly* 187 (September 2006): 659–679.

Gross, Miriam. *Farewell to the God of Plague: Chairman Mao's Campaign to Deworm China*. Berkeley: University of California Press, 2016.

Grusin, Richard. "Introduction." In *The Nonhuman Turn*, edited by Richard Grusin, vii–xxix. Minneapolis: University of Minnesota Press, 2015.

Gu Guohua 顾国华. *Wentan zayi quanbian san* 文坛杂忆 全编三 [Miscellaneous memories about the literary circles, vol. 3]. Shanghai: Shanghai shudian chubanshe, 2015.

Guan, Tiffany T. Y., and Richard A. Holley. *Hog Manure Management, the Environment and Human Health*. New York: Kluwer Academic/Plenum, 2003.

"Guanyu Xihu fengjing qu de diaocha baogao—sheng, shi jingji diaocha zu diaocha cailiao zhi'er" 关于西湖风景区的调查报告— 省、市经济调查组调查材料之二 [Investigative report on the West Lake scenic district—the investigative material of the investigative group of provincial and municipal economy, no. 2]. XHWXJC12, 284–289.

"Guanyu Xihu fengjing qu nei gongchang, danwei banqian qingkuang ji jinhou gongzuo de yijian" 关于西湖风景区内工厂、单位搬迁情况及今后工作的意见 [Opinions on the relocation of factories and units inside the West Lake scenic district and future tasks]. XHWXJC12, 817–821.

"Guanyu Xihu fengjing zhengjian gongzuo jihua de baogao" 关于西湖风景整建工作计划的报告 [A report on refashioning West Lake's landscapes]. XHWXJC12, 216–265.

Guowuyuan fazhi bangongshi 国务院法制办公室. *Zhonghua renmin gongheguo fagui huibian 1958–1959 di 4 juan* 中华人民共和国法规汇编 1958–1959 第4卷 [Collection of laws and regulations in the People's Republic of China, 1958–1959, vol. 4]. Beijing: Zhongguo fazhi chubanshe, 2005.

"Hadini Sujianuo furen daoda Hangzhou, Zhejiang sheng shengzhang Zhou Jianren he furen huanyan Yindunixiya guibin" 哈蒂妮·苏加诺夫人到达杭州，浙江省省长周建人和夫人欢宴印度尼西亚贵宾 [Madam Hartini Sukarno arrives in Hangzhou, and Zhou Jianren, Zhejiang's provincial governor, and his wife hold a banquet for the honorable Indonesian guests]. *Renmin ribao* 人民日报, September 29, 1962.

Haining shi dang'an ju (guan) 海宁市档案局(馆). *Song Yunbin riji (zhongce)* 宋云彬日记(中册) [Song Yunbin's diary (book 2)]. Beijing: Zhonghua shuju, 2016.

———. *Song Yunbin wenji (di'er juan)* 宋云彬文集(第二卷) [Song Yunbin's anthology (vol. 2)]. Beijing: Zhonghua shuju, 2015.

Halbwachs, Maurice. "The Legendary Topography of the Gospels in the Holy Land." In *On Collective Memory*, edited by Lewis Coser, 193–235. Chicago: University of Chicago Press, 1992.

Han Shaohua 韩少华. "Fang Qiu Jin mu" 访秋瑾墓 [A visit to Qiu Jin's tomb]. *Renmin ribao* 人民日报, October 10, 1981.

Hangzhou nongye zhi 杭州农业志 [Annals of agriculture in Hangzhou]. Beijing: Fangzhi chubanshe, 2003.

"Hangzhou shi banyun Xihu ni gongzuo zongjie" 杭州市搬运西湖泥工作总结 [Work summary of Hangzhou city's transportation of silt from West Lake]. XHWXJC12, 571–576.

Hangzhou shi dang'an guan 杭州市档案馆. *Minguo shiqi Hangzhou shi zhengfu dang'an shiliao huibian (yijiu erqi nian—yijiu sijiu nian)* 民国时期杭州市政府档案史料汇编：一九二七年-一九四九年 [Collection of archival materials of the Hangzhou municipal government (1927–1949)]. Hangzhou: Hangzhou dang'an guan, 1990.

Hangzhou shi difangzhi bianzhuan weiyuanhui 杭州市地方志编撰委员会, ed. *Hangzhou shi zhi (disan juan)* 杭州市志(第三卷). [Gazetteer of Hangzhou (vol. 3)]. Beijing: Zhonghua shuju, 1999.

———. *Hangzhou shi zhi (dijiu juan)* 杭州市志(第九卷). [Gazetteer of Hangzhou (vol. 9)]. Beijing: Zhonghua shuju, 1997.

———. *Hangzhou shi zhi (dishi juan)* 杭州市志(第十卷). [Gazetteer of Hangzhou (vol. 10)]. Beijing: Zhonghua shuju, 1999.

"Hangzhou shi fujian 'Su Xiaoxiao mu' he 'Wu Song mu'" 杭州市复建"苏小小墓"和"武松墓" [Hangzhou rebuilds "Su Xiaoxiao's tomb" and "Wu Song's tomb"]. *Renmin ribao* 人民日报, September 15, 2004.

"Hangzhou shi guihua ju, Hangzhou shi wenguan hui guanyu Zhang Taiyan, Zhang Cangshui mu baohu fang'an de han" 杭州市规划局、杭州市文管会关于章太炎、张苍水墓保护方案的函 [A letter from the Hangzhou planning bureau and the Hangzhou bureau of cultural relics administration on the plan to protect tombs of Zhang Taiyan and Zhang Cangshui]. XHWXJC12, 725–726.

"Hangzhou shi jianshe ju yuanlin guanli chu 1950 nian linye gongzuo zongjie baogao (jielu)" 杭州市建设局园林管理处1950年林业工作总结报告(节录) [The 1950 work report of the gardening management office of the Hangzhou bureau of urban construction]. XHWXJC12, 406–418.

Hangzhou shi linye zhi bianzuan weiyuanhui 杭州市林业志编纂委员会. *Hangzhou shi linye zhi* 杭州市林业志 [Chronicle of Forestry in Hangzhou]. Beijing: Zhonghua shuju, 2015.

"Hangzhou shi renmin zhengfu guanyu gongbu *Xihu fengjingqu guanli tiaoli* de tonggao" 杭州市人民政府关于公布《西湖风景区管理条例》的通告 [An announcement by the Hagnzhou people's municipal government on publicizing *The Management Ordinance of the West Lake Scenic District*]. XHWXJC12, 3–4.

"Hangzhou shi renmin zhengfu jianshe ju dui Xihu fengjingqu guanli de yijian" 杭州市人民政府建设局对西湖风景区管理的意见 [Opinions of the construction bureau of the Hangzhou municipal government on management of the West Lake scenic district]. XHWXJC12, 6–7.

Hangzhou shi shuili zhi bianzuan weiyuanhui 《杭州市水利志》编纂委员会. *Hangzhou shuili zhi* 杭州市水利志 [Chronicle of water conservancy of Hangzhou]. Beijing: Zhonghua shuju, 2009.

Hangzhou shi techanju 杭州市特产局. "Xihu gongshe shiyue dui muchan 320 jin longjing cha" 西湖公社十月队亩产320斤龙井茶 [The October brigade of the West Lake commune produces 320 *jin* of *longjing* tea per *mu*]. *Chaye* 茶叶 1 (1960): 13–14.

Hangzhou shi yuanlin guanli ju 杭州市园林管理局. "Yuanlin jiehe shengchan hao, Xihu fengjing mianmao xin" 园林结合生产好, 西湖风景面貌新 [(It's good) to gardening with production; West Lake takes on a completely new look]. In *Hangzhou yuanlin ziliao xuanbian* 杭州园林资料选编 [Selected materials about Hangzhou's gardening], edited by Hangzhou shi yuanlin guanli ju 杭州市园林管理局, 3–11. Beijing: Zhongguo jianzhu gongye chubanshe, 1977.

"Hangzhou shi yuanlin guanli ju wei jiansong 'Shujun Xihu de liangnian guihua' de baogao" 杭州市园林管理局为检送"疏浚西湖的两年规划"的报告 [Report on delivering the Hangzhou Bureau of Gardening Administration's "two-year plan of dredging West Lake"]. XHWXJC12, 576–580.

"Hangzhou shi yuanlin jianshe gongzuo baogao (1949–1955) (jielu)" 杭州市园林建设工作报告(1949–1955) (节录) [Work report on landscape constructions in Hangzhou (1949–1955) (excerpt)]. XHWXJC12, 172–176.

"Hangzhou shi yuanlin jianshe qingkuang he yuanlin hua guihua de chubu yijian" 杭州市园林建设情况和园林化规划的初步意见 [The initial comments on the garden constructions and the planning on the garden-ization in Hangzhou]. XHWXJC12, 99–109.

"Hangzhou shi yuanlin jianshe shinian guihua buchong yijian (jielu)" 杭州市园林建设十年规划补充意见(节录) [Supplementary opinions on the ten-year plan of gardening construction in Hangzhou (excerpt)]. XHWXJC12, 149–155.

"Hangzhou shi yuanlin jianshe shinian lai de zhuyao chengjiu (chugao)" 杭州市园林建设十年来的主要成就(初稿) [Main accomplishments in landscape constructions in Hangzhou in the past one decade (first draft)]. XHWXJC12, 177–187.

"Hangzhou shi zhengxie chengjian weiyuanhui guanyu jianjue shazhu Xihu fengjingqu muzang manyanfeng de jianyi baogao" 杭州市政协城建委员会关于坚决刹住西湖风景区墓葬蔓延风的建议报告 [A suggestive report by the urban construction committee of the Chinese People's Political Consultative Conference of Hangzhou on resolutely stopping the current tendency of building tombs in the West Lake scenic district]. XHWXJC12, 756–761.

Hangzhou shi zhengxie zhi bianzuan weiyuanhui 《杭州市政协志》编纂委员会. *Hangzhou shi zhengxie zhi 1950–2002* 杭州市政协志 1950–2002 [Annals of the Political Consultative Conference in Hangzhou, 1950–2002]. Beijing: Fangzhi chubanshe, 2005.

Harding, Harry. *Organizing China: The Problem of Bureaucracy, 1949–1976.* Stanford, CA: Stanford University Press, 1981.

Harvey, David. "From Managerialism to Entrepreneurialism: The Transformation in Urban Governance in Late Capitalism." *Geografiska Annaler Series B, Human Geography* 71, 1 (1989): 3–17.

———. *Justice, Nature and the Geography of Difference.* Oxford, UK: Blackwell, 1996.

Hayden, Peter. *Russian Parks and Gardens.* London: Frances Lincoln, 2005.

He, Qiliang. "Between Accommodation and Resistance: Pingtan Storytelling in 1960s Shanghai." *Modern Asian Studies,* 48, 03 (May 2014): 524–549.

———. *Gilded Voices: Economics, Politics, and Storytelling in the Yangzi Delta since 1949.* Leiden, the Netherlands: Brill, 2012.

He Yueming 贺越明. "Xihu huimu fengbo yu Hu Qiaomu de yishou ci" 西湖毁墓风波与胡乔木的一首词 [The incident of destroying tombs on West Lake and a ci poem written by Hu Qiaomu]. In *Shijia suibi* 史家随笔 [Random notes of historians], edited by Wang Jiasheng 王家声, 265–274. Beijing: Shijie zhishi chubanshe, 2014.

Hellbeck, Jochen. "Working, Struggling, Becoming: Stalin-Era Autobiographical Texts." In *Stalinism: The Essential Readings,* edited by David L. Hoffmann, 184–209. Malden, MA: Blackwell, 2003.

Hershatter, Gail. *The Gender of Memory: Rural Women and China's Collective Past.* Berkeley: University of California Press, 2011.

Ho, Dahpon David. "To Protect and Preserve: Resisting the Destroy the Four Olds Campaign, 1966–1967. In *The Chinese Cultural Revolution as History,* edited by Joseph W. Esherick, Paul Pickowicz, and Andrew G. Walder, 64–95. Stanford, CA: Stanford University Press, 2006.

Ho, Denise Y. *Curating Revolution: Politics on Display in Mao's China.* Cambridge, UK: Cambridge University Press, 2018.

Hollander, Paul. *Political Pilgrims: Travels of Western Intellectuals to the Soviet Union, China, and Cuba, 1928–1978.* Oxford, UK: Oxford University Press, 1981.

Hong Chunzhe [Hong Sun-ch'ol 洪淳哲]. *Guangrong shuyu nimen: fang Hua shichao* 光荣属于你们: 访华诗抄 [Glory to you: poems of a visit to China]. Beijing: Renmin wenxue chubanshe, 1952.

Hou Jiaxing 侯嘉星. *1930 niandai guomin zhengfu de zaolin shiye: yi Huabei pingyuan wei ge'an yanjiu* 1930 年代国民政府的造林事业: 以华北平原为个案研究 [The afforestation of the Republican government: the case study on the North China plain]. Taipei: Guoshiguan, 2011.

Hu Jiangqing 胡江青. "Zhufei de jiazhi" 猪肥的价值 [The value of pig manure]. *Henan nonglin keji* 河南农林科技 3 (1977): 19.

Hu Mingshu 胡明树. "Yazi he shehui zhuyi, lishi wenwu he mixin, zhu he Xu Xilin" 鸭子和社会主义, 历史文物和迷信, 猪和徐锡麟 [Ducks and socialism; historical relics; pigs and Xu Xilin]. *Wenhui bao* 文汇报, April 13, 1957.

Hu Qiaomu zhuan bianxie zu 《胡乔木传》编写组. *Hu Qiaomu tan wenxue yishu* 胡乔木谈文学艺术 [Hu Qiaomu on literature and arts]. Beijing: Renmin wenxue chubanshe, 2015.

Hu Xiaohai 胡小孩. "Dao shenghuo zhong qu" 到生活中去 [Going to the real life]. In *Tanxi ji* 谈戏集 [Anthology of (essays) on theater], edited by Jiangsu sheng wenhua ju, Zhongguo xijujia xiehui Jiangsu fenhui 江苏省文化局, 中国戏剧家协会江苏分会, 88–112. Nanjing: N.P., 1983.

Hu Xuwei 胡绪渭. "Huagang guanyu gongyuan" 花港观鱼公园 [The public park of Watching Fish at the Flower Harbor]. XHFJYL, 77–83.

Huadong shifan daxue Zhongguo dangdaishi yanjiu zhongxin 华东师范大学中国当代史研究中心. *Zhongguo dangdai minjian shiliao jikan 11 Sha Wenhan gongzuo biji 1949–1954 nian* 中国当代民间史料集刊11沙文汉工作笔记1949–1954年 [Collected works of nongovernmental historical materials in contemporary China, no. 11, Sha Wenhan's work journal, 1949–1954]. Shanghai: Shanghai dongfang chuban zhongxin, 2015.

——. *Zhongguo dangdai minjian shiliao jikan 12 Sha Wenhan gongzuo biji 1955 nian* 中国当代民间史料集刊12沙文汉工作笔记1955年 [Collected works of nongovernmental historical materials in contemporary China, no. 12, Sha Wenhan's work journal, 1955]. Shanghai: Shanghai dongfang chuban zhongxin, 2016.

——. *Zhongguo dangdai minjian shiliao jikan 14 Sha Wenhan gongzuo biji 1957–1958 nian* 中国当代民间史料集刊14沙文汉工作笔记1957–1958年 [Collected works of nongovernmental historical materials in contemporary China, no. 14, Sha Wenhan's work journal, 1957–1958]. Shanghai: Shanghai dongfang chuban zhongxin, 2016.

Huang Fangyi 黄方毅. *Huang Yanpei shiji* 黄炎培诗集 [The anthology of Huang Yanpei's poetry]. Beijing: Renmin chubanshe, 2014.

Huang Shang 黄裳. *Shanchuan, lishi, renwu* 山川, 历史, 人物 [Mountains, history, and figures]. Hong Kong: Shenghuo, dushu, xinzhi sanlian shudian, 1981.

Huang Xintang 黄心唐. "Shuitu baochi shuzhong jieshao zhiqi maweisong" 水土保持树种介绍之七 马尾松 [Notes on tree species that conserve water and soil, no. 7: The horsetail pine]. *Nongtian shuili yu shuitu baochi liyong* 农田水利与水土保持利用 (March 9, 1965): 10.

Huang Yuan 黄源. *Huang Yuan huiyi lu* 黄源回忆录 [Huang Yuan's memoire]. Hangzhou: Zhejiang renmin chubanshe, 2001.

"Huanggang guanyu" 花港观鱼 [Watching fish at the flower harbor]. *Hangzhou ribao* 杭州日报, April 8, 1956.

"Huiyi jiyao" 会议纪要 [Minutes of the meeting]. XHWXJC12, 278–284.

Hung, Chang-tai. *Mao's New World: Political Culture in the Early People's Republic*. Ithaca, NY: Cornell University Press, 2011.

———. *Politics of Control: Creating Red Culture in the Early People's Republic of China*. Honolulu: University of Hawai'i Press, 2021.

Hunt, John Dixon. *Gardens and the Picturesque: Studies in the History of Landscape Architecture*. Cambridge, MA: MIT Press, 1992.

———. *Greater Perfections: The Practice of Garden Theory*. London: Thames & Hudson, 2000.

Isett, Christopher Mills. *State, Peasant, and Merchant in Qing Manchuria, 1644–1862*. Stanford, CA: Stanford University Press, 2007.

Ivanova, K. *Parks of Culture and Rest in the Soviet Union*. Moscow: Foreign Languages Publishing House, 1939

Jiang Wenkui 姜文奎. "Ganxie Sulian zhuanjia dui Zhejiang linye gongzuo de bangzhu" 感谢苏联专家对浙江林业工作的帮助 [Thank Soviet experts' help to Zhejiang's forestry]. *Zhejiang linye tongxun* 浙江林业通讯, 11 (November 1957): 1–2.

"Jiangshan xian Miaolizhen xiang Geshan she kaizhan zhi songmaochong de qingkuang jieshao" 江山县妙里圳乡葛山社开展治松毛虫的情况介绍 [Report on the situation of carrying out (the campaign of) treating pine moth (infestation) in Geshan Cooperative, Miaolizhen Village, Jiangshan County]. *Zhejiang linye tongxun* 浙江林业通讯, 2 (April 1956): 39–41.

Jianguo yilai zhongyao wenxian xuanbian (di 10 ce) (1957 nian) 建国以来重要文献选编 (第10册)(1957年) [Selected collection of important documents since the founding of the nation (book 10) (1957)]. Beijing: Zhongyang wenxian chubanshe, 1995.

"Jiasu shujun Xihu gongcheng zuori kaishi jinxing" 加速疏浚西湖工程昨日开始进行 [The project to accelerate dredging West Lake started yesterday]. *Hangzhou ribao* 杭州日报, January 15, 1956.

"Jiejue Xihu jianshe yu kuozhan chadi de maodun" 解决西湖建设与扩展茶地的矛盾 [Resolving the contradiction between constructing West Lake and expanding tea fields]. *Hangzhou ribao* 杭州日报, May 4, 1957.

Johnson, Hewlett. *China's New Creative Age*. Westport, CT: Greenwood, 1973.

Johnson, Matthew D. "Beneath the Propaganda State: Official and Unofficial Cultural Landscapes in Shanghai, 1949–1965." In *Maoism at the Grassroots: Everyday Life in China's Era of High Socialism*, edited by Jeremy Brown and Matthew D. Johnson, 199–229. Cambridge, MA: Harvard University Press, 2015.

Johnston, Timothy. *Being Soviet: Identity, Rumour, and Everyday Life under Stalin, 1939–1953*. Oxford, UK: Oxford University Press, 2011.

Jones, Owain, and Paul Cloke. "Non-Human Agencies: Trees in Place and Time." In *Material Agency: Towards a Non-Anthropocentric Approach*, edited by Carl Knappett and Lambros Malafouris, 79–96. Berlin: Springer, 2008.

Kahn, Harold, and Albert Feuerwerker. "The Ideology of Scholarship: China's New Historiography." *China Quarterly* 22 (April–June 1965): 1–13.

Kassymbekova, Botakoz. *Despite Cultures: Early Soviet Rule in Tajikistan*. Pittsburgh, PA: University of Pittsburgh Press, 2016.
Kathirithamby-Wells, Jeyamalar. "The Implications of Plantation Agriculture for Biodiversity in Peninsular Malaysia." In *Beyond the Sacred Forest: Complicating Conservation in Southeast Asia,* edited by Michael R. Dove, Percy E. Sajise, and Amity A. Doolittle, 62–90. Durham, NC: Duke University Press, 2011.
Kelliher, Daniel. *Peasant Power in China: The Era of Rural Reform, 1979–1989*. New Haven, CT: Yale University Press, 1992.
Kelman, Ari. *A River and Its City: The Nature of Landscape in New Orleans*. Berkeley: University of California Press, 2003.
Kenez, Peter. *The Birth of the Propaganda State: Soviet Methods of Mass Mobilization, 1917–1929*. Cambridge, UK: Cambridge University Press, 1985.
———. *Cinema and Soviet Society from the Revolution to the Death of Stalin*. London: I. B. Tauris, 2001.
Key, Nigel, William D. McBride, and Marc Ribaudo. *Changes in Manure Management in the Hog Sector: 1998–2004*. Washington, DC: US Department of Agriculture, Economic Research Service, 2009.
Kiaer, Christina, and Eric Naiman. "Introduction." In *Everyday Life in Early Soviet Russia: Taking the Revolution Inside,* edited by Christina Kiaer and Eric Naiman, 1–22. Bloomington: Indiana University Press, 2006.
Knappett, Carl, and Lambros Malafouris. "Material and Nonhuman Agency: An Introduction." In *Material Agency: Towards a Non-Anthropocentric Approach,* edited by Carl Knappett and Lambros Malafouris: ix–xix. Berlin: Springer, 2008.
Kohn, Eduardo. *How Forests Think: Toward an Anthropology beyond the Human*. Berkeley: University of California Press, 2013.
Koss, Daniel. *Where the Party Rules: The Rank and File of China's Communist State*. Cambridge, UK: Cambridge University Press, 2018.
Kotkin, Stephen. *Magnetic Mountain: Stalinism as a Civilization*. Berkeley: University of California Press, 1997.
Kunakhovich, Kyrill. "Ties That Bind, Ties That Divide: Second World Cultural Exchange at the Grassroots." In *Socialist Internationalism in the Cold War: Exploring the Second World,* edited by Patryk Babiracki and Austin Jersild, 135–160. London: Palgrave Macmillan, 2016.
"Laixin zhaodeng" 来信照登 [Publish a letter as it is], *Wenhui bao* 文汇报, May 4, 1957.
Latour, Bruno. *The Pasteurization of France*. Translated by Alan Sheridan and John Law. Cambridge, MA: Harvard University Press, 1988.
———. *Politics of Nature: How to Bring the Sciences into Democracy*. Translated by Catherine Porter. Cambridge, MA: Harvard University Press, 2004.
Laurier, E., and C. Philo. "X-Morphising: Review Essay of Bruno Latour's *Aramis, or the Love of Technology*." *Environment and Planning A* 31 (1999): 1047–1071
Le Bon, Gustave. *The Psychology of Revolution*. Mineola, NY: Dover Publications, 2004.
Lee, Hui-shu (Li Huisu 李慧漱). "*Xihu qingqu tu* yu Lin'an shengjing tuxiang de zaixian" 《西湖清趣图》与临安胜景图像的再现 [Scenic Attractions of West Lake and pictorial

representations of Lin'an's prosperity]. In *"Songdai de shijue jingxiang yu lishi qingjing" huiyi shilu* "宋代的视觉景象与历史情境"会议实录 [A veritable record of the conference of "visual imagery and historical contexts], edited by Li Song 李凇, 172-187. Guilin: Guangxi shifan daxue chubanshe, 2017.

Lee, S. John. "Postwar Pines: The Military and the Expansion of State Forests in Post-Imjin Korea, 1598-1684." *Journal of Asian Studies* 77, 2 (May) 2018: 319-332.

Lehtinen, Ari Aukusti. "Modernization and the Concept of Nature: On the Reproduction of Environmental Stereotypes." In *Encountering the Past in Nature: Essays in Environmental History*, edited by Timo Myllyntaus, and Mikko Saikku, 29-48. Athens: Ohio University Press, 2001.

Leng Xiao 冷晓 and Zhu Dan 朱丹. "Xihu sishi nian de bianqian yu fansi" 西湖四十年的变迁与反思 [The transformations of and reflections on West Lake in the past four decades]. XHFJYL, 416-422.

Levenson, Joseph R. *Confucian China and Its Modern Fate, A Trilogy, Volume One: The Problem of Intellectual Continuity*. Berkeley: University of California Press, 1965.

Leys, Simon. *Chinese Shadows*. New York: Penguin Books, 1978.

Li, Huaiyin. "Everyday Strategies for Team Farming in Collective-Era China: Evidence from Qin Village." *China Journal* 54 (July 2005): 79-98.

———. *Reinventing Modern China: Imagination and Authenticity in Chinese Historical Writing*. Honolulu: University of Hawai'i Press, 2013.

Li Naiwen 李乃文. *Hangzhou tonglan* 杭州通览 [A general guide to Hangzhou]. Shanghai: Zhongguo wenhua chubanshe, 1948.

Li Ruibo 李瑞波 and Wu Shaoquan 吴少全. *Shengwu fuzhisuan feiliao shengchan yu yingyong* 生物腐植酸肥料生产与应用 [The production and application of the biological humic acid fertilizer]. Beijing: Huaxue gongye chubanshe, 2011.

Li Shijun 李士俊. "*Hangzhou ribao* chuangkan de qianqian houhou" 《杭州日报》创刊的前前后后 [Details about the establishing the *Hangzhou Daily*]. In *Hangzhou wenshi ziliao (di 20 ji)* 杭州文史资料(第20辑) [Literary and historical materials of Hangzhou (vol. 20)], edited by Zhengxie Hangzhou shi weiyuanhui wenshi wei 政协杭州市委员会文史委, 191-230. N.P., 1998.

Li Wei 李卫, Wu Chao 吴焯, Li E 厉鹗, Hang Shijun 杭世骏, Zhao Yiqing 赵一清, and Shen Deqian 沈德潜. *Xihu zhi* 西湖志 [Gazetteer of West Lake]. Taipei: Chengwen chubanshe youxian gongsi, 1983.

Li, Yan. *China's Soviet Dream: Propaganda, Culture, and Popular Imagination*. London: Routledge, 2018.

Liang Zhangju 梁章钜. "Langji congtan; xutan; santan" 浪迹丛谈·续谈·三谈 [Discussions on a wandering life; parts 2 and 3]. XHWXJC13, 418-445.

Lieberthal, Kenneth G. *Revolution and Tradition in Tientsin, 1949-1952*. Stanford, CA: Stanford University Press, 1980.

"Liheng he Tiyuchang he jiangke tiqian tianping" 里横河体育场河将可提前填平 [The Liheng River and the Stadium River will be filled and leveled up ahead of schedule]. *Hangzhou ribao* 杭州日报, November 19, 1956.

Lin Fengmian 林风眠. "Meishu de Hangzhou—wei *Shishi xinbao* xin Zhejiang jianshe yundong tekan zuo" 美术的杭州— 为时事新报新浙江建设运动特刊作 [Hangzhou of fine

arts—essay for the *China Times*'s special issue of the new Zhejiang construction movement]. XHWXJC14, 493–501.
Link, Perry. *The Use of Literature: Life in the Socialist Chinese Literary System*. Princeton, NJ: Princeton University Press, 2000.
Liu Beiye 柳北野. *Jiecanglou shichao* 芥藏楼诗钞 [Selected poems from Jiecang chamber]. N.p.: n.d.
Liu Jingyu 刘经雨, Mao Faxin 毛发新, and He Shaoji 何绍箕. "Hangzhou Xihu shuizhi tezheng jiqi zonghe pingjia" 杭州西湖水质特征及其综合评价 [Characteristics and an overall assessment of the aqueous quality of West Lake Hangzhou]. *Hangzhou daxue xuebao* 杭州大学学报 [*Journal of Hangzhou University*] 8, 3 (July 1981): 309–319.
Liu Ming 柳鸣. "Fengjing qu yeyao pojiu lixin" 风景区也要破旧立新 [Eradicating the old and fostering the new is also necessary in scenic sites]. *Zhejiang ribao* 浙江日报, November 12, 1964.
Liu Minggang 刘明钢. *Zhonggong dangshi shangde naxie ren yu shi* 中共党史上的那些人与事 [Individuals and events in the CCP's history]. Beijing: Zhongyang bianyi chubanshe, 2014.
Liu Yanwen 刘彦文. *Gongdi shehui: Yin Tao shangshan shuili gongcheng de gemin, jiti zhuyi yu xiandaihua* 工地社会：引洮上山水利工程的革命、集体主义与现代化 (Revolution, collectivism, and modernization in China: A case study of the Yingtao water conservancy project in Gansu province). Beijing: shehui dexue wenxian chubanshe, 2018.
Liu Yazi 柳亚子. *Su Manshu nianpu ji qita* 苏曼殊年谱及其他 [A chronicle of Su Manshu's life and other matters]. Shanghai: Beixin shuju, 1927.
Löwy, Michael. "What Is Ecosocialism?" Translated by Eric Canepa. *Capitalism, Nature, Socialism* 16, 2 (June 2005): 15–24.
Lu Jia 陆加. "Xihu he haizi men" 西湖和孩子们 [West Lake and children]. *Dangdai ribao* 当代日报, June 1, 1955.
Lu Jiansan 陆鉴三. "Shi nongchuang, bushi 'xuerou'" 是脓疮，不是"血肉" [(They) are abscesses, but not "blood and flesh"]. *Hangzhou ribao* 杭州日报, December 4, 1964.
Lu, Sheldon H. "Introduction: Cinema, Ecology, Modernity." In *Chinese Ecocinema: In the Age of Environmental Challenge*, edited by Sheldon H. Lu and Jiayan Mi, 1–14. Hong Kong: Hong Kong University Press, 2009.
Lu Zhenhao 陆真浩. "Jue buneng yu 'gui' weilinglin" 绝不能与"鬼"为邻 [Never live next to "ghosts"]. *Hangzhou ribao* 杭州日报, December 8, 1964.
"Lühua zuguo" 绿化祖国 [Making green the motherland]. *Renmin ribao* 人民日报, February 17, 1956.
Lynteris, Christos. *The Spirit of Selflessness in Maoist China: Socialist Medicine and the New Man*. London: Palgrave MacMillan, 2013.
Lyons, Thomas P. "Interprovincial Trade and Development in China, 1957–1979." *Economic Development & Cultural Change* 35, 2 (January 1987): 223–256.
Ma Jisen 马继森. *Waijiaobu wenge jishi* 外交部文革纪事 [Account of the Ministry of Foreign Affairs during the Cultural Revolution]. Hong Kong: Xianggang zhongwen daxue chubanshe, 2003.
Malpas, Jeff. "Place and the Problem of Landscape." In *The Place of Landscape: Concepts, Contexts, Studies*, edited by Jeff Malpas, 3–26. Cambridge, MA: MIT Press, 2011.

Manning, Kimberley Ens, and Felix Wemheuer. "Introduction." In *Eating Bitterness: New Perspectives on China's Great Leap Forward and Famine*, edited by Kimberley Ens Manning and Felix Wemheuer, 1–27. Vancouver: UBC Press, 2011.

Mao Cai 茅才. "Zhe bushi shenme mingsheng guji" 这不是什么名胜古迹 [This is not a place of historic interest and scenic beauty]. *Zhejiang ribao* 浙江日报, December 2, 1964.

Mao Faxin 毛发新. "Hangzhou Xihu de huanjing shuiwen tiaojian yu shuiti fuyingyanghua wenti" 杭州西湖的环境水文条件与水体富营养化问题 [Environmental and hydraulic conditions and the issue of water body's eutrophication in West Lake]. *Dili kexue* 地理科学 [*Scientia Geographica Sinica*] 6, 2 (May 1986): 158–166.

"Mao Zedong he hongyang shouzhang tan yuanlin lühua wenti" 毛泽东和中央首长谈园林绿化问题 [Mao Zedong and leading cadres of the center on issues of gardening and greening]. *Yuanlin gemin* 园林革命, 5 (January 1968): 1–2.

Mao Zedong sixiang wansui (1958–1960) [Long live Mao Zedong's thoughts (1958–1960)]. N.P., N.D.

"Mao zhuxi guanhuai yuanlin lühua gongzuo (xu)" 毛主席关怀绿化工作(续) [Chairman Mao shows loving care for work of gardening and greening (part 2)]. *Yuanlin gemin* 园林革命, 4 (September 1967): 1.

Marks, Robert B. *China: Its Environment and History*. Lanham, MD: Rowman & Littlefield, 2012.

"Maweisong de xin haichong—songganjie" 马尾松的新害虫—松干蚧 [The horsetail pine's new destructive insect—*Matsucoccus matsumurae*]. *Keji jianbao* 科技简报, 15 (April 1973): 32.

Meng Zhaozhen 孟兆祯 and Chen Xiaoli 陈晓丽. *Zhongguo fengjing yuanlin mingjia* 中国风景园林名家 [Masters of landscape architecture in China]. Beijing: Zhongguo jianzhu gongye chubanshe, 2010.

Menzies, Nicholas, K. *Forest and Land Management in Imperial China*. London: St. Martin's, 1994.

Merchant, Carolyn. *Autonomous Nature: Problems of Prediction and Control from Ancient Times to the Scientific Revolution*. London: Routledge, 2016.

Mitchell, Timothy. "Everyday Metaphors of Power." *Theory & Society* 19, 5 (October 1990): 545–577.

———. *Rule of Experts: Egypt, Techno-Politics, Modernity*. Berkeley: University of California Press, 2002.

Mitchell, W. J. T. "Introduction." In *Landscape and Power* (2nd ed.), edited by W. J. T. Mitchell, 1–4. Chicago: University of Chicago Press, 2002.

Mittler, Barbara. *A Continuous Revolution: Making Sense of Cultural Revolution*. Cambridge, MA: Harvard University Press, 2016.

Mosse, David. "Introduction: The Social Ecology and Ideology of Water." In *The Rule of Water: Statecraft, Ecology and Collective Action in South India*, edited by David Mosse, 1–27. Oxford, UK: Oxford University Press, 2003.

Murphey, Rhoads. "Man and Nature in China." *Modern Asian Studies* 1, 4 (1967): 313–333.

Murray, Geoffrey, and Ian G. Cook. *Green China: Seeking Ecological Alternatives*. London and New York: Routledge Curzon, 2002.

Muscolino, Micah. *The Ecology of War in China: Henan Province, the Yellow River, and Beyond*. New York: Cambridge University Press, 2015.

Naiman, Eric. "Introduction." In *The Landscape of Stalinism: the Art and Ideology of Soviet Space*, edited by Evgeny Dobrenko and Eric Naiman, xi–xvii. Seattle: University of Washington Press, 2003.

Nanjing linye daxue linye yichan yanjiushi 南京林业大学林业遗产研究室. *Zhongguo jindai linye shi* 中国近代林业史 [History of modern forestry in China]. Beijing: Zhongguo linye chubanshe, 1989.

Nanqu, Xiqu guanlichu 南区、西区管理处. "Xihu shanqu hulin he fengshan yulin de chubu baogao" 西湖山区护林和封山育林的初步报告 [A preliminary report on protecting forests and closing hillsides to facilitate afforestation in the hilly area of West Lake]. In *Hangzhou yuanlin ziliao xuanbian* 杭州园林资料选编 [Selected materials about Hangzhou's gardening], edited by Hangzhou shi yuanlin guanli ju 杭州市园林管理局: 71–79. Beijing: Zhongguo jianzhu gongye chubanshe, 1977.

Nixon, Richard. *RN: The Memoirs of Richard Nixon*. New York: Grosset & Dunlap, 1978.

"Nixon and Chou Stroll and Go Boating in Hangchow." *New York Times*, February 27, 1972.

Nongyebu xumu shouyi si 农业部畜牧兽医司. *Zhongguo dongwu yibing zhi* 中国动物疫病志 [Annals of animal epidemics in China]. Beijing: Kexue chubanshe, 1993.

Nora, Pierre. *Realms of Memory: The Construction of the French Past*, vol. 1, *Conflicts and Divisions*. Translated by Arthur Goldhammer. New York: Columbia University Press, 1996.

Olwig, Kenneth Robert. *Landscape, Nature, and the Body Politic: From Britain's Renaissance to America's New World*. Madison: University of Wisconsin Press, 2002.

Pack, Sasha D. *Tourism and Dictatorship: Europe's Peaceful Invasion of Franco's Spain*. Houndmills, Basingstoke, UK: Palgrave MacMillan, 2006.

Pan, Tsung-yi. "Constructing Tiananmen Square as a Realm of Memory: National Salvation, Revolutionary Tradition, and Political Modernity in Twentieth-Century China." PhD Dissertation, University of Minnesota, 2011.

Pang, Laikwan. *The Art of Cloning: Creative Production during China's Cultural Revolution*. London: Verso, 2017.

Parish, William L. *Village and Family in Contemporary China*. Chicago: The University of Chicago, 1978.

Perkins, Dwight H. *Market Control and Planning in Communist China*. Cambridge, MA: Harvard University Press, 1966.

Perry, Elizabeth J. "Shanghai's Strike Wave of 1957." *China Quarterly* 137 (March 1994): 1–27.

Petrone, Karen. *Life Has Become More Joyous, Comrades: Celebrations in the Time of Stalin*. Bloomington: Indiana University Press, 2000.

Pietz, David A. *The Yellow River: The Problem of Water in Modern China*. Cambridge, MA: Harvard University Press, 2015.

Platte, Erika. "The Private Sector in China's Agriculture: An Appraisal of Recent Changes." *Australian Journal of Chinese Affairs* 10 (July 1983): 81–96.

Powers, Martin J. "When Is a Landscape Like a Body?" In *Landscape, Culture, and Power in Chinese Society,* edited by Wen-hsin Yeh, 1–22. Berkeley: Institute of East Asian Studies, University of California, 1998.

Qin Dong 秦栋 and Ya Ping 亚平. *Sha Wenhan yu Chen Xiuliang* 沙文汉与陈修良 [Sha Wenhan and Chen Xiuliang]. Ningbo: Ningbo chubanshe, 1999.

"Qingnian men wei meihua Xihu de yiwu laodong ri" 青年们为美化西湖的义务劳动日 [A day of voluntary labor for the youth to beautify West Lake]. *Hangzhou ribao* 杭州日报, January 30, 1956.

Qu Yixing 瞿宜兴. "Xihu yuanlin jianshe sishinian" 西湖园林建设四十年 [Gardening construction on West Lake in the past forty years]. XHFJYL, 2–14.

Quanguo nongye zhanlan hui 全国农业展览会. *1957 nian quanguo nongye zhanlan hui ziliao huibian xia* 1957年全国农业会展览会资料汇编下 [Collected materials of the 1957 national agriculture expo, book 2]. Beijing: Nongye chubanshe, 1958.

Que Xiuru 阙秀如. "Fangzhi songmaochong" 防治松毛虫 [Prevention and cure of pine moth infestation]. *Kexue dazhong* 科学大众 (September 27, 1956): 415–416.

Rajan, S. Ravi. *Modernizing Nature: Forestry and Imperial Eco-Development 1800–1950.* Oxford, UK: Clarendon Press, 2006.

Ren Weiyin 任微音. *Meili de Xihu* 美丽的西湖 [The beautiful West Lake]. Shanghai: Shanghai wenhua chubanshe, 1956.

"Riben songganjie de xin tiandi—yinban piaochong de chubu yanjiu" 日本松干蚧的新天敌— 隐斑瓢虫的初步研究 [The new natural enemy of *Matsucoccus matsumurae*—a preliminary study on *Ballia obscurosignata* Liu], *Zhejiang linye keji* 浙江林业科技, 3 (1977): 1–11.

Rofel, Lisa. *Other Modernities: Gendered Yearnings in China after Socialism.* Berkeley: University of California Press, 1999.

Rogaski, Ruth. "Nature, Annihilation, and Modernity: China's Korean War Germ-Warfare Experience Reconsidered." *Journal of Asian Studies* 61, 2 (May 2002): 381–415.

Rotenberg, Robert. *Landscape and Power in Vienna.* Baltimore: Johns Hopkins University Press, 1995.

Roy, Jules. *Journey through China.* Translated by Francis Price. New York: Harper & Row, 1967.

Rugg, Dean S. *Spatial Foundations of Urbanism* (2nd ed.). Dubuque, IA: Wm. C. Brown, 1979.

Saito, Kohei. *Karl Marx's Ecosocialism: Capitalism, Nature, and the Unfinished Critique of Political Economy.* New York: Monthly Review Press, 2017.

Saraiva, Tiago. *Fascist Pigs: Technoscientific Organisms and the History of Fascism.* Cambridge, MA: MIT Press, 2016.

Schell, Orville. *In the People's Republic: An American's First-Hand View of Living and Working in China.* New York: Vintage Books, 1978.

Schmalzer, Sigrid. "Breeding a Better China: Pigs, Practices, and Place in a Chinese County, 1929–1937." *The Geographical Review* 92, 1 (January 2002): 1–22.

———. "On the Appropriate Use of Rose-Colored Glasses: Reflections on Science in Socialist China." In *Mr. Science and Chairman Mao's Cultural Revolution,* edited by Chunjuan Nancy Wei and Darryl E. Brock, 347–361. Lanham, MD: Lexington Books, 2014.

———. *The People's Peking Man: Popular Science and Human Identity in Twentieth-Century China*. Chicago: University of Chicago Press, 2008.

———. *Red Revolution, Green Revolution: Scientific Farming in Socialist China*. Chicago: University of Chicago Press, 2016.

Schwarcz, Vera. *Place and Memory in the Singing Crane Garden*. Philadelphia: University of Pennsylvania Press, 2008.

Scott, James C. *Seeing Like a State: How Certain Schemes to Improve the Human Condition Have Failed*. New Haven and London: Yale University Press, 1998.

Selden, Mark. "Household, Cooperative, and State in the Remaking of China's Countryside." In *Cooperative and Collective in China's Rural Development: Between State and Private Interests*, edited by E. B. Vermeer, F. N. Pieke, and W. L. Chong, 17–45. Armonk, NY: M. E. Sharpe, 1998.

Shang Rong 商容. "Ditou yangzhu haochu duo" 地头养猪好处多 [(There are) many advantages to breed pigs on the edge of a field]. *Chaye* 茶叶 5 (1959): 32.

Shanghai kunchong yanjiusuo 上海昆虫研究所. "Zhongguo de songganjie" 中国的松干蚧 [*Matsucoccus* in China]. *Linye keji ziliao* 林业科技资料 1 (1976): 14–15.

Shapiro, Judith. *Mao's War against Nature: Politics and the Environment in Revolutionary China*. Cambridge, UK: Cambridge University Press, 2001.

Shen Congwen 沈从文. *Shen Congwen quanji 24 shuxin xiudingben* 沈从文全集24书信修订版 [Anthology of Shen Congwen, 24, letters, revised edition]. Taiyuan: Beiyue wenyi chubanshe, 2009.

Shen Deqian 沈德潜. *Xihu zhizuan* 西湖志纂 [Compiled gazetteer of West Lake]. Taipei: Wenhai chubanshe, 1971.

Shen Fu 沈复. *Fusheng liuji* 浮生六记 [Six records of a floating life]. Beijing: Renmin wenxue chubanshe, 2010.

Shen Jianzhong 沈建中. *Zhang Taiyan yu Tang Guoli* 章太炎与汤国梨 [Zhang Taiyan and Tang Guoli]. Hangzhou: Zhejiang daxue chubanshe, 2015.

Shi Diandong 施奠东. *Shijie mingyuan shengjing 1 Yingguo, Aierlan* 世界名园胜景1英国、爱尔兰 [Famous gardens and scenic spots in the world, book 1: UK and Ireland]. Hangzhou: Zhejiang sheying chubanshe, 2014.

———. *Xihu zhi* 西湖志 [Gazetteer of West Lake]. Shanghai: Shanghai guji chubanshe, 1995.

Shi, Tianjian. *Political Participation in Beijing*. Cambridge, MA: Harvard University Press, 1997.

"Shi Xihu hushui bianqing de shiyan baogao" 使西湖湖水变清的试验报告 [Test report on (methods) of purifying West Lake's water]. XHWXJC12, 542–546.

Shlapentokh, Vladimir. *Public and Private Life of the Soviet People: Changing Values in Post-Stalin Russia*. New York: Oxford University Press, 1989.

Shue, Vivienne. *The Reach of the State: Sketches of the Chinese Body Politic*. Stanford, CA: Stanford University Press, 1988.

"Shujun Xihu gongcheng jihua" 疏浚西湖工程计划 [A construction plan to dredge West Lake]. XHWXJC12, 565–568. Hangzhou: Hangzhou chubanshe, 2004.

"Shujun Xihu sheji renwushu" 疏浚西湖设计任务书 [The task statement of dredging West Lake]. XHWXJC12, 569–571.

Siegelbaum, Lewis H. *Stakhanovism and the Politics of Productivity in the USSR, 1935–1941.* Cambridge, UK: Cambridge University Press, 1988.

Sima Chi 司马驰. "Fengjing, shihua he shidai jingshen" 风景、诗画和时代精神 [Landscape, poetry and paintings, and zeitgeist]. *Hangzhou ribao* 杭州日报, November 29, 1964.

Skaria, Ajay. "Timber Conservancy, Desiccationism and Scientific Forestry: The Dangs 1840s–1920s." In *Nature and the Orient: The Environmental History of South and Southeast Asia,* edited by R. H. Grove, D. Damodaran, and S. Sangwan, 596–635. New Delhi: Oxford University Press, 1998.

Skinner, G. William. "Vegetable Supply and Marketing in Chinese Cities." *China Quarterly* 76 (December 1978): 733–793.

Smil, Vaclav. *The Bad Earth: Environmental Degradation in China.* Armonk, NY: M. E. Sharpe, 1984.

———. *China's Environment Crisis: An Inquiry into the Limits of National Development.* Armonk, NY: M. E. Sharpe, 1993.

Smith, Aminda M. *Thought Reform and China's Dangerous Classes: Reeducation, Resistance, and the People.* Lanham, MA: Rowman & Littlefield, 2013.

Smith, Neil. *Uneven Development: Nature, Capital and the Production of Space.* Oxford, UK: Blackwell, 1984.

Song Fansheng 宋凡圣. "Huagang guanyu zongheng tan" 花港观鱼纵横谈 [Full remarks on Watching Fish at the Flower Harbor]. *Zhongguo yuanlin* 中国园林 [*Journal of Chinese Landscape Architecture*] 9, 4 (1993): 28–31.

Song Rongda 宋容大. "Dui renmin gongshe jiti yangzhu ruogan wenti de yijian" 对人民公社集体养猪若干问题的意见 [Opinions on numerous questions regarding publicly raising pigs in the people's communes]. *Zhongguo xumu zazhi* 中国畜牧杂志 4 (April 4, 1959): 121–123.

Song Yunbin 宋云彬. "Xihu shangde san'ge fen" 西湖上的三个坟 [Three graves on West Lake]. *Renmin ribao* 人民日报, April 9, 1957.

Spirn, Anne Whiston. *The Language of Landscape.* New Haven, CT: Yale University Press, 1998.

Stanek, Łukasz. *Henri Lefebvre on Space: Architecture, Urban Research, and the Production of Theory.* Minneapolis: University of Minnesota Press, 2011.

Sun, Peidong. "The Collar Revolution: Everyday Clothing in Guangdong as Resistance in the Cultural Revolution." *China Quarterly* 227 (September 2016): 773–795.

Sun, Xiaoping. "War against the Earth: Military Farming in Communist Manchuria, 1949–75." In *Empire and Environment in the Making of Manchuria,* edited by Norman Smith, 248–275. Vancouver: UBC Press, 2017.

Sun Xiaoxiang 孙筱祥. *Yuanlin yishu yu yuanlin sheji* 园林艺术与园林设计 [Landscaping arts and landscape architecture]. Beijing: Zhongguo jianzhu gongye chubanshe, 2011.

Sun Xiaoxiang 孙筱祥 and Hu Xuwei 胡绪渭. "Hangzhou Huagang guanyu gongyuan guihua sheji" 杭州花港观鱼公园规划设计 [The Planning of "Hua Gang Guan Yu" Park, Hangchow]. *Jianzhu xuebao* [*Architectural Journal*] 5 (1959): 19–24.

Tang Mingxin 汤明信, Ni Lican 倪立灿, Wu Zigang 吴子刚, Tan Boyu 谭伯禹, Yao Yuqiu 姚毓璆, Wang Shounian 王寿年, and Hu Yiming 胡怡明. "Gaishan Xihu shuiti wenti de shijian yu tantao" 改善西湖水体问题的实践与探讨 [Practice and exploration of improving West Lake's water body]. XHFJYL, 433–441.

Tang, Xiaobing. *Chinese Modern: The Heroic and the Quotidian.* Durham, NC: Duke University Press, 2000.

Tang Zhijun 汤志钧. *Zhang Taiyan nianpu changbian (yijiu yijiu nian—yijiu sanliu nian)* 章太炎年谱长编 (一九一九年— 一九三六年) [The full draft of Zhang Taiyan's chronicle (1919–1936)]. Beijing: Zhonghua shuju, 1979.

Thaxton, Ralph A. Jr. *Catastrophe and Contention in Rural China: Mao's Great Leap Forward Famine and the Origins of Righteous Resistance in Da Fo Village.* Cambridge, UK: Cambridge University Press, 2008.

Thomas, Peter A., and John R. Packham. *Ecology of Woodlands and Forests: Description, Dynamics and Diversity.* Cambridge, UK: Cambridge University Press, 2007.

Tian Rucheng 田汝成. "Xihu youlan zhi" 西湖游览志 [A tourist guide to West Lake]. XHWXJC3, 1–250.

Tuan, Yi-fu. "Thought and Landscape: The Eye and the Mind's Eye." In *The Interpretation of Ordinary Landscapes: Geographical Essays,* edited by D. W. Meinig, 89–102. Oxford, UK: Oxford University Press, 1979.

"Tuoshan chuli linmu rushe wenti shi dangqian fangzhi luankan lanfa de guanjian" 妥善处理林木入社问题是当前防止乱砍滥伐的关键 [Properly handling the issue of (villagers') joining cooperatives with woodlands and trees is the key to precluding wanton felling of trees]. *Zhejiang linye tongxun* 浙江林业通讯 4 (July 1956): 1–3.

U, Eddy. *Disorganizing China: Counter-Bureaucracy and the Decline of Socialism.* Stanford, CA: Stanford University Press, 2007.

Uekoetter, Frank. *The Green and the Brown: A History of Conservation in Nazi Germany.* Cambridge, UK: Cambridge University Press, 2006.

Van Fleit Hang, Krista. *Literature the People Love: Reading Chinese Texts from the Early Maoist Period (1949–1966).* London: Palgrave MacMillan, 2013.

Vogel, Ezra F. *Canton under Communism: Programs and Politics in a Provincial Capital, 1949–1968.* Cambridge, MA: Harvard University Press, 1969.

Volland, Nicolai. "Clandestine Cosmopolitanism: Foreign Literature in the People's Republic of China, 1957–1977." *Journal of Asian Studies* 76, 1 (February 2017): 185–210.

———. *Socialist Cosmopolitanism: The Chinese Literary Universe, 1945–1965.* New York: Columbia University Press, 2017.

Wakeman, Frederic Jr. *History and Will: Philosophical Perspectives of Mao Tse-tung's Thought.* Berkeley: University of California Press, 1973.

Walder, Andrew G. *China under Mao: A Revolution Derailed.* Cambridge, MA: Harvard University Press, 2015.

Walker, Kenneth R. *Planning in Chinese Agriculture: Socialisation and the Private Sector, 1956–1962.* London: Frank Cass, 1965.

Wang, Eugene Y. "Tope and Topos: The Leifeng Pagoda and the Discourse of the Demonic." In *Writing and Materiality in China: Essays in Honor of Patrick Hanan,* edited by Judith T. Zeitlin, Lydia H. Liu, with Ellen Widmer, 488–552. Cambridge, MA: Harvard University Press, 2003.

Wang Jingming 王敬铭. *Zhongguo shumu wenhua yuanliu* 中国树木文化源流 [The cultural origins of trees in China]. Wuhan: Huazhong shifan daxue chubanshe, 2014.

Wang Linyun 王林云. "'Yangzhu xiaoqu' bushi 'daban jiti zhuchang'" "养猪小区"不是"大办集体猪场" [The "pig-breeding community" is not to "greatly build the collectively owned pig farm"]. *Zhuye kexue* 猪业科学 3 (March 25, 2007): 23.

Wang, Liping. "Paradise for Sale: Urban Space and Tourism in the Social Transformation of Hangzhou, 1589–1937." PhD Dissertation, University of California, San Diego, 1997.

———. "Tourism and Spatial Change in Hangzhou, 1911–1927." In *Remaking the Chinese City: Modernity and National Identity, 1900–1950,* edited by Joseph W. Esherick, 107–120. Honolulu: University of Hawai'i Press, 2002.

Wang Qi 王起. *Yuan Ming Qing sanwen xuan* 元明清散文选 [Selected proses of the Yuan, Ming, and Qing]. Beijing: Renmin wenxue chubanshe, 2001.

Wang, Shaoguang. "The Politics of Private Time: Changing Leisure Patterns in Urban China." In *Urban Spaces in Contemporary China: The Potential for Autonomy and Community in Post-Mao China,* edited by Deborah Davis, R. Kraus, B. Naughton, and E. J. Perry, 149–172. Cambridge, UK: Cambridge University Press, 1995.

Wang Shaozeng 王绍曾, Lin Guangsi 林广思, and Liu Zhisheng 刘志升. "Guji gengyun, momo fengxian—Sun Xiaoxiang jiaoshou dui 'fengjing yuanlin yu dadi guihua sheji xueke' de juda gongxian jiqi shenyuan yingxiang" 孤寂耕耘 默默奉献— 孙筱祥教授对"风景园林与大地规划设计学科"的巨大贡献及其深远影响 [Solitary cultivation and silent dedication—Prof. Sun Xiaoxiang's great contribution to landscape architecture subject and its profound influence]. *Zhongguo yuanlin* 中国园林 23 (December 2007): 27–40.

Wang Shoubao 王寿宝. *Shuili gongcheng* 水利工程 [Hydraulic engineering]. Shanghai: Shangwu yinshuguan, 1940.

Wang Shuangyang 王双阳 and Wu Gan 吴敢. "Cong wenxue dao huihua: Xihu shijing tu de xingcheng yu fazhan" 从文学到绘画: 西湖十景图的形成与发展 [From literature to paintings: The making and development of paintings about the ten vistas of West Lake]. *Xin meishu* 新美术 1 (2015): 65–72.

Wang Tuizhai 王退斋. *Wang Tuizhai shixuan* 王退斋诗选 [Selected poems of Wang Tuizhai]. Shanghai: Shanghai guji chubanshe, 2016.

Wang Xufeng 王旭烽. "Huagang guanyu" 花港观鱼 [Watching fish at the flower harbor]. *Zhongguo zuojia* 中国作家 9 (2001): 166–188.

Wang Yi 王毅. "Weishenme lingxing shumu buyao rushe?" 为什么另星树木不要入社? [Why shouldn't scattered trees join the collectives?]. *Zhejiang linye tongxun* 浙江林业通讯 3 (May 1956): 1.

Watkins, Charles. *Trees, Woods and Forests: A Social and Cultural History.* London: Reaktion Books, 2014.

Welch, Holmes. *Buddhism under Mao.* Cambridge, MA: Harvard University Press, 1972.

Westboy, Jack C. "'Making Green the Motherland': Forestry in China." In *China's Road to Development,* edited by Neville Maxwell, 231–245. Oxford, UK: Pergamon Press, 1979.

Williams, Raymond. *Culture and Materialism.* London: Verso, 1980.

Wilson, Richard. *The President's Trip to China; A Pictorial Record of the Historic Journey to the People's Republic of China with Text by Members of the American Press Corps.* New York: Bantam Books, 1972.

Winstanley-Chesters, Robert. *Environment, Politics, and Ideology in North Korea: Landscape as Political Project.* Lanham, MD: Lexington Books, 2015.

Wright, Patrick. *Passport to Peking: A Very British Mission to Mao's China.* Oxford, UK: Oxford University Press, 2010.

Wu, Hung. *Remaking Beijing: Tiananmen Square and the Creation of a Political Space.* Chicago: University of Chicago Press, 2005.

Wu Lushun 吴禄顺 and Chen Jiabing 陈家炳. "Xilingqiao pan mianmu yixin" 西泠桥畔面目一新 [A completely new look beside the Xiling bridge]. *Hangzhou ribao* 杭州日报, December 4, 1964.

Wu Sun 伍隼. "Hu Qiaomu he Xihu" 胡乔木和西湖 [Hu Qiaomu and West Lake]. In *Zuozai rensheng de bianshang* 坐在人生的边上 [Sitting beside life], edited by *Wenhui bao* "bihui" bianjibu 文汇报"笔会"编辑部, 154–158. Shanghai: Wenhui chubanshe, 2012.

Wu Xiansong 吴仙松. *Xihu fengjingqu mingsheng bolan* 西湖风景区名胜博览 [A broad view of scenic spots of West Lake]. Hangzhou: Hangzhou chubanshe, 2000.

Wu, Yiching. *The Cultural Revolution at the Margins: Chinese Socialism in Crisis.* Cambridge, MA: Harvard University Press, 2014.

Wu Zigang 吴子刚. "Jianguo chuqi Xihu shujun gongcheng jishi" 建国初期西湖疏浚工程纪实 [An account of the project of dredging West Lake in the early years after founding the PRC]. In *Hangzhou wenshi ziliao (di 23 ji)* 杭州文史资料(第23辑) [Literary and historical materials of Hangzhou (book 23)], edited by Zhengxie Hangzhou shi weiyuanhui wenshi wei, 78–83. N.P., 1999.

Wu Zigang 吴子刚, Tan Boyu 谭伯禹, Yao Yuqiu 姚毓璆, Wang Shounian 王寿年, and Hu Mingyi 胡明怡. "Quanmian zhengxiu Xihu hu'an" 全面整修西湖湖岸 [An overhaul of West Lake's banks]. XHFJYL, 37–41.

———. "Xihu ji huanhu diqu de bianqian he gongyuan lüdi de kaituo" 西湖及环湖地区的变迁和公园绿地的开拓 [The transformations and the opening of public parks in West Lake and the lakeside areas]. In XHFJYL, 64–76.

Xi Chengfan 席承藩. "Zhufen shi hao feiliao" 猪粪是好肥料 [Pig manure is a fine fertilizer]. *Renmin ribao* 人民日报, December 30, 1959.

"Xiang dadi yuanlin hua qianjin" 向大地园林化前进 [March towards the garden-ization of the earth]. *Renmin ribao* 人民日报, March 27, 1959.

Xiao-Planes, Xiaohong. "A Dissenting Voice against Mao Zedong's Agricultural Policy: Deng Zihui—1953–1962." *Études chinoises*, XXXIV-2 (2015): 1–22.

Xihu 西湖 [West Lake]. *Shanghai kexue jiaoyu dianying zhipian chang* 上海科学教育电影制片厂 [Shanghai scientific education film studio], 1958.

"Xihu fengjing jianshe wunian jihua" 西湖风景建设五年计划 [A five-year plan of landscape construction in West Lake]. XHWXJC12, 82–99.

"Xihu fengjingqu dali pojiu lixin" 西湖风景区大力破旧立新 [The West Lake scenic district is making great effort to eradicate the old and foster the new]. *Hangzhou ribao* 杭州日报, December 8, 1964.

"Xihu fengjingqu jianshe jihua dagang (chugao)" 西湖风景区建设计划大纲(初稿) [The outline of the construction plan in the West Lake scenic zone]. XHWXJC12, 71–82.

"Xihu gongshe meimu youzhu yitou duo" 西湖公社每亩有猪一头多 [The People's Commune has more than one pig per one *mu* of land]. *Renmin ribao* 人民日报, November 6, 1959.

"Xihu shanqu zaolin lühua de qingkuang" 西湖山区造林绿化的情况 [On afforestation and (the movement of) making green in the mountainous area of West Lake]. XHWXJC12, 439–447.

Xihu shengji 西湖胜迹 [Famous historic sites of West Lake]. Hangzhou: Zhejiang renmin chubanshe, 1955.

Xin Wei 辛薇. *Dianran jiyi: Hangzhou liushi nian* 点燃记忆：杭州六十年 [Igniting memory: six decades in Hangzhou]. Beijing: Zhongyang wenxian chubanshe, 2009.

Xinhua she xinwen gao 新华社新闻稿 [Press release from the Xinhua News Agency]. N.P., October 20, 1956.

Xu Zhiliang 徐志良, Ruan Qichang 阮其昌, and Chen Gaoming 陈高明. "Lao gongren shuo: women yaowei xiayidai xiangxiang" 老工人说：我们要多为下一代想想 [Old workers say: We shall have (the benefit of) our next generation at heart]. *Hangzhou ribao* 杭州日报, December 3, 1964.

Yang, Dali L. *Calamity and Reform in China: State, Rural Society, and Institutional Change Since the Great Leap Famine*. Stanford, CA: Stanford University Press, 1996.

Yang Su-chi 楊舒淇 and Shinji Isoya 進士五十八. "Chūgoku Kōshū 'Seiko jikkei' no hensen kara mita fūkeichi no seiritsu katei" 中国杭州「西湖十景」の変遷からみた風景地の成立過程 [A study on the formation process of the ten views of West Lake as a scenic spot in Hangzhou, China]. *Randosukēpu kenkyū* ランドスケープ研究 [*Journal of the Japanese Institute of Landscape Architecture*] 60, 5 (1997): 465–470.

Ye Jianxin 叶建新. *Mao Zedong yu Xihu* 毛泽东与西湖 [Mao Zedong and West Lake]. Hangzhou: Hangzhou chubanshe, 2005.

———. *Zhou Enlai yu Xihu* 周恩来与西湖 [Zhou Enlai and West Lake]. Hangzhou: Hangzhou chubanshe, 2006.

Ye Songfu 叶松甫, "Buyao ba songmaochong chiguo de songshu dou kanle" 不要把松毛虫吃过的松树都砍了 [Don't cut down all pine trees eaten by pine moths]. *Zhejiang linye tongxun* 浙江林业通讯 3 (March 1957): back cover.

Yequ 野渠. "Yeyou yougan, xiangcun zaji" 夜游有感，乡村杂记 [Thoughts (occurring to me) during a night out, miscellaneous notes on the countryside]. *Renmin ribao* 人民日报, October 23, 1956.

Yi Xintian 伊心恬 and Gong Jiahua 龚家骅. "Gonshe xianhua yan Xihu—Zhejiang Hangzhou Xihu renmin gongshe xianjing" 公社鲜花艳西湖—浙江杭州西湖人民公社现景 [The flower of the commune beautifies West Lake—the present-day situation of West Lake commune in Hangzhou, Zhejiang]. In *Nongcun renmin gongshe diaocha huibian shangxia* 农村人民公社调查汇编上下 [Collection of investigations into rural people's communes, book I and II], edited by Xinhua tongxunshe 新华通讯社, 729–733. N.P., 1960.

"Yijiuqisan nian songganjie fangzhi yanjiu xiezuo huiyi jiyao" 一九七三年松干蚧防治研究协作会议纪要 [Minutes of the 1973 collaborative meeting on the prevention and curing of *Matsucoccus*]. *Linye keji ziliao* 林业科技资料 1 (1974): 12–14.

Yu Heng 喻衡. *Caozhou mudan* 曹州牡丹 [Peony in Caozhou]. Jinan: Shandong renmin chubanshe, 1959.

Yu Min 于敏. "Xihu jijing" 西湖即景 [The scene of West Lake]. *Renmin ribao* 人民日报, September 10, 1961.

Yu Mingqian 余鸣谦, Qi Yingtao 祈英涛, Du Xianzhou 杜仙洲, Li Fanglan 李方岚, Ji Si 纪思, Zhu Xiyuan 朱希元, and Zhang Zhongyi 张忠义. "Cong 'kuanggu weiyou' tanqi" 从"旷古未有"谈起 [Speaking from "never seen in past history"]. *Wenwu cankao ziliao* 文物参考资料 10 (October 28, 1957): 12–13.

Yu Senwen 余森文. "Hangzhou jiefang hou 17 nianjian de yuanlin jianshe" 杭州解放后17年的园林建设 [The gardening construction in Hangzhou in 17 years after the liberation]. In *Hangzhou wenshi ziliao (di 23 ji)* 杭州文史资料(第23辑) [Literary and historical materials of Hangzhou (vol. 23)], edited by Zhengxie Hangzhou shi weiyuanhui wenshi wei, 149–158. N.P., 1999.

———. "Yu Senwen huiyi lu" 余森文回忆录 [Yu Senwen's memoir]. In *Hangzhou wenshi ziliao (di 20 ji)* 杭州文史资料(第20辑) [Literary and historical materials of Hangzhou (book 20)], edited by Zhengxie Hangzhou shi weiyuanhui wenshi wei, 72–128. N.P., 1998.

Yu, Shuishan. *Chang'an Avenue and the Modernization of Chinese Architecture*. Seattle: University of Washington Press, 2012.

Yuan Yaping 袁亚平. "Bishui qingliu geng yiren—Hangzhou shi zhili shui wuran jishi" 碧水清流更宜人— 杭州市治理水污染纪实 [Pure water and clear streams are more pleasant—An account of water pollution treatment in the Hangzhou city]. *Renmin ribao* 人民日报, November 27, 2000.

Yurchak, Alexei. *Everything Was Forever, Until It Was No More: The Last Soviet Generation*. Princeton, NJ: Princeton University Press, 2005.

"Zai Jiang Jieshi maiguo jituan tongzhi xia de Taiwan" 在蒋介石卖国集团统治下的台湾 [Taiwan ruled by Chiang Kai-shek's traitorous clique]. *Zhejiang ribao* 浙江日报, June 19, 1955.

Zhai Hao 翟灏 and Zhai Han 翟瀚. "Hushan bianlan" 湖山便览 [Guide to lakes and mountains]. XHWXJC8, 593–937.

"Zhanduan Tao Zhu shenjin zhiwuyuan de heishou" 斩断陶铸伸进植物园的黑手 [Cutting off the evil talon Tao Zhu stretches out to the botanical garden]. *Yuanlin gemin* 园林革命 5 (January 1968): 8–10.

Zhang Bing 章兵. "Nanshan she yangde zhu youda youfei" 南山社养的猪又大又肥 [Pigs raised in the Nanshan Cooperative are both numerous and big]. *Hangzhou ribao* 杭州日报, March 29, 1957.

Zhang Dai 张岱. *Tao'an mengyi, Xihu xunmeng* 陶庵梦忆, 西湖寻梦 [Tao'an's memory in the dream; seeking dreams on West Lake]. Beijing: Zhonghua shuju, 2007.

Zhang Henshui 张恨水. "Xihu shi keyan" 西湖十可厌 [Ten detestable (things) on West Lake]. XHWXJC14, 472–473.

Zhang Jialu 章家禄. "Relie yonghu da saochu" 热烈拥护大扫除 [Warmly embrace the great cleanup]. *Zhejiang ribao* 浙江日报, December 3, 1964.

Zhang Jianting 张建庭. *Bibo yingying—Hangzhou Xihu shuiyu zonghe baohu yu zhengzhi* 碧波盈盈：杭州西湖水域综合保护与整治 [The sparkling green wave—comprehensive protection and management of the water body in West Lake]. Hangzhou: Hangzhou chubanshe, 2003.

Zhang, Ling. *The River, the Plain, and the State: An Environmental Drama in Northern Song China*. Cambridge, UK: Cambridge University Press, 2016.

Zhang Shaoyao 章绍尧. "Yuanlin jianshe de qige maodun" 园林建设的七个矛盾 [Seven contradictions in gardening construction]. *Hangzhou ribao* 杭州日报, April 8, 1957.

"Zhang Taiyan xiansheng lingjiu zuori anzang Nanping shan beilu" 章太炎先生灵柩昨日安葬南屏山北麓 [Mr. Zhang Taiyan's coffin was buried at the northern foot of Mt. Nanping]. *Zhejiang ribao* 浙江日报, April 4, 1955.

Zhang Ziyi 张子仪 and Zhang Zhongge 张仲葛. "Dui 'zhu wei liuchu zhishou' ji 'siyang weizhu' de zai renshi" 对"猪为六畜之首"及"私养为主"的再认识 [A new understanding of (the rhetoric of) "pigs taking the leading role in livestock" and "giving priority to private breeding"]. *Zhongguo xumu zazhi* 中国畜牧杂志 30, 5 (1994): 18–19.

Zhao Jijun 赵纪军. *Zhongguo xiandai yuanlin: lishi yu lilun yanjiu* 中国现代园林：历史与理论研究 [Chinese modern landscape architecture: A historical and theoretical study]. Nanjing: Dongnan daxue chubanshe, 2014.

Zhao Shuguang 赵书广. *Zhongguo yangzhu dacheng* 中国养猪大成 [A comprehensive volume on pig rearing in China]. Beijing: Zhongguo nongye chubanshe, 2001.

Zhao Xinyi 赵信毅. "Wang Pingyi tongzhi zai Hangzhou" 王平夷同志在杭州 [Comrade Wang Pingyi in Hangzhou], in *Hangzhou wenshi ziliao (di 7 ji)* 杭州文史资料(第7辑) [Cultural and historical materials of Hangzhou, book 7], edited by Zhengxie Hangzhou shi weiyuanhui wenshi ziliao gongzuo weiyuanhui 政协杭州市委员会文史资料工作委员会, 1–7. Hangzhou: Zhengxie Hangzhou shi weiyuanhui wenshi ziliao yanjiu weiyuanhui, 1986.

"Zhejiang daliang zengyang jiaqin jiachu" 浙江大量增养家禽家畜 [Zhejiang vastly increased the rearing of poultry and livestock]. *Renmin ribao* 人民日报, June 23, 1959.

"Zhejiang sheng Hangzhou shi renmin weiyuanhui guanyu gongbu benshi wenwu baohu danwei ji youguan wenwu baohu gongzuo de tongzhi" 浙江省杭州市人民委员会关于公布本市文物保护单位名单及有关文物保护工作的通知 [Announcement by Hangzhou People's Committee of Zhejiang Province on publicizing the list of heritage site under the protection of Hangzhou and other works about protecting historical relics]. XHWXJC12, 667–676.

Zhejiang sheng linye zhi bianzuan weiyuanhui 浙江省林业志编纂委员会. *Zhejiang sheng linye zhi* 浙江省林业志 [Chronicle of forestry in Zhejiang]. Beijing: Zhonghua shuju, 2001.

"Zhejiang sheng renmin zhengfu wei zhishi baohu Xihu fengjingqu banfa wuxiang you" 浙江省人民政府为指示保护西湖风景区办法五项由 [Five measures issued by the Zhejiang provincial government as the instruction of protecting the West Lake scenic zone]. XHWXJC12, 5–7.

"Zhejiang sheng shengzhang Zhou Jianren juxing yanhui, huanying Xihanuke qinwang deng guibingbin" 浙江省省长周建人举行宴会，欢迎西哈努克亲王等贵宾 [Provincial governor of Zhejiang, Zhou Jianren, held a banquet to greet honored guests, Prince Norodom Sihanouk and his company]. *Renmin ribao* 人民日报, December 23, 1960.

Zhejiang sheng Shuiwen zhi bianzuan weiyuanhui 《浙江省水文志》编纂委员会. *Zhejiang sheng shuiwen zhi* 浙江省水文志 [Annals of the hydrology of Zhejiang]. Beijing: Zhonghua shuju, 2000.

Zhejiang sheng songganjie yanjiu xiezuo zu 浙江省松干蚧研究协作组. "Songganjie de yanjiu" 松干蚧的研究 [Studies on *Matsucoccus matsumurae*]. *Zhejiang linye keji* 浙江林业科技 2 (May 1974): 18–51.

Zhejiang sheng zhengfu zhi xia 浙江省政府志下 [Chronicle of the Zhejiang provincial government, part 2]. Hangzhou: Zhejiang renmin chubanshe, 2014.

Zheng Jin 郑瑾. *Hangzhou Xihu zhili shi yanjiu* 杭州西湖治理史研究 [History of controlling West Lake in Hangzhou]. Hangzhou: Zhejiang daxue chubanshe, 2010.

Zheng, Yongnian. *The Chinese Communist Party as Organizational Emperor: Culture, Reproduction and Transformation*. London: Routledge, 2010.

Zhonggong Zhejiang shengwei xumu shengchan weiyuanhui 中共浙江省委畜牧生产委员会. *Hongse siyang yuan* 红色饲养员 [Red breeders]. Hangzhou: Zhejiang renmin chubanshe, 1960.

Zhonggong zhongyang wenxian yanjiushi, Guojia linye ju 中共中央文献研究室，国家林业局. *Mao Zedong lun linye* 毛泽东论林业 [Mao Zedong on forestry]. Beijing: Zhongyang wenxian chubanshe, 2003.

Zhongguo linye bianji weiyuanhui 《中国林业》编辑委员会. *Xin Zhongguo de linye jianshe* 新中国的林业建设 [The forestry construction in new China]. Beijing: Shenghuo, dushu, xinzhi sanlian shudian, 1953.

Zhongguo xumu shouyi xuehui 中国畜牧兽医学会. *Zhongguo xumu shouyi xuehui cankao ziliao xuanji zhu chuanranbing fangzhi wenti* 中国畜牧兽医学会参考资料选辑猪传染病防治问题 [Selected reference materials of Chinese association for animal husbandry and veterinarians: Issues of the prevention and treatment of pig infectious diseases]. Beijing: Caizheng jingji chubanshe, 1956.

Zhongguo jianzhu wenhua zhongxin 中国建筑文化中心. *Zhongwai jingguan* 中外景观 [Landscape in China and abroad]. Nanjing: Jiangsu renmin chubanshe, 2011.

Zhonghua renmin gongheguo di'er shangyebu shipin shangyeju 中华人民共和国第二商业部食品商业局. *Woguo fazhan yangzhu shengchan de cankao ziliao* 我国发展养猪生产的参考资料 [Reference materials about enhancing pig-rearing production in our country] (2nd ed.). Nanjing: Xumu shouyi tushu chubanshe, 1958.

Zhongyang wenxian yanjiushi 中央文献研究室. *Jianguo yilai Mao Zedong wengao* 建国以来毛泽东文稿 [Mao Zedong's works since the liberation]. Beijing: Zhongyang wenxian chubanshe, 1996.

Zhou Chuming 周初明. "Bu yingdang rang ta jixu sanbu dusu" 不应当让它继续散布毒素 [(We) shall not allow it to continue to spread poisonous elements]. *Zhejiang ribao* 浙江日报, December 2, 1964.

Zhou Haiyan 周海燕. *Jiyi yu zhengzhi* 记忆的政治 [Memory and politics]. Beijing: Zhongguo fazhan chubanshe, 2013.

Zhou Jianren 周建人. "Hangzhou fengwu" 杭州风物 [Sceneries in Hangzhou]. *Renmin ribao* 人民日报, August 20, 1959.

Zhou Xiangpin 周向频 and Chen Zhehua 陈喆华. *Shanghai gongyuan sheji shilue* 上海公园设计史略 [A brief history of park design in Shanghai]. Shanghai: Tongji daxue chubanshe, 2009.

"Zhu Ruixiang shizhan yangzhu benling" 祝瑞香施展养猪本领 [Zhu Ruixiang applies her ability to breed pigs]. *Renmin ribao* 人民日报, November 25, 1959.

Index

Afforestation, 2, 8–10, 16–18, 37, 43, 68–85, 88–89, 142
Agency, 15–16, 31, 42, 45–46, 49, 90, 92, 103, 105, 113; expressive (nonpurposive), 14–17, 23, 45, 88–89, 113, 141–143 (see also *Fan xingwei* [counteraction]); nonhuman, 3, 13–17, 35–36, 45–46, 72, 88–90, 113, 116, 143; voluntaristic, 14, 143
Anti-Rightist Movement (1957), 112, 123

Bai Juyi (777–846), 75, 118
Bureau of Gardening Administration, 25, 32, 42, 80, 83, 112, 120, 122, 131–133

Chen Bing (1920–2008), 103
Chen Xiuliang (1907–1998), 107
Chen Xuezhao (1906–1991), 33, 64, 101
Cold War, 19–20, 47, 141
Collectivization, 8, 15–17, 69, 80–82, 92–97, 100–113, 126, 141–142, 152n109, 159n7, 165n101
Cultural Revolution (1966–1976), 8, 62–63, 67, 81, 105, 124, 127, 137–138

Deng Zihui (1896–1972), 96–98

Fan xingwei (counteraction), 15, 17, 23, 108, 141
Fei Xiaotong (1910–2005), 114, 123, 125
Fertilizer, 2, 43–44, 90–94, 96, 98–99, 102, 105, 109. *See also* Pig manure
"Four Olds," 8, 19, 127

Gao Wangling (1950–2018), 15, 93, 108
Gentrification, 145

Goldfish, 16, 52, 57, 61, 63–64, 67, 143
Gongfen (workpoint), 104, 143, 165n101
"Grassroots science," 40–41
"Great Cultural Cleanup," 19, 125, 131, 134, 138
Guo Moruo (1892–1978), 63
Guomindang (Nationalist Party), 72, 74, 84, 118–119, 127, 134

Hangzhou Daily (*Hangzhou ribao*), 29–30, 96, 104, 126–127, 130–131, 152n13
Hangzhou Hotel (*Hangzhou fandian*), 5, 128
Household contract system, 96, 105
Hu Qiaomu (1912–1992), 126, 131, 133–135
Huagang guanyu (Watching Fish at the Flower Harbor), 2, 5, 16, 18, 41, 44, 47–66, 68, 78, 138, 142

Japanese pine bast scale (*Matsucoccus matsumurae* [Kuwana]), 86–87
Jiang Hua (1907–1999), 124–125, 165n118

Labor, 18–22, 27–28, 43–45, 47, 91, 93, 165n101; labor input, 44, 74, 85, 91, 141, 162n6; organization of, 8, 18, 29–34, 76–77, 85, 89, 141, 153n50; voluntary, 22–23, 30–31, 74, 89, 152n13 (*see also* Voluntarism). *See also* Mass mobilization/mass effort
Latour, Bruno (1947–2022), 13–15, 23
Lin Bu (Lin Hejing, 967 or 968–1028), 116–117, 128–130, 133–136
Liu Estate (*Liuzhuang*), 5, 44, 54, 59, 64
Longjin, 83, 100–102

Index

Manjuelong, 75
Mao Zedong, 4–5, 39, 77, 90–91, 96, 115, 122–126, 128–130, 133–138, 141; Maoism, 11–12, 17–19, 23, 40–41, 62–68, 106, 114–117, 130, 136–141. *see also* Voluntarism
Mass mobilization/mass effort, 8, 11–12, 18, 22–23, 30–31, 44, 60, 74, 76–77, 85, 89, 91, 94, 124, 141, 153n50
Maxim, A. C., 4, 52, 54
Meijiawu, 82–83, 101–102, 107
Memory, 50–51, 63, 116, 139–140, 142, 156n13, 156n23
Microbes/microorganisms, 3, 13–16, 18, 23, 32, 37–39, 45, 116, 143, 146
Model worker (*mofan*), 105–106
Mount Chicken Cage (*Jilong shan*), 123, 132, 134, 139

Nanshan, 5, 92, 96–97, 100, 102–105, 109
Nature, 2–3, 6, 9–13, 16–17, 20, 27, 31, 46, 70, 138, 141–142, 170n6
1911 Revolution, 91–92, 110, 112, 114, 128, 130–131, 133–134, 136, 138–139
Nixon, Richard (1913–1994), 5, 48, 61–62, 67, 143–144
Norodom Sihanouk (1922–2012), 5, 61, 66

"Park of Culture and Rest," 18, 47, 49, 57–58, 68
Peony, 55–57, 63–64
People (*renmin*), 1–3, 19, 53, 64–66, 92, 115, 129–130, 136, 143; laboring, 1, 41, 60, 123, 135
People's Commune of West Lake (*Xihu renmin gongshe*), 80, 83, 92, 97, 100–102, 106–107, 112
People's Daily (*Renmin ribao*), 64, 68, 77–78, 95, 98–102, 105–106, 109, 125, 138, 158n7
Pig farming, 2, 5, 15–17, 19, 90–110, 112–113, 141–143, 164n68. *See also* Pig manure
Pig manure, 19, 90–91, 93–99, 101–102, 162n4. *See also* Fertilizer
Pine, 15, 17, 72–78, 84–88, 142–143, 162n120; pine moth, 16, 84–88
Planning, 3, 9–10, 18, 24–25, 34–39, 45, 49, 53–54, 56, 76, 112; central, 12–13, 16, 67, 88, 93

Political tourism, 20, 48, 61–62, 70, 87, 89, 101, 109
Pollution, 17, 19, 37–39, 79, 99, 109, 144, 155n118
Private plot (*ziliu di*), 19, 93, 95, 108–109, 113, 142–143
Propaganda, 3, 6–12, 16–23, 37, 41–50, 57, 60, 67–72, 76, 81, 103–109, 115, 137; propaganda apparatus, 9, 23, 64, 101–102; propaganda-campaign project, 3, 7–11, 15–22, 29, 44–46, 53, 67–70, 77, 85–92, 103–113, 120–121, 127, 131, 141–145; propaganda state, 6, 9, 48; state propaganda, 3, 12, 17, 31, 48–49, 70–71, 85, 89, 98, 102, 141

Qianlong, 49, 52, 55, 129
Qiantang River, 27, 32
Qing dynasty (1644–1911), 4, 21, 25, 51–57, 92, 110, 119–120, 124, 140, 162n6
Qiu Jin (1875–1907), 123–124, 128, 133–134, 136, 138–139

Red Tide, The (1958), 18, 23, 36–42
Resistance, 3, 9, 14, 16, 45, 67, 85, 92, 108, 141–143, 152n109; resistance-accommodation, 16, 143

Scientific forestry, 69–70, 76, 84, 88
Self-sufficiency, 19, 44, 91, 93, 113, 141, 153n50
Sha Wenhan (1908–1964), 61, 107, 120, 123–124, 165n118
Solitary Hill (*Gushan*), 5, 91, 110–118, 122–125, 127–129, 131–133, 139, 168n82
Song dynasty (960–1270), 3, 18, 51, 75, 116, 137, 156n23
Song Yunbin (1897–1979), 112, 120, 123, 138
Soviet model, 17–18, 57–59
Space, 2, 6, 11, 18–19, 57–67, 78, 82, 90, 109–114, 144, 156n13; political space, 48–50, 60, 62–66, 144, 150n32; spatial practice, 48–50, 60, 66
Stakhanovite. *See* Model worker (*mofan*)
Su Manshu (1884–1918), 124, 128, 133, 139

Su Xiaoxiao, 116, 124–125, 127, 129–136, 138–140, 142, 144
Subjectivity, 10, 16, 70
Sun Xiaoxiang (1921–2018), 18, 49, 56–59, 62–64, 66, 68

Tan Zhenlin (1902–1983), 4, 24, 73, 119
Tao Chengzhang (1878–1912), 128, 133–134
Tea, 3, 15–20, 50, 61–66, 71–73, 81–88, 100–103, 132, 142–143
"Ten Vistas of West Lake," 18, 48, 51–52
Tuan, Yi-fu, 9–10
Two truths, 10, 70, 89

Vaccination, 93, 100, 104, 113, 142
Voluntarism, 17, 22–23, 30–31, 35, 44, 74, 89, 141, 152n13
Voroshilov, Kliment, 5, 61

Wenhui Daily (*Wenhui bao*), 91, 110
"Work in exchange for relief," 27–28, 31, 45, 153n41

Xiaoshan, 33–35
Xu Xilin (1873–1907), 91–92, 110–112, 118, 123–124, 128

Yellow River, 14, 21, 74, 141
Yu Qian (1398–1457), 112, 137–138
Yu Senwen (1904–1992), 22, 24–25, 42–43, 53, 56–57, 59, 63–64, 142
Yuanye (*The Craft of Gardens*), 59
Yue Fei (1103–1142), 110, 118, 125, 133, 137–138
Yunqi, 75

Zhang Cangshui (1620–1664), 119, 122, 138–139
Zhang Taiyan (1869–1936), 119–122, 124, 134, 137–139
Zhejiang Daily (*Zhejiang ribao*), 126–127, 131, 159n22
Zhou Enlai, 82, 94–95, 98, 101, 107, 115, 123–124, 136–137
Zhuangzi (369?–286 BCE), 52, 63, 67

About the Author

QILIANG HE 何其亮 is professor of history at Hong Kong Shue Yan University. He specializes in cultural history, urban history, environmental history, and media studies in modern China. He is the author of numerous books, including *Gilded Voices: Economics, Politics, and Storytelling in the Yangzi Delta since 1949* (Leiden and Boston: Brill, 2012); *Feminism, Women's Agency, and Communication in Early Twentieth-Century China—The Case of the Huang-Lu Elopement* (London: Palgrave Macmillan, 2018); and *Newspapers and the Journalistic Public in Republican China: 1917 as a Significant Year of Journalism* (London: Routledge, 2018).